PET
RYAN

THE INSIDE STORY

Sue Williams is an Australian journalist and columnist who has written for most of the country's leading newspapers and magazines. Born in England, she has also worked in print and TV in the UK and New Zealand and has spent many years travelling extensively around the world.

She has written a travel book, *Getting There – Journeys of an Accidental Adventurer*, co-authored a motivational women's health guide, *Powering Up*, and contributed to a collection of short stories, *Love, Obsession, Secrets & Lies*.

She lives in Sydney with her partner.

PETER RYAN

THE INSIDE STORY

SUE WILLIAMS

VIKING

Viking

Published by the Penguin Group
Penguin Books Australia Ltd
250 Camberwell Road, Camberwell, Victoria 3124, Australia
Penguin Books Ltd
80 Strand, London WC2R 0RL, England
Penguin Putnam Inc.
375 Hudson Street, New York, New York 10014, USA
Penguin Books, a division of Pearson Canada
10 Alcorn Avenue, Toronto, Ontario, Canada M4V 3B2
Penguin Books (NZ) Ltd
Cnr Rosedale and Airborne Roads, Albany, Auckland, New Zealand
Penguin Books (South Africa) (Pty) Ltd
24 Sturdee Avenue, Rosebank, Johannesburg 2196, South Africa
Penguin Books India (P) Ltd
11, Community Centre, Panchsheel Park, New Delhi 110 017, India

First published by Penguin Books Australia 2002

1 3 5 7 9 10 8 6 4 2

Designed by Leonie Stott, Penguin Design Studio
Cover photograph by Rick Stevens, Sydney Morning Herald
Back cover photograph by Jacky Ghossein, The Sun Herald
Typeset in Berkeley by Post Pre-press Group, Brisbane, Australia
Printed and bound in Australia by McPherson's Printing Group,
Maryborough, Victoria

National Library of Australia
Cataloguing-in-Publication data:

Williams, Sue, 1959 Apr. 2– .
Peter Ryan: the inside story.

Includes index.

ISBN 0 670 04077 0.

1. Ryan, Peter (Peter James), 1944– . 2. New South Wales.
Commissioner of Police. 3. Police chiefs – New South Wales – Biography. I. Title.

363.206809944

www.penguin.com.au

*To all those honest, dedicated police officers around the world
who work tirelessly to protect our communities,
and who unstintingly put their lives on the line
in the course of duty.*

There is nothing more difficult to carry out, nor more
doubtful of success, nor more dangerous to handle,
than to initiate a new order of things. For the reformer
has enemies in all those who profit by the old order,
and only lukewarm defenders in all those
who would profit by the new.

– Niccolò Machiavelli,
The Prince, 1515

Contents

Acknowledgements

WITHOUT ADRIENNE RYAN this project would not have been possible. She provided as much background for me as I asked for, and would often gently prod her husband into telling me far more than he ever intended. She kept me in touch with everything as it happened, and was astonishingly frank about her feelings about Peter's work, the life he'd chosen, and the often very difficult position it left her in as a result. She was also exceedingly generous in allowing me to prevail upon their extensive network of friends – and enemies – for comment.

My heartfelt thanks also go to Peter Ryan who was an enormously generous subject for this book, allowing me to interview him even while he was embroiled in the fiercest battles of his tenure as the New South Wales Commissioner of Police, and when he was in the very depths of despair. There were many times I'd turn up at his house, knowing all he really wanted to do was to slam the door on the outside world and spend time alone with his family. Instead, he'd always invite me in, pour himself a beer and then talk me patiently through the day's, week's or month's events. He never resiled from answering the toughest of questions, or from facing every criticism I could throw at him. He'd examine each one carefully in what was, at times, an extremely painful process.

My agent Selwa Anthony, as ever, was a great source of encouragement, support and wisdom. She was always ready to help at any time of the day or night, with advice, guidance and the kind of criticism you hate to have, but know you need.

My partner Jimmy Thomson was an incredible help. He kept me going when I felt overwhelmed by the task, and gave me fabulous feedback on the drafts, even though he was dealing with a mountain of work of his own. The book would have been so much the poorer without him.

I'd also like to thank my mum, Edna Williams, who recently migrated to Australia – just in time to type up some of the transcripts of my interviews with Peter. Even though she must have felt she was entering another world, with places, people and politics so foreign making the task twice as difficult, she was unstinting in her offers to help. Together with my dad, Bill, they turned their house into a refuge for me, where I could sit and write, unbothered by the phone, and be handsomely fed and watered. My dear friend Jane-Anne Lee was a marvellous support, generous in both her time and her patience. I'm grateful too to Sue Bennett, a devoted biography reader, for her insights, and everyone who contributed to the book, particularly Peter's sister, Maureen Chibnall, and Loretta Henson.

Finally, my thanks go to Julie Gibbs, Heather Cam, Catherine Page, Gabrielle Coyne and the fabulous team at Penguin for their guidance, their support and, above all else, their faith.

Sue Williams
Sydney, 2002

'See what you've let yourself in for?'

THE CAVERNOUS FUNCTION room of one of Australia's premier racecourses was packed as Englishman Peter Ryan, sworn-in that morning as chief of the country's largest police force, took his place at the top table. He gazed into the faces of the 350 police officers all sitting expectantly before him. Some stared back with obvious hostility, others looked carefully blank, a few smiled uncertainly.

This was Ryan's first official social function as the New South Wales Police Commissioner, and he was eager to make a good impression. The appointment of an unknown and untested foreigner, he knew, had unleashed bitter controversy from the moment it was first suggested. Politicians, commentators and police officers in New South Wales' corruption-ravaged service had campaigned to have his selection reversed, arguing that only a local could possibly be up to the job. But the annual Commissioned Police Officers' Association dinner at Sydney's Rosehill Racecourse on the evening of 30 August 1996 seemed like a very good place to start to try and change their minds – and win their hearts.

The Police Minister, Paul Whelan, was the first to give a speech. He wanted to extend a warm welcome to the new Commissioner, he said. He wanted everyone to leave the old ways behind, move forward and embrace change. As he sat down, there was a smattering of token applause. Whelan leaned over to Ryan. 'Bastards!' he hissed in his ear.

Next, it was Ryan's turn. 'It's great to be here in Sydney,' he declared jovially. 'It's good to see so many of you here tonight. I'm looking forward to many more similar events, so I can get to know you all so much better.' After a few more general cheery pleasantries, he returned to his seat and there was another, slightly less faint, ripple of applause.

Then the recently retired New South Wales Police Commissioner, Tony Lauer, stood to speak. The applause started immediately, rose steadily to a crescendo and was finally underscored by the clattering of 350 chairs as the audience rose to its feet to give him a thunderous standing ovation. Whelan turned to Ryan. 'See what you've let yourself in for?' he whispered. 'Yes,' said Ryan, his heart sinking, 'I think I do.'

He'd been in Sydney for just three days, but already he was getting the feeling that things weren't quite how he'd imagined. When he and his wife Adrienne had first flown in to accept the top job back on 3 June 1996, they'd been captivated by the beauty of the city, thrilled by the warmth of the welcome and excited by the prospect of the challenges that lay ahead. In turn, New South Wales was charmed by this suave Englishman with his colourful, down-to-earth turn of phrase, his young, glamorous wife and their touching eagerness to give up their lives back in the UK to resettle in Australia with their two small children. The New South Wales police service might well be the best police force money could buy, as the old joke ran, but this new Police Commissioner could well be the best antidote the Australian dollar had ever paid for.

For Ryan, 52, it had been a tough decision to give up his top job at Britain's elite police training establishment at Bramshill in the picturesque Hampshire countryside, turning his back on a hard-earned reputation as one of the most respected police chiefs in the country, the fabulous Jacobean mansion that came with the job and their easy lifestyle. But the idea of turning around a police force so riddled with corruption, plagued by management problems and beset with crises of confidence slowly won him over. 'A number of things attracted me,' he says.

First of all, it was a challenge. Yes, it was difficult, it would be awful; it was a huge organisation in need of root-and-branch reform. But that excited me as that's what I like to do, and *could* do. I was also attracted to the idea of being in charge of security for the 2000 Olympic Games. In terms of a professional police officer's career, that would be a very exciting thing to do . . . I thought, 'This is a place where I can make a difference.' I wanted to give it a go.

Adrienne, 35, was more circumspect. 'I wasn't so sure,' she says. 'It was awkward timing for us. At the time Peter came over for the interview, I had gone to university to study for my degree and was pregnant with twins. The timing couldn't have been worse. I wasn't sure such a big move was a good idea, as we'd moved so much all the time. But Peter was keen to try, and so we agreed, in the end, we'd try.'

There'd been plenty of time for second thoughts, however, in between accepting the position, returning to Britain to work out his notice, and then flying back to Australia to start work as the new Police Commissioner. Ryan had worked hard at tying up all the loose ends in the UK, but it had been difficult to concentrate on the job at hand. His phone had rung constantly, at all times of the day and night, with calls and faxes from Australian politicians, police officers and journalists asking him his plans. He was woken regularly at 1 a.m., 2 a.m. and 3 a.m. by people oblivious of any time difference, and emails banked up with queries on his thoughts on every aspect of the service. A body called the 'Royal Commission Implementation Unit', headed by Jeff Jarratt, was being quizzed by the Royal Commission about how the service saw, or would respond to, certain issues like organisational reform or changes to recruitment and training. Members of the unit therefore called continually, wanting to bounce their responses off Ryan to see what he thought, rather than lock him into something with which he later might not agree. Thick reports thumped on his desk every day. 'While there were good ideas there, no plans were ever laid,' says Ryan. In fact, the only decision actually made during that frenzied period was on the colour of officers' shirts. Previously, commissioned officers wore white shirts, and everyone else blue. The Implementation Unit thought it would be symbolically uniting if everyone wore the same colour, and asked Ryan's opinion. He suggested white; they decided blue. It was the first decision he'd ever made for the service and it was ignored. It was perhaps an omen of what was to come. 'But even today,' Ryan says, 'people joke that, despite all the massive issues of corruption, it was the only decision those people ever made.'

A steady steam of overseas visitors also began casually dropping into his Bramshill police college to meet him, although many, Ryan suspected, had travelled halfway round the world purely to check him out. Among them was Gary Sturgess, a member of the police oversight group, the New South Wales Police Board, who said he was visiting the UK on business, and wanted to come by to say G'day. Ryan had him picked up from his hotel and showed him round. Over lunch, however, the battlelines were drawn. 'He sat in my office and said he did not want me to be the Commissioner, he didn't want a Pommie, and talked of his ancestors who'd been convicts shipped out to Australia in the early days. I knew I was in for trouble with him when I got to Australia . . .' He could never, however, have imagined quite how much.

There were other irritants too. Although Ryan has been vetted in the UK by the Home Office to the level of 'secret and above', because of the confidential security information he had access to, his assessment was up for renewal. The New South Wales Government said he would now have to be vetted to the level of 'top secret', but the British Government said that was not necessary.

It's so unusual, it requires the personal intervention of the Home Secretary. It's sort of nuclear-physicist level, in case you're kidnapped by the Russians, or something. But New South Wales insisted, and eventually [Home Secretary] Michael Howard agreed, and signed the authority for me to be vetted to the level of top secret, including top-secret NATO level! Even then, New South Wales weren't satisfied with that, and the New South Wales Parliamentary Oversight Committee wanted to come to England and interview me some more about my standards. This was stupid – what could these people possibly know about my life in England, and why bother when I'd already been given this level of clearance?

Ultimately, it didn't happen.

The bomb explosion at the Atlanta Olympics in the early hours of 27 July, a month before Ryan's planned departure date, resulted in another flurry of phone calls. As soon as news reached Australia of the explosion in Centennial Olympic Park, in the middle of a crowded concert, which killed one person, gave another a fatal heart attack and wounded 110, Whelan rang Ryan, asking him to go there immediately to find out what had happened. Ryan was dumbfounded by the idea. 'What was I supposed to do?' he asks. 'Atlanta was in a state of complete uproar, and I was meant to go there, and explain that at some point in the future I was going to be the Commissioner of Police in a State in Australia, and now please tell me everything. It was ridiculous.'

These petty nuisances served to fuel Ryan's doubts about the wisdom of accepting the new job. The absolute pinnacle of British policing, the Metropolitan Police Commissioner's job, he'd heard, might be coming up in the not-too-distant future, and he knew he'd be a prime contender. The Home Office, too, was exerting enormous pressure on him to rescind his acceptance of the Sydney offer. A deputy under-secretary at the Home Office one day took him to one side. 'We're very disappointed at the prospect of you leaving, Peter,' he said. 'We would very much like you to reconsider and stay here. It's no secret we have ambitions for you.' In addition, Adrienne was having second thoughts. He'd be departing Bramshill with the job for which he'd been recruited mostly done, and the hard battles behind him. It had become an efficient, well-oiled machine that he'd be leaving for others to enjoy the benefits.

The avalanche of press attention had come as a huge shock, too, especially as he realised it would only get worse with his eventual arrival in Sydney. Daily, he received reports about newspapers, radio presenters and TV current affairs shows questioning his suitability for the job, wondering whether his past would really equip him for the future, claiming that he was more of a pompous pen-pusher than a frontline operations man, and wondering if he was 'mongrel' enough for the task that lay ahead.

I expected the media to look into my past, but I didn't expect it to be so intrusive and to last so long. It was almost as though they were looking for something bad, for some weaknesses, in order to be able to put down this Pommie who was coming. People who were approached by them rang me and told me, and then said, 'Are you sure you really want to take this job? You've still got time to back out!' But what it did was stiffen my resolve that this was going to work. I'd already appeared on [TV current affairs show] '60 Minutes' where I'd spoken about corruption and questioned why the media had never done anything about it when, on the scale it was going on, they must have known about it. I wondered afterwards if that had made me a target, my saying 'You're as much to blame.' It struck me that if journalists had put as much time and effort into exposing corruption as they put into me, there probably wouldn't have been a need for a Royal Commission in the first place.

The Atlanta bombing, however, clinched the deal for him. He realised what an enormous challenge running the security for the Sydney Olympics would be. 'I'd had experience of living in Britain during some of the worst IRA campaigns and thought I could bring some of that knowledge and expertise to a police force that had never, ever experienced that type of terrorism before,' he says. 'I felt I could do a good job in Australia. It was a gamble, but I wanted to try.'

He could have no idea just how much of a gamble the job was to prove. He was to face opposition from politicians eager to prove he couldn't do the job, enmity from corrupt police officers bankrolled by drug-dealers' payoffs, hostility from other officers anxious about the kind of changes he was introducing, antagonism from some members of his top executive team who had all applied for his job – and lost – obstruction from journalists who'd had their own favoured candidates, and from the police unions baulking at the kind of radical upheavals he proposed.

It took only eleven weeks from the day of his swearing-in for war to be officially declared. Between 1500 and 2000 banner-waving police marched through the city in protest at his changes, then stood before the gates of Parliament, chanting, 'Send the Pommie back! Send the Pommie back!'

Ryan, who'd been buoyed by the support voiced by officers he'd met across New South Wales since he'd started, and burning with the passion to make a difference, spoke out angrily about their bullyboy tactics and claimed the campaign of opposition against him had been orchestrated by corrupt cops. In truth, however, he felt absolutely crushed. Their hatred and rage had shocked him to his very core.

Part I

ENGLAND

CHAPTER 1

A taste for trouble

PETER JAMES RYAN came to the attention of the police service early in life. A few days after his sixth birthday, he didn't turn up for tea at his family's tiny terrace house in the old mill town of Lancaster in England's north. As the hours passed, his parents began to worry. When he still hadn't made an appearance by nightfall, they searched the nearby streets and called by at his friends' homes, becoming increasingly frantic. Finally, they called the police.

A major hunt was launched for the missing boy, with all officers in the immediate area put on full alert. His parents were at their wits' end when, much later that evening, a policeman hammered on the family's front door with the news: Peter had been discovered, with a friend, camping out six kilometres away, on the area's commercial quay. The pair had built a makeshift tent out of a blanket and sticks behind the local pub, The Caribou, a rowdy favourite of visiting sailors intent on spending their wages on beer and women. When questioned, Peter had merely shrugged his shoulders. He'd wanted to go camping, he explained. It had simply never occurred to him to mention his plan to his parents.

It was a high-spirited adventure typical of a boy growing up with the confidence that life in a small, tight-knit community in post-war Britain nurtured. Strong-willed, mischievous and bold, Peter was rarely out of trouble, always being unfavourably compared to his older sister who was the model child: bright, quiet and studious. It was only a regime of strict Catholic schooling that finally brought him to heel, the Jesuit disciplinarians instilling in him the firm sense of right and wrong that, even today, often leaves him bewildered when others go so wildly astray. The long, lonely train journeys to school and back, where he daily ran the gauntlet of gangs of older boys, proved the first real test of his mettle. It also produced in him the first stirrings of the self-reliance, wariness and guardedness that was to become his trademark in later life. After knowing him for nearly thirty years, one of his closest friends, Lancaster solicitor David Renwick, still describes him as a 'man of mystery'.

Yet in many ways, Peter had a remarkably ordinary childhood with a loving mother and an astonishingly inventive father, from whom he inherited a burning curiosity about the world and an appetite for working out its mechanics. He also learnt a strong sense of duty, watching his father eaten up with anger and shame at being denied a chance to fight in the war because of the importance of his work at home. Peter grew up gazing into the local army barracks from his bedroom window, longing for the day when he too could button up a smart uniform and march out into the world, to return the conquering hero.

For his parents, Lawrence and Margaret Ryan, however, their son had been trouble since the day of his birth on 18 May 1944. Suffering sudden, excruciating labour pains, Margaret had to rush down the hill to the Lancaster Royal Infirmary, leaning heavily on her mother's arm for support. Just as the pair was about to cross the road to the entrance of the hospital, a convoy of tanks roared out of the army barracks. Margaret could only stand and wait for the long line to pass, all the while fearful she'd give birth, right there in the street.

Peter, named after Lawrence's father and a brother of his dad who'd died early in life, was small, pale and extremely delicate – everything his robust eight-year-old sister Maureen hadn't been. Just a few months after his first birthday, his paternal grandfather died, then the broken-hearted wife Mimi two weeks later, so his parents became even more mindful of their son's frailty. They volunteered him to the new 'sun ray' treatment, a series of sessions under a sun-lamp, something highly recommended at that time for weak children. It did little more than turn him a strange shade of yellow.

But Peter soon became strong, and quickly developed a keen

appetite for adventure and an unhealthy disregard for his own self-preservation. He was always small for his age, but his adventures were somehow much grander than his chums'. Climbing tall trees and falling out of them, and running off as a six-year-old to camp overnight at the back of a sailors' pub were only a few of the headaches he caused his long-suffering parents. 'When they got Peter, they didn't know what hit them,' says Maureen. 'He was a really naughty boy, always getting into all sorts of scrapes. He'd be in short trousers with scarred knees and his shirt hanging out, playing with a peashooter and horrible things in matchboxes.'

Indeed, to his family and friends, Peter was the archetypal scruffy, trouble-prone hero of Richmal Crompton's classic *Just William* novels – the kid with his pockets full of marbles, perpetually up to some kind of mischief. A neighbour angrily marched the four-year-old home to his dad when she discovered him and a friend tossing pebbles into a pair of newly dented milk cans they'd stolen from her front step before the milkman arrived to fill them. A few days later, Lawrence had to drag him to the factory where he worked to scrub him with chemicals when, absentmindedly bowling a tyre along the street, he hadn't noticed the road tar-sprayers approach and ended up caked, head to toe, in sticky black asphalt. From the age of just five, Peter was also constantly disappearing and arriving back home hours later, having caught the bus, by himself, into town. 'He was an adventurous little boy, and completely fearless,' says Maureen. 'He was always out, getting into trouble. Every day was an adventure. In those days, children were allowed to roam, but he would always roam too far.'

But rarely was he in any real danger. Everyone knew everyone else in the community, and all of them looked out for each other and their children. That kind of childhood environment made an enormous impression on Peter. 'It was a real community,' he says today.

All the neighbours knew each other's children so you could never get away with being naughty. They'd tell you off or take you home, literally, by the ear or the scruff of the neck for a smack or to be locked in your room with no pocket money or sweets for a week. If a group of children playing football broke a window, all the parents chipped in to repair it. There was none of this arguing, 'He did it!' or 'She did it!' or 'Someone else did it!' People actually owned up and you got your pocket money stopped to pay for the window. Conversely, if five minutes later you tripped up and hurt yourself or cut your leg or bruised your knee, they'd rush out, pick you up, wash your wounds, give you a cake and carry you home. It really was a society, a society that policed itself and regulated itself, carefully and watchfully. It was quite remarkable.

That old-fashioned caring neighbourhood where everyone pitched in to help, eager to take responsibility for their own wellbeing, has remained Peter's ideal of the kind of community he wishes, somehow, could have survived.

In those days, however, life was a great deal simpler. Those people born in Lancaster in Northern Lancashire usually grew up there, would start their own families nearby, and would die in the same knot of streets, all having lived remarkably similar lives. A cotton-and-wool county famed for being at the forefront of the Industrial Revolution with its 'dark, satanic mills', it was the heartland of working-class Britain; a place of huddled Coronation-Street-type housing, dark streets foggy with fumes belching from local factories and flat caps, Lancashire hot pot and hardship. Families clustered close together. Indeed, Peter's grandmother Mary lived only three doors away in the same street, while his mum's older sister Lizzie, and her younger brother Joe, both lived four streets away. In the immediate neighbourhood alone, Peter had no fewer than eighteen cousins. Neighbours would sit with anyone who was sick (often World War I widows), would help out anyone having difficulties, and those with allotments down the road would give vegetables to anyone going without. In short, the Ryans lived as part of a tight community whose lives had been ravaged by war and economic hardship, yet who displayed a patient endurance of adversity, worked hard, looked after their pennies and made a virtue of doing without.

By the standards of the time, however, Peter's family wasn't too badly off. His father Lawrence had been born in 1910, four years before the start of World War I, and had worked his way up to become the foreman in the spinning department of Lansil, the local silk and rayon works. In his early twenties, he'd met his wife-to-be Margaret, a year younger, at a dance in the ballroom at the back of the local hotel, The Cross Keys. They'd married and moved in together in a modest rented two-up, two-down house on Adelphi Street in the Bowerham district of Lancaster. Margaret was eager to stay home and prepare the house for the family they longed to have. Her own childhood had been immensely unsettled. Her father Albert was a farm labourer from Cumberland, further north, who found work each year, together with the attendant tied cottages for himself, his wife Mary and their growing family, via hiring fairs. Each of the couple's ten children, as a result, was born in a different area of the Lake District. Two of the children were later lost to sickness, and Albert died of TB in his late thirties, leaving Mary battling to make ends meet. Margaret was eager to build a much more stable life for her own family.

Their first child, Maureen, arrived in 1935. A clever girl, well behaved and pretty, dressed always in elaborately smocked dresses made by her mother, she excelled at school and her parents doted on her. 'I was the darling of my mother and father,' she says now.

With the threat of another war looming, the couple put off having more children as Lawrence fully expected to be sent away to fight. At the outbreak of World War II, he immediately volunteered for the Royal Air Force (RAF) but was turned down: his work spinning silk for parachutes made him far too valuable at home. Every few months, he'd make out another application, as more and more friends in other occupations went off to fight. Each time, he was met with a point-blank rejection. Margaret often found him sitting alone in a chair in the front room, weeping with embarrassment and humiliation, over a crumpled official letter. Finally, in despair, he tried the army, yet was refused once again on the same grounds. His misery grew even more acute when the best friend with whom he had applied to the RAF, was accidentally killed running into the propeller of a Lancaster Bomber. As Margaret sat at home, looking after Maureen and knitting jumpers to earn extra money, Lawrence brought up his name regularly, and wept. It was as if he felt somehow he'd let his friend down by allowing him to go off to war alone. It was something for which he never forgave himself. Bitterly disappointed and utterly frustrated, he became a member of the Home Guard, but that never really satisfied the highly developed sense of duty later to be inherited by his son.

The war years hit the area particularly hard, but the Ryans were still better off than most. With Lawrence in his well-paid job and no prospect of going away to the front, he and Margaret decided to try for another child. Peter's arrival towards the end of World War II, when Maureen was eight, shattered the serenity forever in their comfortable little house. Built of honeyed local sandstone two kilometres from Lancaster's city centre, its façade blackened by smog and soot, it opened straight onto a narrow street, with houses lined up identically on the other side. There was a small paved yard to the back, a tiny kitchen, a lounge room just large enough to fit all the family, and an outside toilet. Built into the attic was an extra bedroom that belonged to Maureen at first, and later to Peter when she started at convent school and took over the space under the stairs, converted by Lawrence into a study. Each of the rooms had its own coal fire – and it was one of Peter's chores to break the coal into small, manageable pieces – but the house still tended to be cold and damp, with everyone having chilblained feet inside holed, woollen socks.

From his attic room, Peter used to look straight down onto the Bowerham Barracks at the end of the road, which have today become part of the Lancaster University buildings. Here, Peter would sit and listen to the marching bands drilling on the parade ground, and, seared by his father's anger and shame at having stayed home during the war, daydreamed about one day being one of them. The British Army was still trying to keep the peace in Palestine, with other skirmishes in Cyprus, Aden, Borneo and Malaya, so there was a constant turnover of soldiers through the barracks. He and his mates often sat on the barracks wall watching the soldiers march, or would creep into the barracks and sit quietly behind hedges, peering at the troops and listening to the Sergeant Major. Frequently discovered, they'd be slipped squares of chocolate from the soldiers' ration packs.

The Ryan home was always full of wires, bulbs, pieces of electrical equipment, old radios and the innards of gadgets that Lawrence was repairing or inventing. Often, the family's own appliances didn't work, as he'd cannibalised them for repairs he did as a sideline from his factory work. His inventions, inspired by magazine or newspaper articles he'd read, included a working TV set that he made long before most other people had TV, and a clock that worked off a huge pendulum swinging over a magnet that hung on the shed door outside the house. Among his most spectacular failures was an attempt to make, for Margaret, a contraption that would froth the milk on the top of her hot chocolate and Horlicks. After a few days fiddling in the shed, he proudly presented her with the device. She poured in the milk, turned it on and then leapt back out of the way as the milk shot up out of the machine, hit the ceiling and sprayed down over the entire kitchen.

Yet Lawrence was a brilliant man who, like many at that time, was never quite able to fulfil his potential. Later on, he read about the change of car ignitions from points and the distributor to transistorised ignition, and he went along, bought all the parts and made a transistorised ignition system. He put it into a small, lidded tin and fixed it under the bonnet of the car, which smoothed out the engine beautifully. Another time, he built an electrical railway set, complete with sidings, hills, bridges, stations and level crossings that, he told his wistfully admiring small son, he was making for a friend. Peter discovered it at the end of his bed that Christmas. His father's ingenuity excited, in Peter, a natural curiosity about how things worked, a hunger for new ways of doing things and a fearlessness about experimenting with them. While Lawrence rarely played soccer or cricket with his son, like the other dads, he did teach him about radios, electricity and the value of lateral thinking and good ideas – and the confidence to go with them, in the face of scepticism from other people. Years later, that passion for technical innovation still burning fiercely, Peter would determinedly overhaul the way police forces around Britain, and then New South Wales, operated, introducing bigger and better crime-fighting computer systems wherever he went.

From an early age Peter's mother Margaret tried to instil a sense of responsibility in him, sending him off with a shopping list and leaving him to walk the one and a half kilometres back alone, laden with heavy bags. And evenings he often spent helping her with the knitting, rolling hanks of wool provided by the neighbours into balls, as she made clothing to order, in return for butter, bacon, eggs, or their rationed meat coupons. They were even able to afford the occasional holiday in the seaside resorts of Blackpool and Fleetwood, about twenty-five kilometres away – a penny journey that would take two buses and around an hour and a half along the meandering route through the villages – or later in their own motorcycle and double sidecar. The family would stay in cheap bed-and-breakfast boarding houses, which kicked everyone out after breakfast and only allowed them back again for lunch or in time for tea – hail, rain or shine. There'd be Punch 'n' Judy shows, candy floss and, if the weather wasn't too bad, the kids would sit on the beach in their coats, digging in the sand for winkles and cockles or building sandcastles. But they would always avoid the icy sea.

Peter and his sister Maureen were never terribly chummy. The eight-year age gap left them little in common, and she could not often be bothered with a mischievous kid brother who always seemed to be sniffing, coughing and scratching the eczema on his top lip – later discovered to be an allergy to the family cat and her frequent litters of kittens. Besides, her life was surging ahead. She passed her eleven-plus school exam two years early but waited till she was twelve before she went off to convent school in Preston. Any spare time at home, she spent in her study.

Peter was left very much to his own devices, which he took to with gusto, not least his tendency to champion causes. He and a friend were eventually warned off by the RSPCA after calling on them continually with their concerns about the animals at the permanent fairground at Heysham Head, saying that the monkey was looking a bit sad that day, or that they feared the elephant might not be getting enough to eat. One Christmas, everyone suffered on account of his burgeoning sense of righteousness. The chicken the family had been paying all year to be fattened up by the neighbours over the road, who kept and fed everyone's chickens, had to be allowed to live, he demanded. He'd grown too fond of it to stand by and watch it be killed.

It was an idyllic time for a carefree boy, so school came as a rude awakening. Peter's father was Catholic, and his mother had converted on their marriage so, at the age of five, Peter started at the primary school just behind and attached to St Peter's Cathedral. A sombre brick building, with high arched windows and echoing polished parquet floors, it could hold around 250 children in classes of thirty-five to forty. In the early days, before the school bus service started, Peter walked the eight kilometres there and back, running the gauntlet of children from other schools wanting to pick fights.

All the teachers there had known Maureen and talked fondly about her academic ability. For her younger brother, it was a daunting reputation to have to live up to, and he tried not to attract undue attention. 'They'd always be saying, "He's not as good as Maureen, is he?"' says Peter. Even today, it's Maureen the surviving teachers remember more than Peter. 'Maureen worked very hard and she was a very bright girl,' says Gertie Sowerby, who taught at the school for forty years until she retired. 'She was very good. Peter . . . I remember him as a quiet little boy, never any trouble.' The school, with a fair complement of nuns teaching, was presided over by the terrifying Mother Mary Agatha, a tiny woman with such massive feet that the children giggled about her being L-shaped. She ruled with a rod of iron. Standing in front of the statue of Mary, she'd demand to know each Monday morning who had not been to Mass.

Once, a child who had suffered a bad accident was discovered not to have been christened and was picked up and rushed through to Mother Mary's office by a nun screeching in terror at the risk of eternal damnation. The priest was called from the rectory next door, and an emergency christening was held on the spot. Peter struggled to curb his high spirits, but he didn't always manage it. His mother was overcome with shame the day Mother Mary wrote her a letter suggesting she try to send her son to school a little tidier, rather than looking as if he'd been dragged through several hedges backwards.

Peter muddled through junior school, always feeling in the shadow of his brilliant sister. Constantly, he found himself being compared with her, and never favourably. A few times, she'd help him with his homework. 'But she lost her temper quickly and had no patience with me at all,' says Peter. 'She was a teenage girl, after all.'

The birth of his brother Geoffrey in 1950 seems barely to have touched him. Geoffrey was very much an accident and, while a lovely child with a sunny disposition, he never received the kind of attention from his parents that had been lavished on his siblings. 'It was as if,' says Maureen, 'they'd simply run out of steam by the time Geoffrey had come along.' The six-year age gap meant Peter was never that close to his brother, either.

When Peter finished at junior school, he wanted desperately to go to the local grammar school, the Royal Lancaster Grammar (RLG), one of the best schools in England, and just a short bicycle ride away. He passed the requisite exams, but his parents instead insisted he should go to the grant-assisted 700-boy Preston Catholic College run by the Jesuits (since renamed Cardinal Newman College). To send Peter to the RLG required special permission from the bishop, and it simply never occurred to the couple to ask. In those days, people tended to just do as they were told by their church. For Peter, that decision proved disastrous. Instead of attending a good school close to home, he found himself travelling every day on a bus to the train station at Lancaster, then on the train to Preston, then on another bus to the school, in the centre of the city. It was only a thirty-eight-kilometre journey and should, in theory, have taken an hour and a half, door to door. But in reality, it could take hours, especially in the winter. At the slightest trace of fog, ice or snow, the steam train would become hopelessly delayed. Frequently, he wouldn't even be let onto the train when it arrived as, being the main London-to-Glasgow train, it was sometimes too crowded for any more passengers. Similarly, the buses from Lancaster station to Bowerham were too full of workers clocking off to allow schoolboys on, and then he'd be faced with an additional hour-long trudge home.

Often, Peter wouldn't get home from school at night until 8.30 in the evening frozen and exhausted after hours waiting on the station platform, desperately trying to do his homework by the light of the one fly-blown lamp in the filthy, freezing waiting room, or hours spent on the delayed train, wreathed in smoke and steam. His education suffered. Even today, it doesn't take much to stir his anger over the stupidity of the decision to send him to such a distant school. Yet, ultimately, it proved a seminal period in his life. At the time, he was miserable about not being able to fulfil the kind of academic potential he undeniably had, particularly when he was so eager to replicate his sister Maureen's success. Subsequently he was resentful that no one else could see as clearly as he the handicap he had to face. On the other hand, this did trigger the ambition that has driven him all his life, often far beyond the point of personal happiness or simple career fulfilment. The image of that little boy, struggling against the odds to do his schoolwork, and dreaming of the day when he'd make everyone sit up and notice just how clever he really was, is hard to ignore.

Still small for his age, Peter also became a target for the school bullies on the train. The younger children always tried to travel in the same carriage, so they'd have strength in numbers if they were picked on, but that wasn't always possible. After a few months of variously being hung through an open window as an oncoming train roared towards him, being burned on the back of his neck with the hot metal of the carriage light bulb, and having his head pushed down the toilet while it was flushed, Peter made a decision.

> I was already going to a boys' club and learning how to box, so I went more often and learnt how to box better and how to take blows. One day, I was on my own on the train when two of the older, bigger boys got on and started punching and pushing me. I was trapped in the carriage with them, but I turned around and got stuck into one of them and gave him a good hiding. The word got around about what had happened and they left me alone from that day on.

The experience made a profound impact on him. He found himself in demand from the other younger boys as their protector, and tried to teach them to stand up for themselves too.

> I realised that all bullying is cowardice and that you have to stand up for yourself and show that you're not prepared to put up with it. The confidence that gave me meant I developed a kind of aura where people would leave me alone. Since that time, I've never had any time for bullying at all. I won't be terrorised by bullies. It started at that point, but has been reinforced at various stages of my life, in the Territorial Army, in the police. You have to cope.

Those unending school journeys had a long-term effect in other ways as well. Peter became a bit of a loner, self-reliant and self-possessed, only prepared to socialise on his terms, when *he* wanted to. It is a quality that has stayed with him all his life, and one that seems to make others even keener to get to know him. At school, starting times were staggered, so the boys wouldn't bump into the girls who studied at the sister school, the convent, further down on the square. Both sets of pupils were banned from speaking to each other, or even walking on the same side of the road. Despite that, Peter is remembered by schoolmate Tony Halliwell (now a chartered surveyor in Preston) as knowing a fair few of the girls.

> He had a very sociable personality and was popular and well-liked. He could charm the teachers in a way that could get him out of scrapes. He was very bright and always ended up in the top part of the class, even though he never seemed to make much effort. He was always very particular about what he wore, too. He'd have a fashionable sweater that he'd insist on wearing to school, although he'd often have to take it off because it wasn't part of the school uniform. He wasn't very keen on authority at that time. He obviously got over that one.

The Jesuits, dressed in black suits over which they wore a long tailored smock, were hard taskmasters. They believed in moulding their charges, imbuing them with a strong sense of right and wrong, and punishing them if they didn't respond to their strict regime. 'Give me the boy until he is seven,' is the refrain, 'and I will give you the man.' The boy they took over in Peter rebelled at first to the demands of unquestioning obedience. He frequently received a printed note detailing the punishment to be meted out for failing to finish homework (a daily danger for him) or for not learning the catechism, or for breaking a rule. He would then have to go along to another teacher to redeem the note within twenty-four hours, or risk the punishment being doubled. It usually consisted of a number of strokes with a ferrule, a whalebone wrapped in leather about two-foot long, either on the hand or on the backside. If anyone was sentenced to more than twelve strokes, the headmaster Rev. Father

Carty would elect to deliver it personally. He was a man feared so much as he strode around the school in a black hat and flowing black gown that the mass of pupils would part like the Red Sea before him. His victim would be forced to kneel on a cushion, pray for forgiveness from God and then bend over an old Jacobean table in his office to receive his strokes.

Peter soon, however, began to respond to the authoritarian regime 'I remember Peter as a fresh-faced, small, good-looking young lad. I tended to blackmail people into appearing in our annual school plays and I managed to push him into one too,' says former teacher Arthur Malone. 'He had the ideal build for tights. I would invite likely lads along to an audition, and God help them if they didn't come. He was cast as Macduff in our production of *Macbeth* and he did very well. I remember him being very excited by the prospect of being involved in swordfights.' Indeed, the play ended up a triumph, with Peter receiving a glowing review in the school newsletter. 'Macduff was not too well served by the costumier and had to wear clothes of a sobriety near to drabness,' wrote the school reviewer. 'Thus P.J. Ryan had to rely on his own resources to portray the stern, upright character of Macduff. He did this extremely well and was perhaps the toughest and strongest of the anti-Macbeth faction, a worthy avenger of evil.' It was a role he adored.

During this period, the family moved house – albeit only three streets away – buying a bigger terrace on Coulston Road, for the grand sum of £650. It had three bedrooms, a much larger lounge room and a small garden at the front of the house, on a wider road. At this time, Lawrence also bought his first car, much to Peter's delight, and Maureen married, at the age of 22, teacher John Chibnall, with Peter in attendance as one of her groomsmen. She set up home just one street away, but afterwards, the newly-weds moved 350 kilometres away to Welwyn Garden City.

Despite his difficulties, Peter passed five O-Levels the first time around, and three more when he resat the exams a few months later. He decided to stay on for A-Levels, needed for university. He didn't know, however, what he wanted to do. The employment counsellors were little help. They simply told students what jobs there were available at the time, particularly in the army, and encouraged them to apply for those vacancies, rather than steering them towards any idea of vocations.

Peter's mother was keen for him to opt for a solid occupation, like a clerk in the town hall, or to train as a teacher, as Maureen had done. Lawrence told him that whatever he did, he shouldn't follow him into the textiles trade since mills were closing all around Britain, and India and Pakistan were winning an ever-greater slice of the market. Besides, he had his own theories about what Peter would end up doing. He'd smiled at his son's fascination with the soldiers down the road. He'd watched him become an enthusiastic member of the St John Ambulance Brigade. He'd agreed to his joining the part-time Territorial Army, even appearing as an extra in the 1960 Laurence Olivier movie *The Entertainer*, as one of the soldiers welcoming home Albert Finney's character on his return from Suez. But he drew the line when Peter started talking about joining the White Fathers, part of a missionary group that went about the country dressed (obviously) in white.

From a largely untroubled childhood, a surprisingly complex youth had emerged. Ambitious, self-reliant, drawn to defending those weaker than himself, but reticent in personal relationships, he had a strong sense of duty, and a firm view of right and wrong, as well as a passion for innovation. But somewhere, etched indelibly in his young mind, was the image of his frustrated father at home, and ruler-straight lines of fine young men, marching off to serve Queen and country.

As he watched Peter grow up, Lawrence knew where his son's ambitions lay. 'If it's got a bloody uniform,' he said in despair, 'he'll be in it.'

CHAPTER 2

From
A to Z cars

THE POLICE WASN'T Peter Ryan's first choice of career. Or his second. Or even his third. He really wanted to be an airline pilot, but that seemed an ambition totally beyond the modest world he knew. He would have liked to be a doctor, yet his disrupted schooling meant his grades weren't good enough. Becoming a solicitor appealed, and he was accepted by two law firms to train as an articled clerk. The only problem was that he wouldn't get paid until he qualified, so his parents would have to keep him. His father's response was unequivocal when he raised the subject: No.

Halfway through sixth form, Ryan knew, however, that he was heartily sick of travelling to school and back every day. He longed to escape the tyranny of such long hours and itched to earn some money. So, at the age of 16½, he told his parents he was finished. He found a job as an apprentice architect at a local Lancaster firm. But it didn't take long for boredom and impatience to set in. 'I was just tracing other people's drawings and they were as bland as hell,' he says. 'Nobody was building St Paul's Cathedral; they were building sheds and warehouses and junk like that.' The long-term prospects didn't seem particularly good, either, with Government grants to companies taking on apprentices stopping when they reached 21, which meant they were then often abruptly turfed out.

Ryan looked around once again, and this time set his sights on the police service. It looked the kind of job where there'd be excitement, interesting people, a purpose, prospects, a regular wage and, of course, a uniform. Maureen wasn't in the least surprised by his decision. 'He wasn't very academic, and the police did seem to offer opportunities,' she says. 'Peter probably realised that his schooling was going to hold him back, but that the police had a lot of different careers.' Ryan joined the Lancashire Constabulary on 16 January 1961 as a police cadet, at the princely weekly wage of £2 9s 4d a week.

In those days, Lancashire had the biggest provincial police force in Britain, second in size only to the Metropolitan Police (the Met) in London, covering areas like the current Merseyside, Manchester and Cumbria. It was a thriving force with 2900 police officers and growing fast under the watchful command of the fiercely efficient and innovative Chief Constable, Colonel Eric St Johnston, nick-named 'The Saint' for his debonair style as much as for his name. In an odd coincidence, ten years after Ryan joined, St Johnston, by then Sir Eric, was invited over to Australia to report on how police ser-vices could be reorganised to make them more effective. His report was eventually filed in the too-hard basket, says one of Ryan's old bosses, Tommy Watkinson, who was later to retire as Lancashire's Assistant Chief Constable.

In contrast, the Lancashire force had a reputation as a sleek, effi-cient, go-ahead organisation. Former local officer-turned-author Bob Dobson says St Johnston spent two spells in the USA looking at how the police worked, and returned each time determined to introduce new ways of doing things to his force. They were the first to paint their police cars white, with day-glo orange stripes, and had the first transistorised radios for motorcycle police, fitted into the rider's helmet. A new BBC TV show in 1960 had also caught the nation's attention: 'Z Cars', a dashing police drama based on the Lancashire Constabulary's own ground-breaking system of fighting crime with patrols in large, fast saloon cars. Set in the mythical town of New-town, which was in fact Kirkby, an overspill housing estate sixteen kilometres east of Liverpool, it was the precursor of all the realistic police shows to follow. It proved highly controversial not only for its thrills and spills, with big Ford Zephyr Mk III cars racing up and down the motorways, but also for its no-holds-barred portrayal of low-life, both criminal and police. 'It seemed to have all the hall-marks of the new realism,' says revered TV and movie critic Leslie

Halliwell; 'the influence on other crime series was immense.' Indeed, in recent years it's been revealed that the creator of the 1980s multi-Emmy-Award-winning American series 'Hill Street Blues', Steven Bochco, showed early episodes of 'Z Cars' to his original cast before they started making their own show.

At the start of work on 'Z Cars', St Johnston had been enthusiastic about the concept, cooperating fully with its writers and producers, believing it would bring new recognition and kudos for his officers and himself. But he quickly moved to distance himself when it went to air, portraying officers sleeping with other people's wives and flouting the rules to catch their prey. 'As soon as he'd seen the first episodes, he tried to stop it,' says Watkinson. 'He said, "Our policemen don't behave like that!"' He immediately went to London to face the music at the Home Office about the show. 'Then he went to see the producers of the program,' says Watkinson. 'But they wouldn't take it off. But in the end they did agree to drop references to the Lancashire Constabulary from the credits.'

It was in this atmosphere of excitement and innovation that Ryan started right at the bottom of the force. He sailed through his first two weeks training, was kitted out with a uniform, and took the bus off to his posting in Morecambe, a large seaside town eight kilometres west of Lancaster, and a favourite holiday spot for all the major mill towns of the county. It was a typical resort area, with candy floss, sticks of rock, penny amusements, 'Kiss Me Quick' hats, two wooden piers, and a stone jetty for the ferries to Ireland. A long promenade wound its way around the shoreline, which looked beautiful when the tide was in, particularly at sunset, but when it went out was exposed as a kilometre and a half of boggy, muddy salt marsh. The town once had a thriving export business in mussels – more than 2000 tonnes were sent off annually by train between 1900 and 1905 – until sewage contaminated the area, and the mussels had to be boiled rather than eaten raw. Now it relied mostly on tourists for its livelihood.

The police station was a large sandstone building by the bus terminal with a busy front desk where Ryan mostly worked. It was a world away from the thrills of TV cop shows – his days full of lost wallets and dropped keys – but he liked the job for its human interaction. 'I remember he used to get genuinely upset when old ladies lost purses,' says Maureen. 'He got very bothered about that, and about lost children. He used to tell us about them at the dinner table.'

The main crimes in the town were theft, the occasional house or shop break-in, a car being stolen, and drunkenness among holiday-makers hell-bent on a good time. One night, a massive brawl broke out in The Ship pub and every officer in the area was called in to help separate the fighters. Ryan, who had been doing a dull evening shift behind the station desk making sure the Wanted records were up-to-date, jumped into the station's big old Austin van and arrived to find officers dragging people out of the pub. He helped them throw their prisoners into the van but, when everyone had been arrested and flung inside, they realised someone had stolen the keys. 'So we had to push this van, full of shouting and fighting prisoners about half a mile to the police station,' says Ryan. 'It was either that or let them go because no one knew where the spare keys were. Everybody stood on the pavement cheering and laughing at us. It was very embarrassing. Real Keystone Kops stuff.'

At times, that was as close to real crime he seemed destined ever to come. When a body of a young murder victim was found on the beach, his job was merely keeping the detectives from HQ in cups of tea. And when in December that year he was moved to divisional HQ in Lancaster, his main duties turned out to be filing, typing, keeping ledgers up to date, working the switchboard, supervising the delivery of coal to the station and stoking the ancient coke boiler in the fume-filled basement when the boilerman wasn't there. It got worse. When a local landowner sent a brace of pheasants to the Chief Superintendent in thanks for catching a poacher, it turned out to be Ryan's job to clean and pluck them.

That year, there was a firearms amnesty, when the Government asked anyone with an unlicensed weapon to surrender them and avoid prosecution. Ryan stood stunned at the counter, looking at the World War I and World War II armouries people brought in: machine guns with belts of ammunition, gas masks, live hand grenades, and mortars, all carried for miles on the local bus, and pre-sented to police in shoeboxes or paper carrier bags. Every one of them was carefully stored in the police station cell – although if they exploded, that would have been no protection at all. 'It was all so different in those days,' Ryan says. 'Relations with the public were good. People still fought you, especially drunks, and robbers would try to escape and beat you, but there were very few firearms ever used. The occasional knife would be produced in a crime and police would sometimes be attacked with a stick or iron bar, but the mood felt very different.'

At the age of 17, Ryan abandoned the bus for his first car, a 1937 Morris 8 Tourer, bought for £25. It sparked the beginning of a life-long passion for cars. As soon as he could afford it, he'd sell one car and buy a bigger or better model. His father Lawrence taught him all about engines, and Ryan completely stripped and rebuilt two cars, including a Mini Cooper, over the next couple of years. He felt it would prepare him well for his next career step, and it came in the middle of 1962 when, at the age of 18, Ryan got his big break as a cadet: he was allowed to join the highway patrol. For every young recruit, this was the dream job – being able to drive a car. It didn't quite work out as he'd imagined, however. Most of the time he simply cleaned the cars, checked the oil and water levels, poured paraffin into the red warning lamps, and made sure all vehicles were equipped with their traffic cones, torch, towrope and bag of tools. The sergeant in charge took great delight in hauling the new boys off the traffic roster and making them instead fill out the tiresome petrol, mileage and oil ledgers. Unintentionally he did Ryan a good turn one day by banning him from going out with a young woman officer on patrol in her open-top MG sports car. A few hours later, she was killed racing to the scene of a road accident.

After a few months, Ryan was moved into CID (the Criminal Investigation Department), again looking after the files. But these files were a great deal more compelling. Among them were photographs of crime scenes, dead bodies and the gruesome aftermath of accidents. 'It came as something of a shock to realise just how cruel people were to other people,' says Ryan.

Serious assaults between friends and lovers, the incest complaints that were sort of taboo and never spoken about anywhere at any time, and the murders where people didn't just kill somebody, they actually mutilated them, hacked them with axes. I was quite innocent, I'd had a normal upbringing; it was all a shock. One was a picture of a couple in bed who'd been attacked by their son with an axe whilst they were sleeping, and it was quite horrendous. It was like the whole place had been sprayed with blood. Then there were photos of people on mortuary slabs. It was really quite upsetting. You felt the churning sensation of shock, horror really, absolutely awful. It was fascinating reading the files, but I never went to anything other than road accidents or house break-ins at that stage.

As a break from the routine of menial duties expected of any junior, Ryan was sent to the training school, an old American air-force base, at Bruche in Warrington on the sixteen-week course to become a fully-fledged police officer. Due to rising crime, the Government had in early 1963 embarked on a major recruiting campaign to double the size of the force countrywide – Lancashire's was set to increase to 7500 by 1969 – and the fledgling officers were squeezed six to a room, head to toe, in the dorms. Yet lowering the recruitment standards wasn't a great success. Of Ryan's six, only two finally became police officers. While Ryan finished the course with close to top marks, his greatest lesson happened outside the classroom. The last morning of the course, he threw all his energy into his final cross-country run and was pleased to note he'd finished at a personal best time. Hot and sweaty, he dived into the shower block and straight under the cold water. As he was soaping up, one of the course leaders came in. 'Ryan!' he bellowed. 'What are you doing here? Skiving off are you?' Ryan explained he'd just finished his run in record time. But the tutor was having none of it. 'No, you've been having a lie-in and then come straight in here,' he insisted. 'I know it. You haven't been for a run at all.' He was deaf to Ryan's protests, and ordered that he be put on patrol duty after graduation and the passing-out parade as his punishment. The injustice burned, and Ryan made a mental note that there would always be those determined not to let others succeed. And a little more of his innocence had gone.

After graduation to a fully-fledged probationer on 19 May 1963, Ryan was posted as a beat policeman to Little Hulton, a new town near Bolton built to accommodate the overspill from Manchester's crumbling slums. He moved into digs in Walkden, near Manchester, with a deeply religious couple who viewed their lodger as a long-lost son, and he went back home only at weekends. His brother Geoffrey didn't miss him much, as he recalls.

> I suppose we just used to pass in the night. We had an OK relationship, but there was still that age difference. I'd sometimes go out with him when he was out and about with the boys, and he was always quite sociable. But we were extremely different people. I was always very easy-going, and he became a bit serious. He started always looking ahead.

For Ryan had already begun to start attracting attention from those above him in the service. He was an enthusiastic young officer. He bought his own bicycle for patrol duty – for which you earned an extra sevenpence allowance a week – and his own typewriter to the office for an additional sixpence, and soon found that all that time spent on the most routine, boring duties as a cadet was standing him in excellent stead. He knew all the forms and documentation for every single incident that could possibly happen. He'd typed and filed so many statements and reports, he could quickly tell the difference between the good and the bad. And then, on his very first day out on patrol with his tutor learning his beat, he spotted someone struggling to carry his lunch bag, asked to see inside, and discovered a haul of copper cabling and wire stolen from a nearby factory. 'Making an arrest on your first day is pretty well unheard of,' says Ryan. 'I was very excited – my first arrest and my name on a charge sheet. I felt sorry for the man, of course, because the guy was trying to make a living, trying to keep his family going, but it was good to be doing the job.'

Ken Bennett, who was the managing director of the area's largest copper fabricator at that time, agrees that such a coup would have marked Ryan out from the very beginning. Since stealing from the factory was an offence that, if discovered, carried the penalty of instant dismissal and no future references, which made subsequent jobs extremely hard to find, thieves tended to conceal their loot carefully. 'It was usually your surveillance guards at the gate that would catch anyone stealing,' says Bennett, who ran Frederick Smith & Co, which made copper wire for electrical engineering, cables and domestic appliances.

> They'd be watching the work force at whatever time they went out. They'd look out for someone with an elongated right arm from carrying heavy materials, or with a thick waist from copper wiring wrapped round it. It was comparatively rare for the police to pick someone up; they'd tend only to be called in to check someone's home if they were caught stealing by the guards. So that was pretty smart of him to have noticed someone struggling down the road with a heavy bag.

On their normal police rounds on the beat, local shopkeepers used to chat, and an elderly woman would beckon Ryan inside to help her change light bulbs or do other little odd jobs. Even then, some police would take advantage of the warm welcome. Two days after Ryan's first arrest, a constable was introducing him to a few of the locals when he disappeared upstairs at the butcher's shop. Ryan was left downstairs drinking tea with the butcher until his re-emergence half an hour later, his face curiously flushed. Ryan learned later he'd been having a passionate affair with the butcher's wife.

With the factories churning out thick black smoke, and most homes burning coal fires, the air could be extremely polluted, and officers were often advised to wear masks to walk their beat. They also had to go down the mines whenever there was an accident, to record the incident or describe deaths for the coroner, down among bodies crushed beneath great slippages of coal or earth or people who'd lost arms or legs.

The main railway line between Manchester and Liverpool was also a source of grisly memories. Very early one cold, drizzly, foggy morning, a train pulled into Little Hulton with a severed arm hanging over the buffer at the front. Ryan and two other officers were called to the suicide scene. There was nothing for it but to walk back down the rails, picking up all the pieces of mangled flesh scattered when the train ploughed into the man who'd stood in front of it. Ryan was sent in search of something to hold all the bits of the body, and went into the local shop, begging for bags or boxes. The owner emptied a giant cardboard box that had been holding Kellogg's Cornflakes packets, and the three men walked slowly down the railway line, tossing bloodied chunks of the man's torn body into the box they dragged behind them. They put the box in a hearse to go to the mortuary, and then went back to the police station for breakfast. In those days, there was no such thing as a trauma debrief team waiting back at the station. 'The thing is, if you didn't put experiences to one side you'd never get over them,' says Ryan. 'I think today we encourage stress with all this counselling and welfare. It can have the effect of making people think they're ill or under stress when they're not. We give them this stress; we deliver it to them with the welfare packet.'

Instead, the three men ate breakfast, then simply stood, warming themselves by the coal fire. The sergeant, Joe Seddon, then went off to make the tea – his way of showing he cared, since tea-making always fell to the junior officer. Over the radio came the news bulletin, topped by Parliament's vote the night before to give police a pay rise of three shillings and fourpence a week. Then the item cut to an MP questioning whether the police were worth the pay rise. The two men stood and looked at each other. 'I wonder,' Ryan said finally, 'if that man would have done what we have just been doing with those cornflakes boxes for an extra three and fourpence.'

But there were moments of black comedy, too. A man dropped dead of a heart attack on his kitchen floor, and Ryan accompanied a younger constable to report the death and then went to the mortuary at Bolton District Hospital to see the body laid-out. When the pathologist snapped on his rubber gloves, the officer gasped, fainted and smashed through an instrument cabinet, cutting his face on the glass. Passers-by could only stand, open-mouthed, as a body on a trolley was rushed *out* of the mortuary at top-speed and into the casualty section. There was much muttering about how this one couldn't have been dead at all, with onlookers devoutly crossing themselves. Another day, Ryan was walking through when, out of the corner of his eye, he thought he saw a body's hand twitch. As he approached the body, suddenly a loud groan rent the air and, white-faced and frozen to the spot, he watched as the body slowly sat up. It was one of his fellow officers, inducting him into the time-honoured tradition of the mortuary practical joke.

Yet despite his attempts to look unfazed by his mortuary visits, his sister Maureen says they did affect him. I remember the day he went to a post mortem for the first time,' she says. 'He was very upset when they put the organs back inside the body. They didn't rearrange them where they should have been, they just shoved them back in. I can remember the horror on his face as he told us about it.'

His sergeants, Seddon and Albert Jordan, tried to pass on to the handsome young constable everything learned in decades in the job. But, first, Seddon took Ryan out for a drive. Telling him to pull over, suddenly, he pointed out two pretty girls walking on the opposite side of the road. 'They're nice girls,' he said. 'What do you think of them?' When Ryan, confused, nodded, Seddon turned to face him. 'They're my daughters,' he said. 'They're nice girls, and I want them to stay that way. I don't want you or any of your mates anywhere near them.' At the same time, Seddon was also fiercely protective of his men. He wasn't happy to hear one of his officers, John Blake, talking about his impending wedding, at which Ryan was due to be best man. He felt they were far too young to be getting married, and did his best to per-suade them so. Women were only after their money, he declared, and they had to escape them in any way they could – and the more dis-tance they put between themselves and marriage, the better. 'I'll tell you something,' he said. 'As soon as money goes out of the door, love goes out of the window.' He put a ten-shilling note in front of John and another ten in front of Ryan. 'I'll give you ten shillings,' he said. 'That's all you need to get to Australia.'

While that might have provided a handy shortcut to his later life, Ryan wasn't tempted. He was enjoying his job too much. His time away from work wasn't quite so satisfying, however. The couple in whose house he lived were so devout, they'd frequently give his bed to a visiting priest or nun, and leave him a note at night to sleep on the sofa downstairs. He couldn't do much about it. At that stage, the police service controlled nearly every aspect of its officers' lives, from where they lived to what they did in their spare time. Getting a girlfriend pregnant was a sackable offence, says Watkinson, and you weren't allowed to marry until you were 25 or had completed two years' service, whichever came first. Weekends, Ryan would go back home to Lancaster, and visit his girlfriend Barbara, an accounts clerk whom he'd met at 18 at a dance at Morecambe Pier. Each time, it seemed, he arrived back in a different car. It used to be a source of great amusement to Maureen.

He used continually to be buying old cars. He once had three Jags in quick succession. Once, he took me for a ride in one that had belonged to a businessman in Manchester and had a bar in the back. He started off, then stopped at a garage and asked for one single gallon of petrol. All his money had gone into the car. He couldn't even afford to fill it up.

At work, his arrest figures increased steadily. Everyone at that point was broke, and he discovered he could stand outside any factory and stop virtually anyone and find they were stealing something. One man wheeling out his bicycle had tyres almost flattened from the weight of what it was carrying – Ryan discovered the frame had been filled with mercury. At night, you could go to the coal heaps at the back of the mines and just listen to people shovelling coal into sacks to lug home. He even pursued, on his big, heavy old bicycle, a local character he thought might have stolen the motor scooter he was riding with his friend on the back. Ryan was peddling furiously, and losing ground, when the pair skidded and fell off in a heap. The driver ran away, but he managed to catch and arrest his pillion passenger. There seemed to be nothing for it but to handcuff his prisoner to the bicycle and make him push it back to the station. When the pair arrived, however, the sergeant in charge ordered Ryan to walk back to the scooter, pick it up and drive it back to the station. Of course, it wouldn't start, so he had to push it all the way back. By the time he got round to the man's house he'd initially suspected of stealing the scooter, it was 1 a.m. and his mother said he was asleep in bed. Ryan went up to his room, marched over to his bed and pulled back the covers – to find the man fully dressed, covered in mud and grass, underneath.

I could actually smell a crook and I could spot people who were acting wrongly. I could almost say that this car coming down the street has been stolen. I just had that feeling, I don't know what it was, I just had this instinct. Often when I stopped a car, if the people inside hadn't stolen it, they'd have just broken into a house and had everything in the boot. So I had a very high arrest rate and, before you knew where you were, I was seconded to the detectives, even though I was still a trainee probationary constable.

He was given a chilling introduction to his new job, investigating the murder of a young woman who'd been walking home at night across the building sites that marked out the new town. Her killer was eventually caught when he attacked another woman who escaped his clutches. Ryan won a fresh round of kudos after he investigated a case where a woman, high on drugs and drunk on port wine, had stepped out in front of a train on the railway line and been instantly killed. Others tried to close the case as an accident, but Ryan insisted there was far more to her death than caught the eye. The trail took him to a Manchester club, where he uncovered the fact that she'd been forced to work as a sex slave in a bizarre racket run by a Jamaican man. Six weeks later, detectives from the Manchester City police called to say they had a similar case, and that they'd be taking over his. A couple of months later, the *News of the World* newspaper ran a huge centrespread on the bust of a Jamaican and his drugs and sex-slavery organisation, praising the Manchester city detectives for their skill at uncovering the scandal.

It was a good time to be part of what was an extraordinarily innovative Lancashire Constabulary. Police radios, at the time, looked like huge backpacks with an aerial on the top. They were as clumsy as they were impractical, but the Lancashire force came up with a portable radio, the LANCON, about the same size as a cigarette packet, worn on a harness under the uniform with an earpiece and microphone that came up the side. By 1964, says Bob Dobson, every officer in the county carried one – and forces throughout the UK were eagerly putting in orders. It made an incredible difference to police effectiveness. Previously, each police officer would have to nominate a time they'd be passing a particular public phone box so the station could ring the officer to give them a job. An incident would take up to an hour to elicit a response. Suddenly, officers were available and immediately contactable. At about the same time phones became more generally available, with a corresponding sharp rise in the number of reports of problems to police. In the early 1960s too, there were experiments with a mix of foot and car patrols. This mix was so spectacularly successful, that 175 Ford Anglias, dubbed by St John's deputy Bill Palfrey 'pandas' for their broad blue stripes and white patches, were put into commission in Lancashire in 1966.

The year before, in 1965, Ryan had achieved every young policeman's dream: a spot in the divisional patrol-car unit. This was the high-profile real-life Z Cars, a squad of detectives and uniform police with high-powered, unmarked cars, with the radio call sign 'Zed Kilo One'. It was a thrilling time. This unit was the only one where police had cars (the six-cylinder Zephyr Zodiacs) and the only ones with radios in the cars, and so they were sent to all the major crime jobs, from potential suicides to murders, from assaults to robberies, anything that required immediate action. There were patrols to guard the wages going from banks to industry, which were, in those times, always paid in cash. There were murder scenes to race to. There were assaults, especially domestics, including the one when a policeman arrived home unexpectedly from work to find his wife in bed with a fellow officer.

It could be dangerous for the team, too. One night, a Z Car was chasing a car full of armed robbers who'd been wanted for months. Ryan's car was heading towards them from the opposite direction. As he came out of a side road, the robbers' car hit a traffic island, took off, sailed through the air straight over his car, touching the roof with its wheels, and then crashed to the ground, rolled over and ended up in a men's clothes shop window among all the dummies. Everyone involved, including Ryan and his colleagues, could easily have been killed.

But Ryan was in his element. 'It was the job everyone wanted,' he says. 'We were the real glamour boys of the force. We had a big, fast, powerful car, all the exciting jobs and total free range. It was what I'd always imagined life in the police would be like.'

They were halcyon days for an ambitious young copper with a taste for flash cars and the road ahead seemed filled with excitement and adventure. But in his private life, trouble was just around the corner.

CHAPTER 3

Love fails to conquer all

THE CAR CAME out of nowhere. Absolutely nowhere. One minute, Ryan and his mate Reg Robinson were barrelling down a clear country road, third in a rally for the police versus the army in North Wales. The next, they rounded a bend to see a car turn out of a farm track right in front of them, there was a thunderclap of an explosion and their car crumpled like a cigarette packet around them.

The next thing Ryan knew, they were surrounded by blue flashing lights, being cut out of the wreckage. His arms were covered in blood and pinned down by the side of the caved-in car, and his legs and knees were badly cut. Robinson, his co-driver who'd been navigating at the time, was, however, lying quite still. 'Reg! Reg!' cried Ryan, unable to move his arms even to touch him. 'Please don't leave me!'

Happily he didn't, and both men were eventually freed and rushed from the accident site at, appropriately enough, World's End, near Holywell, to hospital. They spent the next two weeks there, being X-rayed, stitched up and recovering from their injuries. The smash proved a turning point in Ryan's life, however. Until then, he'd loved nothing more than indulging his passion for both cars and speed, competing in car rallies across the country. He'd been good at it, too. But while he'd won a number of minor events, it was proving an expensive hobby on a constable's wage and without any form of sponsorship. A serious crash would also mean insurance would probably prove impossible in the future. And then there was his girlfriend Barbara. She was adamant: this was the end.

It was bad enough for Barbara going out with a police officer who was only back in town at weekends – and only then if he wasn't at a rally. She wanted a more serious, committed relationship. Ryan felt ready, too. It wasn't easy for a young man to live in digs all week with a couple who were zealous Christians, however kindly they were, and then spend weekends back at his parents'. It was 1965 and he was 21, about the sort of age most of his friends were getting married. She was also 21, and thinking it was time to settle down, just like everyone else. They had a good time together and had plenty of friends in common. Also, the police service was so autocratic at that time that it prohibited single people from setting up home on their own until they'd completed at least five years in the force. When you married, on the other hand, you were given a police house in the area where you worked.

Still, Ryan's parents weren't all that keen. They thought he was too young and really ought to wait a few years. 'But you're foolish when you're young,' says Ryan. 'We actually got on very well with each other. Barbara was an extremely nice person, very gentle, very quiet, spoke in a very quiet way, and had a very pretty face and a very good figure.' They ended up drifting into marriage, exchanging vows in late 1965.

Things didn't work out quite how they planned, however. There was a brand new police house available on a council estate in the middle of Little Hulton but, at the last minute, the couple were told the sergeant wanted it instead. They'd have to move into digs together, as there weren't any other police houses available locally. Barbara was distraught. She hadn't really ever wanted to move away from her tight-knit family in the first place; but to go to live as a newlywed in someone else's house seemed the worst of all available options. Besides, the one house they found, although it was warm and neat, was far from satisfactory. The elderly woman who lived there routinely burst into their bedroom in the middle of the night shrieking, 'Bill! Bill! You've got to get up! It's time to say Mass!' Her long-dead brother, a priest called Bill, was apparently the spitting image of Ryan. After three weeks, the couple could take it no more and fled, moving in temporarily with some friends of Barbara's, while Ryan searched for a place for them to live.

Barbara found a job organising orders for production at a local food factory, which she enjoyed, but she was fast losing patience at having to camp at her friends'. Salvation, however, seemed close at hand. Finally, the police service realised it would have to buy more houses to accommodate the officers that had been taken on in the big recruitment drive, and sent Ryan along to look at a place they were considering buying. It was a lovely, semi-detached house in a nice part of town. Australia was once again to the fore. The owner was emigrating and offered to sell Ryan everything, from the bed linen to the cutlery. It seemed ideal for a couple just starting out on life together. Ryan went back to the station and said he'd like to take the house, so the police force agreed to buy. But two weeks later, just as he and Barbara were on the point of moving in, they were told there'd been a change of plan. The sergeant who'd taken the police house preferred the new house instead. His wife hadn't liked the council estate at all. She'd wanted something grander. So instead, Ryan and Barbara moved into the original police house.

From the very first, Barbara hated it. She started going home every weekend to her mother's. Ryan was working long, long hours and was virtually on nightshift for a six-month stretch. Officers weren't paid any overtime; they were just expected to work when-ever they were needed. Barbara felt as if she hardly saw him. For Ryan, it was a great deal easier. After eighteen months with Z Cars, the experiment was broadened and the squadron was renamed 'Task Force', covering a wider area, across the whole of north Manchester, Liverpool, Ashton-under-Lyme and Oldham. The glamour factor remained. Another TV series, 'Softly Softly', a spin-off from 'Z Cars', began shortly after. It lasted for ten years, although later renamed 'Softly, Softly: Task Force'.

Ryan loved the job. Well, mostly. While he enjoyed racing around the country catching crooks, there were also mountains of paper-work to fill in every night, and the more tiresome operational duties to perform. Roger Farrington, a sergeant working with him, remem-bers the long days working together in the operations room, sitting at the twenty-foot-long desk with its telephones, switchboards, radios and the two communications boxes placed at the foot and the head of the table into which calls from the emergency phones on the

M6 motorway came. One morning, everyone but he and Ryan had gone to breakfast when all hell broke loose during the 8 a.m. to 9 a.m. peak hour. Farrington was answering the phone from the divisions and domestic calls, while Ryan was sitting at one of the boxes, logging all the problems that were being called in. Then the emergency box at the other end of the table started ringing with details of an accident. Immediately, the box at the other end rang to report a breakdown. Ryan raced between the two for a solid hour, asking one to hold on while he dealt with the other, then asking the other to call back in five minutes while he solved another problem. The phones rang and rang and rang, and Ryan dashed backwards and forwards, backwards and forwards.

After work, he'd often go drinking with detectives when they'd swap stories of their exciting days – or nights. It was infinitely preferable to going home to a bleak house and an unhappy wife. He and Barbara drifted further and further apart. About the same time, Barbara started complaining of feeling ill and would sometimes be so sick, she could barely get out of bed. She'd be bad for a few days, then would be fine again. After visiting the doctor for tests, she found she had a kidney disease.

A move for Ryan to Preston, much closer to home in Lancaster, couldn't have come at a better time. He'd applied for a new scheme of police scholarships to university, and been accepted in the second intake for a three-year degree course. When the new University of Lancaster was being built, Lancashire Chief Constable Eric St Johnston had twisted the arms of each divisional superintendent to give a donation, says police historian Bob Dobson. That paved the way for special arrangements between the university and the force, which had decided it wanted to increase the number of officers who had degrees. It was a tough scholarship to win, however. Apart from a written exam, there were a series of interviews, first with the Police Board and only then with the university itself. Tommy Watkinson was one of the officers on the board.

We were looking for officers who were going to be leader material. When we were interviewing officers you'd ask them to come into the room and then if they sat down, we'd say, 'Who

gave you permission to sit? Go back and start again.' If an inter-
viewee pulled their chair closer to the desk we'd ask them why
they think we put the chair in that position in the first place.
They might have a short temper – it was one way of finding that
out. They might wear jeans for the university interview, but we
refused to see them if they weren't dressed properly.

Ryan was chosen to be part of the first-ever intake of officers, and was
moved to Preston to give him a taste of life at the Lancashire Police
HQ. Barbara was delighted. A house in Preston, even though it was
just another police house, was so much nearer to her family. They
moved in, but immediately she fell ill again. This time, it was serious.
Ryan rushed her to hospital where the surgeon told Ryan she'd have
to have a kidney removed. He was sorry, but it would mean she'd
never be able to have children. 'She'll be all right, though, won't she?'
asked Ryan, wondering how long she'd be under anaesthetic. The
surgeon looked grim. 'She's got a 50–50 chance of recovery.'
  He sent Ryan back home and told him to return later that afternoon after the operation. He came back to the hospital as soon as he
was allowed, and raced to Barbara's bedside. He sat there, holding
her hand as she lay sleeping, terrified she'd never recover, and wondering how she'd cope with the news that she'd never be a mother.
The hours ticked by. Finally, the doctor called by just as Barbara was
coming round. 'Oh,' he said airily, 'we didn't have to do that operation after all. We did a laparoscopy instead and we can treat the
damaged kidney with antibiotics.'
  The ordeal brought Ryan and Barbara closer together, and the
prospect of moving close to the university, living back in Lancaster,
cheered Barbara immensely. This time too, Ryan pleaded with his
bosses to let him buy a home. There were no police houses available
near the university, he told them, and he was having huge difficulties finding a place to rent. If they allowed him to buy a house, he
promised to sell it the minute he finished his course. Finally, his
supervisors relented, and the couple bought for £2500 a pretty four-
bedroom bungalow in Lancaster. Barbara found a new job with her
family's car-parts business nearby. Everything seemed rosy. But that
second honeymoon wasn't to last.

Ryan was thrilled at the chance to go to university and, as only the fourth officer to be accepted, was determined to make a go of it. He was allowed to study whatever he liked, and he threw himself wholeheartedly into his course in politics, philosophy and history. But it wasn't always easy. Ryan was a 24 year old studying with people who were generally just 18. While everyone else was growing their hair long and wearing baggy, hippie clothes Ryan, according to his old schoolfriend Tony Halliwell, 'still liked to dress smartly. He didn't have any of the scruffiness that most students did. He was still very particular about what he wore.' His casual dress at the time was sports jacket, shirt and tie. At one of his first tutorials, a student stood up and gave him his chair when he walked in. Puzzled, he thanked him and sat down, but it was only when everyone else shuffled their chairs around to face him that he realised they thought he was the lecturer.

The late 1960s were a period of unprecedented student unrest around the world, and Lancaster was no exception. There were major demonstrations across the country against the Vietnam War, there were sit-ins, love-ins, pickets and pot-smoking, and occasionally lectures would be disrupted by students rushing in, setting off firecrackers, claiming they were bombs. That placed Ryan frequently in the odd position of being a lone police officer in a crowd of rebellious students. Sometimes, he was even accused of working at the university as a spy for the authorities. He tended then to keep his distance, feeling sure that even the most outspoken ones would eventually cut their hair, shave off their beards and knuckle-down to earning a wage. One of the firecracker throwers, who often dressed in a white sheet daubed with red ink, was far too busy demonstrating to attend lectures. He was always friendly nevertheless. On one of the final exam days, he stumbled into the hall high on pot, sat down, wrote the words, 'I know Fuck All' on the paper and stood back up again. For a moment he stayed still, looking around the room, until he happened to catch Ryan's eye. The two men gazed at each other in a moment of quiet understanding. Then, he waved, shouted a cheery, 'See you, Pete!' across the bent heads of all the other students, and marched straight out.

A couple of years later, Ryan was called to an emergency at one of the high bridges arching over the River Lune near Lancaster. A man was dangling from the parapets of the bridge, yelling that he was about to let go; he wanted to die. Ryan took a deep breath and started to speak to him quietly, desperately hoping to persuade him to climb back up to safety. The man grew silent and twisted around to face him. Ryan was shocked to the core to see that same 'firecracker man'. It had only been five years since they'd started out as eager students at the university, both filled with the hope, dreams and idealism of the young. What strange tricks fate could play. 'You're Peter Ryan,' the man said to him quietly. The man eventually agreed to climb down from the bridge. Ryan touched him lightly on the shoulder and led him to a car that would drive him to the local detox centre.

Most students, in any case, seemed to enjoy having an older colleague around, and Ryan was regularly approached for help and advice when things got tough. Counselling took up a fair bit of his free time, as did the usual university student rounds of dances, concerts, reviews and late-night discussions about the meaning of life with fellow students. He joined the Conservative Association, more for the social aspect than anything else, particularly because they tended to invite good speakers along to address the students. He also became involved in the student union, then called the Student Council, finishing up as president of his college. In his final year – quite amazingly for a police officer during such a radicalised student time – he stood for president of the union, then the Student Representative Council. Ten days before the election, however, he decided he should concentrate on his degree, and stopped campaigning. With his heart in his mouth, he discovered he was still only beaten by three votes. The successful candidate went on to fail his degree.

All this time, Ryan was drifting further and further from Barbara. A cosy domestic life seemed a world away from the excitement of university, and it was continually difficult to bridge the gap between the two. 'I think she felt threatened by me moving intellectually in a different direction, if you like,' says Ryan. 'Becoming a student meant you took part in all the student activities and I think she felt different and separate and not part of the gang. When we went to student functions, she was obviously out of it. These were all silly

students and she was a woman now. Tensions began to creep in.'
Graduating with his degree, however, now as a sergeant, meant the
pair would both be back leading a normal life. They hoped things
would settle back into their old pattern.

Ryan was slotted into the fast-track career development program
and put to work in Lancaster, first in uniform, then as a detective
and finally back – much to his horror – on highway patrol. He'd
already done that, he felt, and while he tried to reassure himself that
it was to make sure his policing experience was well-rounded, he
secretly suspected it was because there was a real backlash from the
rest of the force against the few who'd been paid to go off to university. His sister Maureen, watching on the sidelines, had her own
opinion. 'It was a good time to be in the police as these were their
first degrees,' she says. 'But it can't have been easy for him. It must
have made him many enemies. He probably *had* to learn to be thick-
skinned.' It was to prove a valuable lesson.

Ryan knuckled back down, and soon started attracting attention all
over again for the long hours he put in, and the way he organised the
people under him. His team was just an eighth of the total strength of
the station, but he was proud to have chalked up one-third its number of arrests – more than the whole of CID put together.

It was the way I ran the team and let the lads work through our
problems and deployment. Our arrest record, as a result, was
extraordinarily high. A lot of officers wanted to get on our team.
My people were always being poached to CID or promoted to
other teams. I was ambitious. When I started, I realised I could
do pretty well because the competition wasn't all that hot. By the
time I was doing my final course as a probationer, my colleagues
could see I was a bit different. I was tough. I put in hard yakka
to get promoted, to get established. I was always watching my
back, always looking to see how the boss operates, what does he
do? What do I need to know to do it? I set myself targets.

Watkinson was deputy in charge of Ryan's division at the time, and
remembers being impressed. 'He was a very intelligent, hard-working,
very presentable fellow,' he says. 'He was a good-looking man. I used

to say, "Lock up your daughters!" He showed a lot of promise early on. He was a very good organiser.'

Ryan was also playing to a home-team advantage. Because he'd grown up in Lancaster, many people knew him, and he was often in the newspapers. He became known as the sergeant who locked everyone up – popular among many of the law-abiding townsfolk, less so among others. He began to get used to making enemies. One day, he went to the rescue of a traffic officer who'd been almost strangled with his own tie by a local scrap-metal dealer he'd stopped to breathalyse. Going round to the dealer's house later to arrest him, Ryan was set upon by the man in his bedroom, while his wife called his mates on the phone for reinforcements. He had just managed to overpower the man when the wife threw her six-month-old baby at him, so he let go of his prisoner to catch the child. In the meantime, the wife dragged her husband from the room by his hair. Ryan then put the baby down, leapt over the bed and managed to grab the man again, handcuff him, and drag him down the stairs. A crowd had gathered outside, and Ryan ran a gauntlet of sticks, rocks and abuse as he pulled the man into his van. Later, the man was jailed for six months for grievous bodily harm to the traffic officer, resisting arrest and assaulting Ryan. His wife and her sisters, outside the courthouse, screamed over to Ryan, 'You're going to die! You're going to die!'

A week later, Ryan was told a contract had been put out to have him beaten up. He asked a couple of his officers to come with him, then strolled down to the family's stronghold, a noisy, smoke-filled pub in the backstreets of Lancaster. As he walked in, the pub fell silent. Ryan walked over to the bar and turned around to face the room. 'Right,' he said. 'I understand someone wants to come and do me over. Who's going to be the first?' He took off his police hat and placed it carefully on the bar. 'Let's start again shall we?' he said in a louder voice, this time. 'I believe money's going to be paid to beat me up. Now, who's going to be the first one?' There was a soft murmur of voices around the room, but nobody did anything. Ryan held his breath. Still nothing. Finally, he picked his hat back up. 'Right!' he said. 'Let this be the end!' He walked out. After that, he received a number of abusive phone calls at home, and threats. But nothing happened, and soon they too died out. 'I got a reputation for being a hard man, someone who faces down criminals,' says Ryan. 'But it was always a gamble. Do you handle it that way or ignore it? I took the choice I've taken more or less my whole life: to go in and face up to it, and say, "Let's do it now." You should never let such things fester.'

When Ryan was moved on to highway patrol, he used the experience he'd gleaned on the Z Cars to turn a group of officers who had been all about radar traps and catching speeding motorists into a proper crime-fighting force. What was the point of the traffic division having the best radios, blue lights, fast cars and great equipment merely to catch people committing minor traffic offences? he reasoned. While the unit was becoming more and more important because of the motorways opening in Lancashire – Britain's first being the Preston bypass in 1958 – Ryan used to take selected men out on patrol at night, and teach them how to spot stolen cars, or the signs of people returning from housebreaking or robbery. He'd instruct them on how to think ahead in high-speed chases, working out where offenders might drive to, where they could give their pursuers the slip, where to position cars to best catch them if they drove up a dead-end and tried to run away. It completely transformed the unit. For the first time, they became a pro-active force, arresting people for theft, and getting involved in high-speed chases if motorists driving eccentrically, and thus suspiciously, failed to stop when flashed with police headlights. At the same time, he was known as an officer who knew the law inside out, another legacy of his years filing, which meant he could write charge sheets up without having to refer to books at all, significantly speeding up the whole process.

But it was a double-edged sword. He was popular with his team, but less so with some of his superior officers. Graduating from his five-week advanced driving course, Assistant Chief Constable Jack Allen quizzed him on how many speeders he'd caught that month. 'Probably a couple, sir,' said Ryan, 'but twelve people for housebreaking, car-stealing and assault.' Allen merely frowned. 'But what have you done to keep road traffic offences down?' he barked. 'I'm not interested in criminals. There you have a traffic sergeant and he hasn't booked many people. Typical! What a short-sighted hare-brain!' Embarrassed and annoyed, it made Ryan all the more determined to climb the ladder. Certainly, he was confident and self-opinionated to the point some might think him brash and pushy, but he tended to see it more in terms of being an innovator eager to improve the force, despite sometimes having stick-in-the-mud idiots above him. It was the kind of clash between the old and the new that would occur many more times in the future.

In 1972, Chief Constable Bill Palfrey dropped into the station, and proved himself a supporter. In front of everyone, he called Ryan over and asked, 'How would you feel about being inspector?' Ryan could only nod, dumbly. The only vacancy, however, was in Barrow-in-Furness, a small shipbuilding town on the Cumbrian coast in the far north-west of England. He declined, politely. The rumours about an imminent police service reorganisation were growing in strength, and Ryan didn't want to end up, because of boundary changes, in the Cumbrian force instead of the Lancashire one. Instead, he waited on and, six months later, over Allen's opposition, was promoted to an inspector in Lancashire HQ in Preston.

He was thrilled at this huge jump in rank; Barbara was appalled. Even though Preston was only thirty-seven kilometres away on the motorway, and the motorway was just five minutes away from their house, officers, at that time, weren't allowed to travel more than a few miles from their home to their station. The couple would have to move house again, this time back into a police house as only exceptional circumstances last time had allowed them to buy, leaving their beautiful home in Lancaster – and Barbara's family and job – behind. Besides, there was still a fair amount of resentment around that they had such a pleasant home in the first place. Allen insisted they move. Watkinson, aware that Barbara didn't want to shift, had a private chat with Ryan. 'You'll do as you're told,' he recalls telling Ryan. 'My job was to get use out of the men who came back from university. The control room always needed good people, and it was a chance to do well in head office.'

Barbara did everything she could to dissuade Ryan from taking the position. Her sister's husband, Peter Gardiner, had gone into business with his brother David when their father retired, buying a haulage company to move cattle around Britain. She talked to him, and Gardiner asked Ryan to join the business, overseeing the operational side, while he and his brother worked the books and touted for more clients. The company was expanding rapidly, and Ryan knew it would afford him a good living and a comfortable life in a big stone house on the moors, with a nice car and a happy wife. But, suddenly, he could see a bright future in the police service, and he wanted to keep going to see how close he could get. He turned Gardiner down and accepted Preston.

Barbara couldn't come to terms with his decision. When he took her to see their new home, a cold, damp, grim, rundown house on a bad bend in a narrow lane, close to the police dog-training centre, with dogs barking all hours, and dogs and their handlers often slinking through the back garden in the dead of night on various training exercises, she was appalled. 'You must be joking!' she exclaimed. 'There's no way I'm going to leave where we're living for this. And you call this a promotion!' She wouldn't budge. He couldn't really blame her. The house, unlike their home in Lancaster, had no central heating, and on some bitterly cold nights ice would form on the *inside* of the windows. Ryan had to keep the windows open to let the warmer air from outside, in. The bath was so rusty it had eaten away all the enamel. The woodwork outside the house even had teethmarks where the police dogs had exercised their jaws as they passed. In the end, Barbara stayed in Lancaster and Ryan only partly furnished the Preston house, just enough to make it look as though they'd moved in, while he continued to spend most nights with her.

Only occasionally did he sleep in Preston, when the hours made it too difficult to drive back home again, for his new job was demanding. He'd been posted to the control room in charge of the whole of the communications service, a position seen as an excellent stepping-stone for officers' careers. A few weeks after he'd started the new job in 1973, he joined four other young officers on a Rotary Club exchange program to see how parallel professions work overseas. His nemesis Allen had protested that he'd only just begun as an inspector and shouldn't go, but it was too late. Ryan's group had already been allocated a trip to North Carolina for eight weeks to see how American officers did the job and he had to take six weeks' leave to be allowed to go. It opened his eyes not only to policing overseas, but the kind of experiences he'd never imagined he might have. Even the trip over was eventful. The BOAC jet landed in New

York, there was a helicopter troop carrier waiting with a group of Vietnam War soldiers for the short trip to Newark, then there was the flight to North Carolina. On board, everyone was asked to vote on whether they were happy to land in the midst of a massive storm sweeping across from the coast, bearing in mind there was a handsome reception waiting. They agreed and the plane seemed to fall like a stone out of the sky to land with a bang on the ground. 'My God!' said the pilot, turning to his ashen-faced passengers. 'I nearly chickened out there at the last few yards. Careful when you get out – the wind will blow you over.'

Ryan was shocked to see prisoners in ankle shackles mopping out one local jail and police station, and amazed to accompany officers on 'moonshine' patrols, trying to catch people making illicit liquor in the woods of the State. The moonshiners' cars had tanks in the doors, or would have tanks slung underneath the chassis. It felt strangely like the 1920s of the Prohibition, rather than the 1970s. There were other dark sides too. One night, he was invited out for a few beers with the boys. It turned out to be a Ku Klux Klan meeting, full of people wearing hoods and swearing allegiance to each other. 'What's it like,' one person asked Ryan, 'living in a country twenty-five years behind the times?' 'I don't know,' he replied. 'I'm not going to be here long enough to find out.' No one laughed.

But Allen, still smarting over Ryan's promotion, had a miserable surprise waiting on his return. He'd noticed while driving past that the grass at the front of the Preston house hadn't been cut. He ordered a superintendent to check Ryan's dustbins. Finally, Ryan was exposed as disobeying the rules, and not living in the house which he'd been allocated. He was hauled up before the Deputy Chief Constable, John Moody, disciplined, and ordered to stay in the house. It was just before Christmas 1973, but it was the beginning of the end of his marriage. Ryan and Barbara began living quite separate lives, he in Preston and she in Lancaster. They both found new circles of friends, they did different things, and they even started seeing other people. It was heartbreaking, but it wasn't going to be the last time he sacrificed love for his career.

Maureen wasn't in the least surprised about the separation. She liked Barbara, but she didn't see the pair as particularly well matched.

She was very nice and very sweet. But my view was that she was very much a family girl, wanting to be at home with her mum and her sisters. Peter definitely wouldn't have got where he is today with Barbara; she didn't want to leave home, really. Still lives there, in the same area. She was probably way behind his aspirations. She didn't have the confidence or education to be there.

Yet the couple managed to stay on good terms. One day, Barbara phoned Ryan to tell him a storm had blown up overnight and had torn down the high fence around the house. He got together with a few friends and went over, tidied up the debris and built a new wall with sixteen tonnes of bricks, all of which he moved by hand in a day. That night, Barbara asked him if he'd like to stay – in the spare bedroom. He said he would, but why didn't they go out to dinner beforehand, just for old time's sake? At 3 a.m., an hour after they'd got back, the phone rang. Barbara flew into Ryan's room and shook him awake. 'My mother's dead,' she told him, flatly. 'They were looking for me when I was out with you. If I'd been here, I would have gone straight to the hospital. I might have seen her before she died . . .' Any chance of a reconciliation, they both knew, had died with her mother. The next morning, Ryan packed his clothes silently, walked out of the house, and never saw her again. After eight years of marriage, they were divorced by mutual consent a year later.

CHAPTER 4

On the
up and up

IT WAS A quiet evening in the control room at Lancashire Police HQ when the switchboard lit up with news that shattered peace on mainland Britain. It was 21 November 1974, and two massive explosions had gone off simultaneously, ripping through two crowded Birmingham pubs, just 300 metres apart. The pubs had been full of people having a drink on their way home from work or stopping off before they started their nightshift. Twenty-one people were killed and 162 injured, either directly from the blasts or from being crushed by falling masonry. In The Tavern in the Town, the ceiling had collapsed, the bar was blown against a wall and a fireball had screamed up the stairs. At The Mulberry Bush, great chunks of the building had come smashing to the ground.

A group of four or five men had been seen immediately afterwards walking away from the bloodied scenes of carnage, and could have boarded the Irish boat train that stopped at the port of Heysham just near Lancaster, the main ferry port to Belfast. These men were urgently needed for questioning. Ryan, supervising the control room, reacted quickly. He circulated the description of the men to the special units on duty at the ports, and passed on the order to arrest them on sight. Just minutes later, a group of men answering the description were spotted and taken into custody.

These men were part of the group who later became known as the 'Birmingham Six', alleged to have been responsible for the worst-ever IRA bombing campaign against civilians in history. The following year, the men – Hugh Callaghan, Patrick Hill, Robert Hunter, Noel McIlkenny, William Power and John Walker – were convicted and each sentenced to twenty-one terms of life imprisonment at the end of Britain's then longest and most expensive murder trial. After serving sixteen years behind bars, they were released in 1991 on appeal, when the forensic evidence against them was discredited. The traces of a substance found on their hands, which had originally been analysed as gelignite, could also have come, it was revealed, from handling playing cards, cigarette packets, or soap.

It was Ryan's first brush with the IRA, but it wasn't to be his last. The IRA had stepped up its bombing campaign on mainland Britain, and terrorist threats and warnings were on the increase. Later, Ryan would play a much more active role in trying to foil IRA activity, and would be rewarded for his efforts by being named as a target on their own hit list.

But, at that stage, he was still finding his way in his new job as an inspector in the control room at Lancashire Police HQ and, newly divorced at only 29, he threw himself into his work. It was a position of great responsibility. If there was any major incident anywhere in the county, his task was to co-ordinate the police and emergency response. If there was a murder, he had to alert investigators, pathologists, forensic staff and organise everyone's transport. And, on top of that, there was all the routine stuff to manage in one of the busiest counties in England.

'He did very well there,' says Tommy Watkinson. 'He was a good organiser, he was intelligent and he was popular. He was also ambitious. He always had an eye to the main chance. Some people would reach a certain level and were happy to stay there. Others were always looking around, showing an interest in everything going on. I knew he'd go higher, and he did.'

Out of work, he lived hard, too. He made firm friends with a group of three other male officers and met them every Friday night for a drink. Often, they'd all end up at his police house – after all, he didn't have a wife they might disturb – for a curry and a chat. They were happy days, a group of mates together with no responsibilities, but often they didn't stay alone for long. One time, Ryan formed a relationship with Linda, a receptionist who worked with them in the control room. Another time they were all out when Ryan started talking to a pretty young woman, Elaine, at the bar. They started going out together, and he helped her restore her old farmhouse in the Lancashire countryside. Then there was the local newspaper reporter Gillian.

'He was never without a lady friend,' says David Holt, whose daughter, Jessica, is Ryan's god-daughter. 'He was good looking and he was charming, and girls just fell for him.' It was a long-established pattern. Maureen remembers that, even as a kid, he was in a group of boys who had lots of girlfriends, and was always the romantic. 'There were so many evenings he'd spend in his bedroom with a friend, playing the Everly Brothers over and over again, "Dream, dream, dream".' Time only added to his charms, says Holt. His ex, Barbara, had obviously loved him deeply. Even today, remarried, she refuses to talk about their split, she found it so painful. 'It's a long time ago now,' she says. 'It's now a closed book. It wasn't the happiest time. A break-up in a marriage is always difficult, but it's now part of my life that's over. I'm very, very happy now. I've never been happier.' She still lives very close to her family in Ellel, an area six kilometres south of Lancaster and a kilometre and a half away from Galgate, where she grew up.

Holt says that kind of female attachment to Ryan was very much par for the course. Linda was besotted with him and would have done anything for him. So was Gillian. And Elaine. And they seemed always to overlap, and he'd invariably have another in tow before he finished with the last. 'He even got quite friendly with his housekeeper too,' says Holt. 'She would have only been in her twenties. I think she offered him some home comforts. Why else would you appoint a twenty-year-old housekeeper? They usually come in their fifties or sixties, some old dear.'

Another close friend, plastics entrepreneur Malcolm Bowry, says those single days, post-Barbara, were happy for Ryan, uncomplicated and fun. 'He's always preferred mixed company to going out with the chaps,' he says. 'He's very charming, enjoyed being a free agent, and had an eye for women, with maybe two, three, even four girlfriends at the same time.' Holt agrees. 'He was a bit of a womaniser. He liked women. He never told you much about whom he was seeing, though. He didn't talk about his marriage break-up either. He'd never really opened up.'

When Holt married his wife Brenda, the three used to go on shopping trips together. Ryan took great pride in the way he looked and always made a point of ironing his own shirts – despite his girlfriends or housekeeper offering – and liked buying new clothes. Coming from a modest background, he took great pleasure in spending money on the finer things in life and, because of his career ambitions, felt it was always important to look smart and well groomed. First impressions were important, particularly, perhaps, in a vocation where it was a distinct advantage for a man to look imposing. Brenda Holt holds a different opinion. 'I think it was vanity,' she says. 'We all used to go to the sales together, he always needed something. We'd buy household stuff and suits and shirts. He was always meticulous about his appearance, even when he was dressed casually. He was a bit of a social climber in a way. He liked to mix with people like solicitors.' Her husband, who is now retired from the force, but still lives in Preston, agrees. 'He had brilliant ideas, but it's all contacts, that's part of how he's got where he is today.'

Solicitor David Renwick is still a good friend of Ryan's. The two met when Ryan joined the local South Ribble Round Table club, a fundraising social group for professional men up to the age of 40. During Ryan's year as chairman in 1984 he stunned everyone by, instead of bringing along a local comedian or minor sportsman as speaker at the club's birthday function, he persuaded Manchester United manager Tommy Docherty to come along. Never quite sure how he'd managed to pull that off, Renwick nicknamed Ryan 'man of mystery'.

It's a tag he still finds pertinent today. In part, that kind of reserve is a characteristic typical of the bluff Lancashire personality. Men wouldn't dream of discussing anything remotely important to them, and only really achieve any degree of intimacy with other men via vague general discussions about football, jobs or jokes. In Ryan's case, Renwick believes, it's a trait even more deep-set because of his career and the guardedness it encourages. 'He was always a very private person,' says Renwick, who still acts as his solicitor.

He doesn't open himself up to people; he's very reserved. He doesn't like to reveal much of himself to people. Although we know each other well, he's never discussed his first wife with me. It was a place not to go. But he's someone who likes to be liked, very personable and he's always prepared to have a go at anything if it fires his imagination. And he's always been ambitious. He was always going to go far in the police service.

Even though Ryan could be reserved and aware of appearances, he didn't mind making a fool of himself if it was in a good cause. He wholeheartedly entered the spirit of the annual Round Table sponsored pram race, where everyone dressed up either as the baby or the pram-pushing mother, stopping off at pubs along the way to raise money for charity. At the Christmas party when he served as chairman, he was asked to perform a 'flasher' joke on stage, and volunteered to take his trousers off under the dirty mac he was given to wear. When, later that evening, he became the butt of an extended 'This Is Your Life' skit, with everyone joining in to take the micky out of him, he took it in good part. 'He had a cracking sense of humour,' says friend Tony Halliwell, who was also a Round Table member. While he was ribbed mercilessly for his predilection for wearing coordinating clothes, he was happy to laugh along. 'He's not someone who stands on his own dignity,' says Renwick.

Back at work, he was also making some friends in powerful places. As well as being conscientious and full of ideas for improving the way the force worked, he was also quite dogged about having them accepted. 'He was always very determined,' says Watkinson. 'In fact, he could be an awkward bugger. Sometimes, he made me want to hit him. But to move up, you have to have strength and not be frightened of taking chances. The boss thought a lot of Ryan.'

The boss was Joe Mounsey, the Detective Chief Superintendent in charge of CID. Under his command, the CID in the five years to 1974, says Bob Dobson, had dealt with a total of 181 murders – and solved 180 of them. Nationally, Mounsey had achieved an awesome reputation in 1965 when he led the team that found the remote graves nestling in the bleak Pennine hills in which notorious Moors Murderers Ian Brady and Myra Hindley had buried two of their brutalised young victims. His tireless work was instrumental in convicting the pair responsible for the torture and murders of five young children, and seeing them jailed for life. While Brady was declared clinically insane in 1987, Hindley, now a devout Christian, is still challenging the ruling of successive Home Secretaries that she should never be freed.

Later, Mounsey was to play a major role too in the 1975 capture of the 'Black Panther', Donald Neilson, the psychopathic killer of four, including the young heiress Lesley Whittle. A few years on, Mounsey conducted a top-secret mission to Northern Ireland to locate security leaks that led to the deaths of informers in 1982, and after his retirement in 1988, was awarded an OBE for his work. In Ryan's time, Mounsey had been instrumental, together with Chief Constable Bill Palfrey, in creating the Task Force system, and inspired tremendous respect, loyalty and reverence from his officers. In 1974, he was promoted to Assistant Chief Constable, and started looking around for an aide. He chose Ryan.

It was a turning point in Ryan's career. Suddenly, the sky was the limit. During the next eighteen months, he laboured all the hours he could, drawing up the first anti-terrorist plans to protect Lancashire, which had several ports that fed Northern Ireland. He formulated tactics on how to deal with terrorists taking hostages. He planned arms strategies to use against them, and worked with firearms teams to start building the first of the special anti-terrorism response groups. It was a massive rethink of the role of the police. The traditional amiable British bobby, solving domestic situations, rounding up mad cows, or even occasionally tackling an armed robber was now expected to deal with a new and very real terrorist threat.

This was also increasingly a time of major demonstrations around the country, from the Anti-Apartheid Movement and Vietnam War protestors to the National Front. Ryan devised different ways to manage such potentially imflammatory events. The old mill towns of Preston, Blackburn and Lancaster, with their large populations of Indians, Pakistanis and Bangladeshis, were centres for frequent National Front demos, where participants used often to try and provoke a reaction from the watching crowds. Ryan's experience at university proved immensely helpful; there he'd seen how the police handled demonstrations and how students had responded. It was a time too when all the major political parties started having their big Party Conferences at Lancashire seaside towns like Blackpool, Brighton and Scarborough, so he came up with strategies on how to manage these as well.

In his spare time, he went back to the University of Lancaster to study part-time for his Master of Business Administration. For the next three years he swapped shifts with other officers so he'd have time to attend classes two days and two evenings a week without skipping any of his police work. It was tough, but Ryan felt the sacrifice would eventually be worth it. The course introduced him to new methods of strategic planning, thinking through processes and budgeting and personnel management. He felt it was a great investment in his future. In the meantime, he watched and learned from Mounsey.

> I learnt a lot from Joe. He was a hard taskmaster and took me around everywhere. He was a tough man to work for. He demanded loyalty and absolute discretion and professionalism. He expected you to perform and didn't forgive people easily. We had a good relationship, punctuated by the odd shouting match. Often he'd throw you out of his office and call you useless and worthless. I'd stand outside for a while, then he'd ask me back in. It was a way he had of getting things off his chest, and using you as a sounding board. He later became a champion of mine and a good support. He was the best detective I've ever known.

Indeed, Mounsey even helped Ryan overcome his old adversary, Jack Allen. Their relationship had hit an all-time low, and Allen was openly rude and hostile, to the point where some of their fellow officers were avoiding being seen in public with Ryan. One day, everyone was in the officers' mess, having a lunchtime drink, when Allen decided to have some sport. 'Hey Ryan!' he called over. 'Aren't you going to buy your father a drink?' Ryan shook his head. Even though it was customary that junior officers always bought their bosses a drink, he had no intention of giving Allen that satisfaction. Allen's face darkened, and he let fly a tirade of abuse. 'You're a useless pillock!' he cried. 'Just because you've been to university . . .'

Mounsey was also in the bar and, after listening for a few minutes to the exchange, told Allen to stop. 'Just leave the lad alone,' he said. 'He works for me. He's doing a good job. He's one of the best inspectors we've got; he's got a great future. You leave him alone, Jack.'

Allen reddened, then turned on Mounsey. What did he know about it? He had nothing to do with it. He shouldn't poke his nose in where it didn't belong. The trading of insults built up into a blazing row about how junior officers should be treated. Finally, Allen stopped and looked around at the horrified expressions on everyone's faces at the hushed bar. His shoulders slumped as suddenly he seemed to realise he'd overstepped the mark by attacking Mounsey, his superior and the force's icon. As the hostility registered, he took a deep breath. 'If that's what you all think . . .' he spat to the room, 'I'm going!' He returned only on the Saturday morning to empty his desk. Within a week, he'd retired. Ryan was hugely relieved. Suddenly, there were no major barriers remaining to his progress.

In 1976, Ryan was promoted to Chief Inspector, moving from Mounsey's area to organisational planning. Once again, it was away from the excitement of being on the frontline, but he didn't mind. This would give him a valuable insight into how the police service worked, and how it was preparing itself for the challenges of the future. Watkinson, ever a valuable ally, told him what a good move this would be. 'The police force these days it all about good organisation,' says Watkinson. 'These days, it's being pushed towards being a business, and it's only half about being a good policeman; the rest is about having good ideas and making them blossom. Ryan was always a very good organiser; I knew he'd at least get to be a Superintendent.'

In his new job, he looked again at all the counter-terrorism plans he'd previously worked on, and revised and devised new tactics. He drew up schemes for protecting Britain's water supply, and for protecting companies that might become major targets, like British Aerospace, from terrorist attack. He did the groundwork for new legislation and examined new laws about to be put in place, drawing up papers on how they might affect the police and how they operated. All the time, he was attending courses at the Police Staff College at Bramshill on police management and new techniques of crime-fighting. It was important to learn there, and to be seen to be learning, in order to move on and up.

Eighteen months later, Ryan was made Detective Chief Inspector, and was put in charge of Lancashire HQ's CID support service, looking after criminal records, scenes of crime and forensics, criminal intelligence and major incidents response. It was a move back into real crime-fighting, and Ryan loved it. But even more, he liked finding ways to improve how the police responded to trouble, and developing new systems for intelligence, so they could avoid trouble happening or, at least, know when it was about to occur.

The police service was still using manual typewriters at that time, and punch cards for data processing. The system was slow and laborious, and it was becoming more and more obvious that a national criminal record database was becoming essential. The Home Office decided to harness rapidly developing information technology to try and start a database, and set up a number of working parties to research the task and advise them the best way to go about it. Ryan received the call in 1978: he was to be promoted to Superintendent and was wanted down at the Home Office in London to compile all the research being done by the various police forces around the country and help work out the way forward. He was thrilled. London felt like the big time at last. Before, the Home Office had loomed as the big, mysterious presence at the head of the organisation, full of shadowy figures issuing directives to be filtered down the ranks. Suddenly, Ryan was there, at the heart of it all, liaising with all the top advisors to the service, and watching how the Central Government, the Civil Service and the police all meshed together.

The work of the Home Office Police Research Services Unit was fascinating. He was in a group of six, pulling together the research on systems and operations, and helping develop the identikit photofit and computerised facial-recognition systems. He was working both with frontline police officers and scientists behind the scenes. He was also sent overseas to check how criminal intelligence worked there. The first trip was to the Bundes Kriminal Ampte at Viesbaden, near Frankfurt. The second was to Northern Ireland.

Just eighteen months before, the IRA had restructured its organisation dramatically because of the combined toll of war weariness, mounting losses and successive British successes in capturing leaders. The battalion system was changed into a rigid cell structure with specialist groups dedicated to bombings, robberies, executions or sniping, and younger, unknown figures moved into positions of responsibility, with the older leaders becoming merely the public spokesmen. The aim was to rebuild the IRA into a more secretive, disciplined, dangerous force. And it was working.

Only hours after the Queen left Northern Ireland's Coleraine University late in 1977 during her Silver Jubilee celebrations, a bomb exploded there, showing just how vulnerable the security forces had become. A British Army document said that the Provisionals were acquiring weapons at a faster rate than the army could take them away from them, and predicted that they might be gearing up to buy a number of SA7s – Soviet-designed anti-aircraft missiles. The IRA felt it had good reason to step up direct action. Their anger was mounting steadily over the 1976 declaration that convicted terrorists would no longer be housed together in barbed-wire camps, but together with other inmates, whatever their crimes, in the new, innovatively designed cells in the Maze prison which became known as the 'H-Blocks'. It was the effective end of IRA prisoners being accorded special status as de facto prisoners-of-war. They were furious; they were being treated as common criminals. They responded in a way that was by now becoming increasingly familiar, with the deadliest blow of the troubles so far: the assassination of Lord Mountbatten on his launch at Mullaghmore in the West of Ireland on 27 August 1979.

There was hardly time for Britain to recover from the shock when there was another horrific murder. Eighteen members of the Second Battalion Parachute Regiment were blown up on the northeast coast at Narrow Water Castle in County Down. It was at this time of crisis that Ryan was dispatched to Belfast to take a look at how criminal intelligence was gathered in the province. The atmosphere was tense, and there was a brooding feeling of imminent disaster. A routine 'Troops Out' march in the province attracted an unprecedented 10 000 supporters. British soldiers and members of the police force were warned to be constantly on their guard. Ryan's first impressions, in stark contrast to the horrors he'd heard so much about, were the beauty of the countryside and the magnificent rolling green hills dotted with picturesque villages. Then he felt his heart sink as he caught his first sight of the barbed-wire barricades of the city, with its armed guards at each check-point, slogans daubed on the walls and kerbstones painted to mark Catholic territory from Protestant.

'You had to be so careful where you went and who you spoke to,' he says. 'You had to be guarded about what you said and who you told. Life was so difficult, every day.' In the evenings, everyone would congregate in the local bars and hotels for a drink. There were always a lot of single women coming in, looking to meet people. 'But the trouble was, you didn't know who they were, or what they wanted,' says Ryan. 'So I would go down for a meal, get a couple of beers, then go back to my hotel room and watch TV. Beer and then whisky would stop you remembering some of the things you'd seen during the days, and help you forget.'

One night, he was staying with a friend from Northern Ireland's own police force, the Royal Ulster Constabulary, when the friend suggested they go out for the evening with his wife. The three dressed in casual clothes, and drove to a local club in the countryside, by an immensely circuitous route. When they finally arrived, they entered through great iron gates set in a high wall topped with coiled barbed wire all the way around. They were all frisked for weapons before being allowed through, but at least they felt safe. They were in the middle of nowhere, and in a club that obviously had the tightest security.

The trio went up to the bar and bought drinks, then wandered over to find a seat in the main part of the club to listen to the band, and watch people on the dance floor. They'd just sat down, when a stunning young woman walked over to Ryan. 'Would you like to dance?' she asked him. Ryan looked over to his friend. He nodded, once. She seemed a safe enough bet. Ryan stood up and was led over to the dance floor. As soon as they started dancing, she leaned over and whispered in his ear. He didn't catch what she was saying, shook his head and asked her to repeat it. 'You're that English policeman!' she yelled. 'Aren't you?' Ryan reeled back. How could she possibly know that? He'd never been to this club before, had kept an exceed-ingly low profile, and was wearing an innocuous open-necked shirt and sports jacket. It felt like time to go.

CHAPTER 5

Murder, mayhem and a shock move

AT FIRST, THEY thought it was a dressmaker's dummy. Lying wedged beneath a jutting rock six metres from the surface of the remote quarry pool, it bobbed in the icy water as the two scuba divers, out for a practice on a bleak Sunday afternoon, swam up. As they took a closer look, however, they reeled back in horror. It was the naked body of a man, half gutted, with both his hands hacked off, his face battered to a pulp, his teeth smashed, and his legs tied down with two twenty-six-kilogram cast-iron weights.

The police were immediately called in, and the painstaking investigation launched into who the victim could possibly be. Peter Ryan was contacted immediately. Late in 1979, just before the body was discovered, he'd been brought back from Northern Ireland and London to Lancashire as the Commander of the district of Leyland and Central. The gruesome find had been in the village of Ecclestone, slap-bang in the middle of his patch.

The only clue to identity lay in the medallion that had slipped around to the back of the man's body. As his killers were systematically brutalising him to erase every distinguishing feature, they'd obviously missed the fine gold chain under the torrents of blood. Ironically, it was inscribed with the Chinese long-life symbol. A photograph of the medallion was published in the local newspaper and an anonymous caller rang offering information. The mystery was solved. The victim was New Zealand-born Christopher 'Marty' Johnstone, better known worldwide as the notorious 'Mr Asia', the lynchpin of a multimillion-dollar heroin-trafficking ring.

With networks across Asia, Australasia and the UK, Johnstone was thought to be the chief of the global drugs syndicate, a man who lived the high life, with a network of companies in a number of different countries, stylish homes, flashy cars, beautiful clothes and a small army of drug-runners who did the hard work for him. But it had all suddenly started going wrong. 'Marty Johnstone, who had lived a charmed life of success, had hit a bad patch,' says Pat Booth in his book, *The Mr Asia File*. His attempts at investments weren't working, he was spending copious amounts of money, and he had messed up a half-million-dollar drug deal in Thailand. 'He was costing the drug ring and his partners money,' says Booth.

Revenge was swift. While his girlfriend Julie Smith and her friend Barbara Pilkington were on holiday together in Spain, Johnstone had been shot in a car, dragged out and shot again, then taken to a garage nearby where his hands were chopped off and an attempt made to gut his body with a spade. The mutilated corpse was then driven to the quarry, tied with weights and rolled into the lake. Unfortunately for his killer, it had caught on a ledge and lay there until discovered that quiet weekend by the two members of the Merseyside Sub-Aqua Club.

The identification of the 27-year-old's body caused a flurry of excitement among police in Britain, Australia, New Zealand and Asia, who had been trying to unravel the Mr Asia dealings for years. Responsible for the explosion in the amount of heroin on the streets in many countries, he had been the focal point of a massive investigation and the discovery of his body was a golden opportunity to unpick the threads of his worldwide crime network. For Ryan, however, the discovery eventually caused enormous practical problems.

One of the men subsequently arrested in London and charged with Johnstone's murder, his partner Terry Clark (alias Alexander Sinclair) was taken to Manchester's Strangeways Prison on remand. But he refused to go quietly. He openly declared that he'd pay £1 million reward to anyone who freed him from prison. After all, he was a valuable prisoner – involved in five murders and later revealed to be the true head of the drugs syndicate rather than Johnstone. Clark was thought to be responsible for importing, into Australia alone, some eighty-five kilograms of heroin, worth about $170 million. But the investigation had repercussions way beyond the cartel members themselves. As far away as Queensland, Australia, for instance, it highlighted how the cancer of corruption eating away at the police service had led to the drug baron's escape from their clutches. Fitzgerald's public inquiry into corruption would later reveal that in 1978 Clark, arrested only days after murdering one of his couriers, had been allowed to walk free on the instructions of an unidentified 'senior police figure' before Federal authorities had a chance to lay charges. Ryan would, of course, understand much more clearly that culture of police corruption when he was brought in to tackle similar problems in New South Wales sixteen years later.

But back then, the problems were more practical if not just complex. Transporting such a man from the jail to court and back again for the various hearings entailed a huge security operation every day and Ryan was in charge of the convoys. Twice they were buzzed by helicopters they were unable to identify, and twice high-powered cars tried to break into the convoy. One was being driven by a woman, thought to be Clark's girlfriend, who hung out of the car's window, screaming, 'I love you! I love you!' at the prison van. When Clark was eventually committed to Crown Court for trial, things didn't get any easier. Lancaster Crown Court was chosen for his trial because of its location in the middle of the town's Norman castle, with turrets that proved perfect for placing police snipers, and a passageway that used to be part of the old dungeons leading directly into Lancaster Gaol.

That should have been the end of the affair for Ryan, but it wasn't. He was left with Smith and Pilkington, the two women who had eventually identified Johnstone's body. Clark was believed already to have ordered Smith's death; Pilkington was the de facto of his accomplice Andrew Maher who'd helped kill Johnstone. Both women were placed in protective custody until the trial, which looked like being months away, so they'd be able to testify. They were set up in a house somewhere in Leyland – the exact location still can't be revealed for fear of possible reprisals – and lived there under twenty-four-hour armed guard, in constant fear that one of Clark's associates might try to kidnap, kill, or at least intimidate them into refusing to act as witnesses. 'It was my responsibility to make sure they were safe, but at the same time you can't keep two people in a house for months at a time,' says Ryan. 'They had to be taken out from time to time so they could live fairly normal lives. But it was always extremely difficult.'

The two women were taken under armed escort to visit their relatives living nearby, but never at any prearranged time in case details were leaked to other members of the drugs syndicate. They were also occasionally taken out shopping, and to pubs, clubs and for meals. Their presence proved a constant headache, however. The women were young, beautiful and restless. Frequently, the police officers guarding them were young, handsome and not impervious to their charms. There were frequent allegations of wild parties being held at the house and liaisons between the women and their guards. Every time the officers at the house were changed, a new group of police would fall for them. 'I'm sure some of it was true, and some of it would be exaggerated, but it was an additional problem,' says Ryan. 'My chief asked why wasn't I keeping it under control, but I couldn't stay in the house twenty-four hours a day with them.' When Clark and Maher were eventually convicted and sentenced to life imprisonment in July 1981 – Clark later died of a heart attack in prison in August 1983 – no one was happier than Ryan. 'I was relieved eventually to see the back of them, and have things return to normal,' he says.

Ryan had no inkling, of course, that the far-ranging repercussions of the Mr Asia case would one day end up dictating the direction of his life. In September 1984, a former member of the Mr Asia drug syndicate in Australia told ABC TV's 'Four Corners' that he knew of seven New South Wales detectives who were actively involved in heroin trafficking. A few days later the shock allegation was confirmed by the Australian Federal Police: they had extensive evidence, drawn from phone taps, of New South Wales officers mixed up in the drug trade. A few months on, when John Avery was appointed New South Wales Police Commissioner, he reviewed the tapes and formed an elite squad, the Internal Security Unit, with a brief to 'actively seek out institutionalised corruption'. Tony Lauer was selected by Avery to be one of the four team leaders of the new unit, and ended up spearheading action against the high-profile detective Roger Rogerson and the figure at the centre of the tapes, Lebanese businessman Frank Hakim. Those tapes led to action against almost sixty New South Wales police officers, and the revelations it threw up of the existence of entrenched and systemic corruption in the New South Wales police service eventually played a major role in the decision to set up the 1994 Royal Commission.

And as revelation after revelation of corruption and illegalities shocked the Australian public, Peter Ryan was recruited to head up the service as an outside 'cleanskin' – the only chance, it was felt, of rebuilding public trust in its police service.

Back then, however, Ryan returned to his normal work, although normal wasn't terribly normal, in any case. Ever since Ryan had returned to Lancashire at the end of his Home Office secondment, he'd been, in truth, itching to get back to London, where all the major decisions in the police service were made. Still, he tried to make the best of it, and used his time in Lancashire to introduce some of the operating methods he'd been researching. Everything he did, and observed his officers doing, he'd question and then try to come up with a better way of achieving the same end. 'Community policing' was becoming a fashionable catchword, but Ryan had doubts about its efficacy. Good criminal intelligence and smarter ways of working seemed far more important. He began to spend longer and longer days at work. He'd return to his police house around 5 p.m. in the evening, eat a quick dinner, and then go straight back to the station to meet detectives and talk them through some of his ideas.

Occasionally, he'd drop into his local pub for a drink or a meal or a game of pool or darts, or sometimes he'd go to the cinema or the theatre with a girlfriend, but generally he was consumed by his work. 'I was working very hard all the time,' says Ryan. 'As a Superintendent, I was already thinking I wanted to be assistant chief and chief. But I knew I'd have to work for it. I was always one of the youngest at my rank, and I looked particularly youthful too. There was a lot of jealousy around, and I had to keep myself on top of everything.'

In June 1981, Ryan took a holiday to Florida with his girlfriend of the time, Elaine. Malcolm Bowry lived there for a period, and Ryan used his home as an occasional bolthole. 'He'd unwind there, sitting by the pool with a book, or we'd go out on the boat, or play golf,' says Bowry. 'He's always been a man basically wary of people wanting to be his friend and, as he went up in the force, he became more guarded over time, particularly after Northern Ireland. A lot of people think Peter is hard and cold, but it's more that he's a very self-reliant person. He can't afford to show his vulnerable side in his job. I've always been one of his few trusted friends among dozens of his acquaintances. He doesn't let a lot of people in.' Ryan and Elaine had a great time with Bowry, then drove down through Miami and up to Palm Beach and Fort Lauderdale.

The couple became close, and Ryan even proposed to her at one point. 'He was very much into Elaine,' says Bowry. According to David Renwick, 'Elaine was his first proper girlfriend after his marriage ended, and she was a very, very nice girl indeed. I thought he would marry her. I think he asked her, and she said No. It devastated him for a while, I think. But she didn't want a career moving around with all that insecurity.'

Yet when Ryan flew back in early July to Manchester and picked up his car at the airport, he was as relaxed as he had been for a long time. As he pulled up on the driveway of his home on Saturday, 5 July, he could hear his phone ringing. He raced inside. It was HQ. They were sorry, they knew he was still on holiday, but could he report to the station as soon as possible? He'd be leading a contingent of 400 Lancashire police officers over to Merseyside at about 5 o'clock that afternoon. They were expecting trouble at a place called Toxteth.

A run-down inner-city area of Liverpool, with 45 per cent of the population unemployed, many of the rest on low incomes, a large black community and a stronghold for a number of well-known criminals, Toxteth had always been a difficult area. A favourite trick of some of the local youths would be to steal a car and drive it furiously around Liverpool city centre until they'd attracted the attention of police. The police would then give chase into a Toxteth housing estate and, as soon as the officers had got out of their car to accost the driver, a gang would emerge from the shadows and start

stoning the police, smashing car windows and trying to turn the car
over and set it alight. The previous week, the police had mounted a
crackdown on the area. Some of the locals had hit back. And, every
night since, the atmosphere had been heavy with tension, with spor-
adic incidents flaring up between police and the youth of the area.

Three months before, in April, the south-east London suburb of
Brixton had exploded into bloody riots which left 165 people
injured and more than £5.6 million ($10 million at the rate of the
time) worth of damage, with an inquiry chaired by Lord Scarman
having started on 15 June. Just two weeks later, 500 black and white
youths had clashed in Peckham, nearby. The night before in Toxteth,
police had tried to arrest a black youth on a motorcycle and a crowd
of about fifty youths, both black and white, had joined forces to
attack the police. Sources had told the police that tonight could be
much worse. They were expecting a full-scale riot.

Ryan went into HQ, and found the 400 officers waiting ready for
him. They climbed into a convoy of coaches, and set off with a truck
following, stacked with the few riot shields and other equipment
they had available. The officers had been briefed about the importance of tolerance and patience in such situations, but the mood was
belligerent. A couple of officers had been injured in the trouble the
previous evening, and conversations centred on the need to teach
these troublemakers a lesson. 'They're not going to get us,' shouted
one man above the hubbub. 'No,' came the enthusiastic reply. 'We're
going to get them.'

The coaches arrived in Liverpool and were told to report to the
old HQ around the corner. As Ryan walked into the briefing room,
his heart sank. The Liverpool City Police had been merged with the
county police into Merseyside Police in the reorganisation of 1974,
so in essence it had moved from being an inner-city force to becoming a typical county rural service, with very little experience of the
demands of city policing. The briefing reflected this. In fact, there
was no real briefing at all. Instead, a few officers were asking everyone where they were from, and dividing everyone up to move into
different areas. Ryan was unimpressed. 'Why don't you leave us
together as one group?' he suggested. 'Everybody here knows me.
We have a proper structure of inspectors and sergeants to give orders

down the line. We're already broken down into units. We've even brought our own mobile canteen to feed my officers. We're totally self-sufficient. I think it would work a lot better that way.'

The man who appeared to be in charge fixed him with a steely gaze. 'We haven't time for any of that,' he said. 'You'll go where you're told and do as you're told. Now, let's get on with it!' Ryan's officers were divided up and sent with different coachloads all over Liverpool. He was left with a group of officers under the command of an elderly, grey-haired Chief Superintendent who'd previously been with the rural Cheshire Police, to go into Upper Parliament Street, a strong black area two kilometres from the city centre, lined with graceful Victorian terraces that had been subdivided into flats and nightclubs, overlooked by high-rise council flats. He went back to the commanding officer to voice one last complaint. 'This guy doesn't have a clue!' he protested. 'He's a rural officer. He's not up to this.' His protest fell on deaf ears. 'You'll do as you're told,' his boss said sternly. 'Now, get out there!'

It was a hot, sultry night and out on the streets, everything was eerily silent. Ryan stood with the other officers, waiting for something to happen. They didn't have to wait for long. At about 7.30 p.m. an army of local youths appeared over the horizon with a veritable arsenal of weapons. Everyone tensed, and immediately their Chief Superintendent ordered them to form lines across the street. The hail of stones, bricks and bottles came first, and officers started falling like bowling pins. Still, they were told to stand firm. Officers from the back moved up to the front to replace those who had been injured and dragged away. Next, came metal railings the gangs had pulled from front gardens. They started lighting fires all the way down the street, held the metal in the flames until they were white-hot and then used them as spears to hurl at the police. Then came the petrol bombs, exploding in a deadly shower of flames throughout the police lines.

One group stole a mechanical digger, poured petrol all over it, set it alight and drove it straight at the police. Cars they'd previously stolen were fitted with petrol bombs, knocked into gear, had bricks placed on the accelerator pedal and were sent hurtling straight into the police. Within half an hour, something like 30 per cent of the officers were lying on the ground, covered in blood from serious injuries, nursing faces that had been slashed by bottles and iron tools, and rolling around in agony as their uniforms blazed on their backs.

It was like World War I. It was a case of lions led by donkeys. They were ordering us to push men further up into the front-line and I was arguing that this is quite stupid. I wanted to go around the back with a group of volunteers to act as a pincer movement. I was saying, 'Let me go in there, I can sort this gang out.' But I was told, 'No, you do as you're told. Stay here and make sure the line doesn't break.' It was absolutely stupid. And all the time, ambulances were carting more and more of my officers away.

But the rioters still weren't finished. They advanced with burning torches and set light to a number of buildings along the street. Two police transit vans that the Chief Superintendent had ordered be pushed into the crowd to disperse them were simply set on fire and destroyed. It was an inferno. One by one, the flames caught and roared through houses, shops, the old Rialto cinema. Fire engines came screaming to the scene. Right in the middle of the street was a nursing home, and soon smoke started billowing from there, too. The nurses inside were screaming for help; many of the elderly residents were trapped. Finally, a hasty truce was negotiated to allow the ninety-six old people to be evacuated from their beds, on stretchers, in chairs, anything Ryan and his men could lay their hands on.

The battle erupted again immediately they were out of the way. Now, the fire brigade became the target. They were pelted with bricks and bombs as Upper Parliament Street steadily burnt to the ground. Ryan was beside himself with anger. The whole exercise had been a tactical disaster. At first light, the true extent of the damage became shockingly apparent. With so many men having been carted away to hospital, Ryan was left standing with a raggle-taggle army of exhausted, blood-stained police, dressed in filthy, burnt uniforms, with smoke-blackened faces and bandages around their heads. Everyone who could climbed wearily into coaches and was driven back to Preston. They arrived and filed off into the canteen for breakfast and a debrief. The Chief Constable, Albert Laugharne, stood watching them limp in, and his eyes filled with tears. 'What happened?' he asked Ryan. 'I saw some of it on the television news. But I didn't realise it was that bad.'

Ryan took a deep breath. He explained what had gone on, and how badly the whole police operation had been organised. 'Look, you'll have to do something,' he pleaded. Laugharne nodded his head. 'Yes,' he replied. 'I'll speak to them today.' The toll had been immense: 220 people had been treated in hospital; 259 police had been injured, including one left with a fractured skull; more than forty buildings had been burned down, and many more looted; 75 people had been arrested, 21 of them 16 years old and younger. A local councillor estimated there was not a single shop in Toxteth that had not been smashed and looted. And the whole of Britain was reeling with shock.

That night, Ryan set off again with a fresh battalion of men. The mood was, however, quite different. This time, the threats had been taken seriously, and protective equipment had been fastened on to the police transit vans to make them better able to withstand attack, and many of the men had been issued with crash helmets and protective clothing begged from defence institutes and army suppliers. Ryan was given a Range Rover as a command vehicle, which meant he'd be able to drive over the rubble, devastated gardens and parkland to get to his men. His officers were sober, quiet, anxious about what the night might bring. Ryan was hopeful that the Liverpool command might have started to see sense about their tactics.

But when they arrived, he found there was no noticeable change. Once again, the command broke his team up and scattered them all over the city centre. The same crusty Chief Superintendent was in charge of Ryan's team, this time looking absolutely exhausted. At about 8 p.m. the trouble started again. Stones, bricks, bottles and petrol bombs came whistling off the tops of the buildings. There were fires, but no buildings left to burn. The rioters had retreated to a plot of open land, from which they sent burning cars again into the police lines. The Chief Superintendent again ordered that transit vans be driven at the rioters at full speed to disperse them, a tactic of riot control long employed by the Royal Ulster Constabulary (RUC) in Northern Ireland. It became a complete repeat of the previous night. Nothing seemed to be working. 'Hold the line!' was all the Chief Superintendent seemed to be able to order. 'Hold the line!'

Ryan was incensed. 'This is ridiculous,' he yelled. 'This is just absolutely stupid being here like this. We've got nearly 1000 police here. We should easily be able to go into the crowd and get rid of them.' But still, the Chief Superintendent wouldn't budge. 'Do as you're told,' he shouted back at Ryan. 'I'm the one in charge here.' Five minutes later, a brick flying over from the rioters hit the Chief Superintendent full in the face and he crumpled to the ground. It broke his nose, cut his face and he lay bleeding where he'd fallen. Ryan couldn't help feeling a stab of relief. 'I immediately thought, "Here's my chance! Let's get him out of the way. This is it!"' he says. But it wasn't to be. 'No, this fellow wouldn't lie down,' says Ryan. 'He gets up again and he's still giving orders and I said, "You're not in a fit state!" The man was clearly dazed and in a hell of a mess, but he was still giving these orders about hold the line, hold the line.' Again, the line didn't hold, and there were dozens more casualties. In frustration, Ryan marched off and drove around the smoky, dark streets to check on his officers who'd been placed in other units. There had been skirmishes and injuries all over the city. He called into the hospital to check on those who'd been taken away injured.

Ryan's anger grew as the next weeks fell into a grim pattern of driving into Liverpool every night to prepare for a beating. It was a good exercise in self-control. 'It's one of his strengths that he can be calculating and unsentimental when the occasion demands it,' says Bowry. 'He can be hard in his own business, and he's not afraid to take tough decisions and the responsibility. He would shoot someone without thinking of it if it had to be done. He's totally capable of turning off and doing what needs to be done. He has a soft centre, but can adjust accordingly, and be ruthless. He doesn't suffer fools gladly, either.'

One night, Ryan and a group of officers chased a gang of rioters into a block of apartments and were lured down into the courtyard in the middle of a group of flats. As they appeared, residents hurled TV sets, sofas, chairs, everything from their homes down from the balconies onto the men. The police beat a hasty retreat. If these people wanted to trash their homes, was Ryan's thinking, it was up to them. No one wanted to end up fighting on the stairwells of apartment blocks.

Ryan still found it hard to hide his frustration at the way the police were operating. He was adamant that they needed to work better, smarter and vary the nonsensical 'holding the line' idea. Indeed, he started asking his Lancashire officers to come in early at 4 p.m. with a couple of hours to spare before the trip to Liverpool. Then, he'd rehearse his officers in how to hold a baton and shield, and run forward in the field, hold the line, and run forward again, so they'd actually be progressing and taking ground. At certain points, they'd suddenly open the line for a special hand-picked arrest squad to dart out, snatch rioters, and drag them back behind the lines, effectively taking them out of the action. No other police force in the country was working on such advanced tactics. 'We began to think more like Spartan soldiers in the Peloponnesian War,' says Ryan. Indeed, the kind of manoeuvres he was developing formed the basis of national police strategy in all the British riots and public disturbances to follow, such as in the later rioting that changed the face of Brixton.

Large numbers of Lancashire officers were sent daily until 19 July when the rioting died down, and then from 28 July to 3 August when it flared up again. The last riot of all degenerated into a ferocious hand-to-hand battle. By then, however, the police were better organised, with protective gear issued for everyone. Their tactics hadn't advanced much, though. Officers still stood in line like Aunt Sallies, waiting to be hit by the rioters' bricks and iron bars. Riots also broke out in Manchester, Leeds, Leicester, and Southall in west London, just as the Liverpool troubles were at their height, and copycat gangs caused trouble all over the UK. On Ryan's days off from Liverpool, he was actually out on the streets of towns around Lancashire quashing similar mini-riots.

During the days, the detectives were on the ground trying to hunt down the ringleaders. Politicians on all sides were appealing for calm. Inquiries were launched into the causes of the riots, and everyone was being given a chance to have a say. Prime Minister Margaret Thatcher appointed Environment Secretary Michael Heseltine to conduct an investigation into the effectiveness of inner-city policies of local and central Government in Liverpool, as a pilot inquiry to be used Britain-wide. The hot weather finally broke. Interest was rising in the imminent royal wedding between Prince Charles and Lady Diana Spencer. Whatever the real reason, the rioting finally simply melted away.

The cost, however, had been enormous. There were times when significant sections of Liverpool had been completely out of police control. The third day of the Toxteth riots had only been brought to a close when a policeman fired tear gas into a mob – the first time CS gas had ever been used on the British mainland. One man was injured when a police officer picked up the wrong kind of bullet and ended up shooting a 'ferret', a bullet fitted with a capsule of CS gas intended for firing through doors in the event of a siege, into the crowd. It hit him in the stomach, exploded and burnt him badly. Another, a crippled bystander, was killed when a police Land Rover was driven at high speed through a mob. David Moore, 23, was too slow to get out of the way and was dragged twelve metres by the vehicle, dying of his injuries. Two police officers were later charged with unlawful killing. Teenager Paul Conroy received severe spinal injuries when he was run down by a police van. Feelings had run so high against the police that an official inquiry was set up into alleged abuses of their powers. Experts estimated that the damage throughout Britain of the riots would top £45 million (A$71.1 million, at the rate of the time).

The analysis after the Toxteth riots followed a number of different strands. Merseyside Chief Constable Kenneth Oxford blamed local hooliganism. Right-wing MP Enoch Powell doggedly pursued the line that large-scale immigration had inevitably led to racial strife, and that the trouble was largely race-based. Most, however, felt that the riots were the result of steadily increasing unemployment, particularly among the young and disadvantaged, concentrated in run-down, neglected urban areas, who were venting their frustrations on the authorities via the police. Among black people in Toxteth, the average rate of unemployment was 47 per cent; among whites 43 per cent. 'If you have half a million young people hanging around on the streets all day, you will have a massive increase in juvenile crime,' said former Tory Prime Minister Ted Heath in a strong critique of Thatcher's policies. 'Of course, you will get racial tension when you have young blacks with less chance of getting jobs.' Others blamed the police for sparking the riots with heavy-handed tactics against local youths, and institutionalised racism within the force. Indeed, Lord Scarman said police procedure in dealing with the rioters had been 'awfully haphazard' with few lessons learned from experiences in Northern Ireland, and had probably only served to inflame problems. Ryan took a harder line, believing the essence of the troubles lay in antisocial behaviour.

> Maybe the police could have operated better in normal circum-stances before the riots. Maybe. Maybe they might have displayed some racist attitudes to people by making derogatory comments, but Toxteth was well known for having a large crim-inal element. There were parts that were nice from the old merchant town, but in the 1970s and 1980s it was a pretty tough spot. And what you can't do is pussyfoot around with criminals who are baiting the police by hooning round in their cars, doing wheelies and goading the police into a trap, only then to stone the police, turn the car over and burn it. So there were always people, apologists, looking for reasons instead of saying these people are criminals. Yes, maybe the police did operate a bit heavy-handedly, but there is no excuse for this sort of behaviour.

On the morning after the last night of rioting, 29 July, Ryan drove tiredly home and nearly fell out of his car. His neighbour, coming out of his house to pick up the newspaper, looked shocked to see him. 'Oh my God!' he said. 'You're as white as your car.' Ryan looked at himself in the wing mirror. Only twenty-four days before, he'd looked happy, tanned and relaxed after his holiday. Now his face was ashen, his skin was grey and his eyes were red-rimmed from lack of sleep. His uniform was stained and torn. He felt shattered and utterly exhausted. 'Come inside,' said the neighbour, taking him by the arm. 'Sit down and we'll make you some breakfast.'

Ryan obediently allowed himself to be ushered into the house, and sat drinking coffee until bacon and eggs arrived. The TV was snapped on. On the screen were the crowds lining the streets of London, celebrating the royal wedding. If ever he was asked in future, he thought, what he was doing that day, he'd never have to think twice.

The future – his own future – was never far from his mind. The period spent in Toxteth had made him even more determined to rise up through the force to a position where he could make decisions and issue orders, rather than having blindly to follow those from senior officers who sometimes seemed far less qualified to do so. 'Peter could be extremely calculating and unsentimental when he needed to be,' says Bowry. He phoned up his old mentor Tommy Watkinson and asked him what he thought his chances might be of getting onto the prestigious Senior Commanders' course, held at the police staff college at Bramshill. He knew only the officers earmarked as real high-fliers were ever considered. Watkinson didn't hesitate. 'I think you should try,' he told him.

Only one six-month course a year was held at the college in Hampshire, southern England and, in 1983, only fifteen officers were to be taken on. More than 250 officers applied. Ryan wrote out the forms, and waited to hear. Finally, he was told he'd been selected to take part in the three-day interview process, which included a whole range of physical, mental and psychological tests. Despite the sadness of his father's death earlier that year, he was overjoyed when he was eventually chosen as one of the fifteen – aged 39, he was one of the youngest officers ever to take the course.

The course was rigorous, physically, academically and psychologically, with speakers ranging from the Home Secretary William Whitelaw to captains of industry and community leaders. It could also be enormous fun. One week, a group of officers went over to Berlin to see how the West German police force operated, and were allowed through the Brandenburg Gate to see the East-German side. That visit nearly ended in disaster when, after a talk from the hosts about people attempting to cross from one side to the other, one of the American officers also taking part pointed to the busts of Queen Charlotte mounted on pillars all the way along the no-man's corridor between the two countries and asked, in an extremely loud drawl, 'Hey! Are those the heads of the ones who never made it?'

Ryan managed to pacify the German guards only after promises of copious quantities of free beer back at their hotel.

Less enjoyable was an exchange program with the US police. Ryan was posted, along with three others, to Charlotte in North Carolina on the east coast, a police district which was pursuing new strategies in criminal intelligence, and had drawn up an innovative call-priority system – rating calls in terms of their urgency so as to send police out first on those that needed immediate attention – which was just beginning to be studied in the UK. They also had innovative programs for dealing with domestic violence and sexual assault. The contrast with British policing was quite staggering. The first day Ryan went on patrol with a US officer, he was amazed to note the man was armed to the teeth, whereas all he'd have in a similar situation in the UK was his trusty truncheon. Then he was handed a key to the lock of a shotgun that was strapped to the dashboard, between the driver and front passenger seat. 'If I go down, get the gun!' said the officer. 'But don't worry, I've got another gun strapped to my ankle.'

A routine car accident that would simply be noted in Britain, necessitated a mountain of paperwork, and a fight at a nightclub was quashed with the help of the bouncer at the door who happened to be an off-duty policeman in his full police uniform – something that never would have been allowed in the UK. The approach to incidents too was often much more gung-ho. Later that night, they were called to a house with a report of a hostage and shots having been fired. While the US officer and those from other patrol cars raced around the back of the house intent on smashing their way in, Ryan tried to calm down the woman who had called the police in the first place. She explained that her male lodger had got drunk, grabbed one of her friends who'd been visiting and disappeared into his room, locking the door behind him. When she'd shouted at him to leave the girl alone, he'd responded by firing off a volley of shots through the door. Ryan was then able to creep into the house, find the room where the man was hiding out, and call the American cops to the scene. They kicked the door down and rescued the girl, who'd obviously been bashed and raped.

After completing the course successfully, Ryan was impatient for a new challenge. He'd been posted back to Lancashire, but he knew it wouldn't be long before his next move. When the call eventually came, the offer was a shock. He was being invited to take up the post of Chief Superintendent in London's Metropolitan Police, stationed in the Royal Borough of Chelsea and Kensington, from 31 October 1983. It was far more than he'd ever dared dream of; it was an absolutely plum job. The area included institutions like the British Museum, the HQ of the Royal Household Cavalry and the Guards' Barracks, as well as fashionable King's Road, exclusive Pimlico and a swag of embassies. It was one of the best postings anyone could hope to have. But there was a downside. There were so many buildings and people in the area considered prime IRA targets that security was a nightmare. In addition, the Met, an organisation with its own tight-knit culture, was beset with terrible morale problems after years of corruption allegations. And Ryan knew the appointment of a northern outsider to the pick of the Met jobs was likely to invite a certain amount of resentment, if not open hostility. A poisoned chalice? He had no idea how deadly it would prove.

CHAPTER 6

A massacre at Christmas

IT WAS THE last weekend before Christmas 1983 and the London Underground trains were packed with excited and exhausted families doing the last of their Christmas shopping in the city's West End. Peter Ryan had been in his new job as the Chief Superintendent of the Chelsea division of the London Met for six weeks and, as he jostled for space in the crush of his train to Marble Arch, he reflected on how much he'd been looking forward to a rare day off.

That six weeks had been among the longest, and hardest, of his life. As he'd expected, he'd been made to feel like an outsider from Day One. His appointment had been a surprise not only to him, but to most of the 350 police officers he found himself commanding. They'd become used, over the years, to a strict line of succession, with a series of bosses brought up in the tight culture of the Metropolitan Police and with a clear interest in continuing to see it flourish. Ryan was another prospect entirely. Not only was he a northerner, who'd done his time in what they considered a small, provincial, country force, but here was someone with no experience of the ways things were done at the Met and, even worse, no apparent intention of preserving those traditions.

Obviously, Ryan had been appointed for a reason: to cast a fresh eye over a force that had been shaken to its core by series of revelations of corruption, public inquiries and overhauls, and in which public confidence was at an all-time low. It was also a move intended to answer criticism that the Met's in-house promotions system had allowed nepotism and corruption to thrive. It wouldn't have been much comfort at the time, but it was to prove the perfect training ground for his later move to Australia.

'He was like a fish out of water,' says Mike Bell, a fellow northerner who'd been transferred to Chelsea eight years before.

> He was the first non-Met guv'nor the station had ever had and so, in everyone's eyes, he was a 'foreigner'. They wouldn't treat him immediately with the respect they would have given to any other Met Super. The Met has its own customs and practice and they're quite different from country forces. It's like an alien country. Officers aren't subservient at all; they speak their minds. He would have been a big person in a country force, but in the Met he was treated like just one of many. Outsiders just aren't, generally, accepted.

Another officer under him, ex-soldier Barry Greenhalgh, was also originally from Lancashire. 'But I was older, so they treated me better,' he says. 'His predecessors weren't all they should have been. I wouldn't be surprised if he came to sort the place out.' Says Roger Lashbrook, who'd been at Chelsea for twenty-three years before Ryan's arrival, 'When we heard we were getting someone from Lancashire, we all thought, "Oh God!"'

For Ryan, the culture shock had been exhausting. Not only was he suddenly right in the thick of a force that, with 26 000 officers and 13 000 full-time civilians, was easily Britain's biggest, more than three times the size of its nearest rival, the Greater Manchester Police, but he was coming in at a point when morale was at one of its lowest ebbs. A year before, nearly half the Londoners polled by London Weekend Television felt the Met should be controlled by the Greater London Council (GLC) or an elected police authority. Public dissatisfaction had been buoyed by the failure of Operation Countryman, investigating allegations of corruption in the Met and city forces, rises in recorded crime and the failure of the Met to solve more than 17 per cent of those crimes reported. The Government's answer was to bring in Sir Kenneth Newman, formerly the Chief Constable of the Royal Ulster Constabulary, charged with the task of restoring public confidence in the force, and dealing with its internal problems.

It was likely to be a long, hard haul, however. The independent educational charity, the Policy Studies Institute, brought out a damning report, 'Police and People in London', two weeks after Ryan's arrival, following the most extensive study ever done into the Met. It suggested that the abuse of police powers continued to be widespread. The GLC report shortly afterwards, 'Policing London', was equally critical. The newspaper headlines were damning. 'SHAMING OF LONDON'S POLICE . . . Racialist, sexist, drunken and bullying, says own report,' shouted London's evening newspaper *The Standard* on 18 November 1983. The same day's national *Daily Telegraph* was just as outraged: 'RACIALISM IS FASHIONABLE IN THE MET,' it said. 'London police "racist and bullies".'

On a personal level, the job had its petty irritations too. Bell remembers Ryan comparing the way, back in Lancashire, he'd be driven to work, where tea and biscuits were laid out for him, ready for his arrival, on his desk. In the Met he had to shout for tea before it would come. One of his first weeks, he'd been angry that, when he'd called the station to be picked up from a meeting at Scotland Yard, he'd been told by a junior on the switch to catch the Tube. It wasn't until Ryan exploded that finally a police van was sent for him. Any residual naivety was quickly being knocked out of him. His old mate David Renwick remembers Ryan proudly showing him his new numberplate for his BMW: GOV 1. When Renwick pointed out this might not exactly endear him to his new workmates, he went out the next day and changed it.

He didn't make his position easier for himself, in other ways, though. Right from the beginning, he showed he was quite unwilling to compromise any of his own ideas about the way a division should be run in return for enhancing his own popularity. One of his first moves had been to ban the usual Friday afternoon drinks at the station, insisting the premises be dry and that officers sign off duty and go to the pub if they wanted to drink. It wasn't a move that went down terribly well. Then, he started to impose strict financial and budgetary constraints on his command to minimise the overtime bills that were spiralling out of control among police divisions all over London due to the explosion in the number of weekend demon-stration marches.

That hardly endeared him to the commanders of the other divi-sions in his London area, forced to listen at the weekly commanders' conferences to him being praised by the area boss for cutting his overtime bills so dramatically. Gradually, their suspicion of this young upstart began to spill over into open resentment. Regularly, he found himself sitting at one side of the table, while all the other commanders sat ranged along the other. It became worse when he declined to join in their long Friday night Scotch sessions and adjournments to the pub.

I'd thought Lancs was tough. I'd had to fight my way up through the ranks there. But they weren't as tough in terms of slyness and underhandedness as these guys were in the Met. There was a huge Masonic influence in the Met. It quickly became apparent I wasn't a freemason, which made me even more of an outsider. The guys I was working with were all from one lodge. One or two, trying to be friendly, were whispering in my ear, 'You've got to make the boss sweet, and you're not a Mason.' But I thought, 'To hell with that! Why bother? I've got a job to do and I'm doing it well.'

Not for the last time, it was that failure to indulge in the mateship of an organisation that was making him enemies. Some saw it as stand-offishness, the vanity of a man who clearly thought he was better than his colleagues. He saw it as the only way to do a good job.

Others at the station, however, were starting to re-evaluate him, par-ticularly in comparison to his far-more-authoritarian, old-fashioned predecessor. Inspector Mike Jukes, who'd been at the station for nine years when Ryan arrived, said his management style was quite differ-ent. 'The previous management had been about doing it their way, with no one allowed to complain,' he says. 'Peter knew where he was going, and knew what he wanted done, but he spared time to speak to you and listen to what you had to say. He had authority as well as the experience and focus.'

But those first two weeks of December had been particularly

arduous. The whole of London in the run-up to Christmas had been put on a heightened alert for IRA activity, with the Chelsea division especially vigilant because of the number of 'prime target' buildings on their patch. Since the hunger strikes of IRA prisoners in 1980 and 1981, there had been an upsurge in the number of IRA operations in Britain. Ten Republican prisoners had died in the hunger strikes protesting against the abolition of their 'special' status by Prime Minister Margaret Thatcher's Government. The most famous, Bobby Sands, died on 5 May 1981 after sixty-six days without food. The IRA vowed revenge. In October 1981, a nail bomb exploded outside Chelsea Barracks, injuring forty soldiers and civilians and killing a female passer-by and a teenage boy. In July 1982 two further bombs were detonated in central London, one another vicious gelignite-and-nails device in an ambush of the Household Cavalry at Hyde Park, the other an explosion at Regents Park. Together, they killed a total of eleven soldiers, four of them members of the Household Cavalry, and seven members of a band of the Royal Greenjackets, as well as killing a number of horses and injuring fifty-three other people.

The following year, just days after Ryan took up his posting, 35-year-old Gerry Adams became President of the Sinn Fein. He denied membership of the organisation's paramilitary side, the provisional wing of the IRA, but was said by sources to have an 'impeccable' record in 'the war zone'. On his promotion, he addressed assembled members with a speech that cast ice into the hearts of those on the British mainland. 'Armed struggle is a recognised and morally correct form of resistance . . . against a Government whose presence is rejected by the vast majority of Irish people,' he said. The bloody spiral of IRA violence immediately began to gather momentum. In mid November, IRA gunmen burst into a Pentecostal church hall in Darkley, South Armagh, opening fire on the defenceless congregation. Then came the murder of prominent Unionist politician Edgar Graham, a spate of sectarian killings and the kidnapping of English chainstore executive Don Tidey. Britain became gripped by fears of a Christmas bombing blitz on the mainland.

Ryan had raced into the station on that Saturday morning of his day off, 17 December 1983, to check all was well. One squad was out patrolling with dogs specially trained to sniff out explosives. Every officer on the beat was primed to report any suspicious packages or objects. On only the previous Wednesday, police from his station had been called to examine a lone satchel left hanging over a parking meter in nearby Onslow Gardens, off Kensington High Street, one of London's busiest shopping strips. It turned out to contain a potentially devastating five-kilogram bomb, which was detonated by using a robot to fire a shot into the bag. Less than half an hour later, three further suspect packages were found nearby. They turned out to be bags left by forgetful shoppers. By the Thursday and Friday, reports of suspicious objects by the public were running at eight a day. Over in south-east London, a bomb exploded at Woolwich army barracks, injuring four. Everyone was on tenterhooks. A few days before, Ryan had been advised there was an active service unit armed with explosives somewhere on the mainland. The unit had entered the country via ferry from the Irish port of Larne to Stranraer in Scotland and travelled down through Lancashire, where they'd been spotted. The information was sketchy as they'd given police the slip and nobody knew where they were. Yet all was quiet at the station. Ryan did his rounds and then stole away to catch up on Christmas shopping.

He'd been particularly looking forward to that afternoon. Earlier in the week, he'd summoned up the courage to ask out an attractive young police officer who had been working with his policy advisor group. Startled, she'd disappeared out of his office to consider his offer. When she returned to say she'd be delighted to go on a date with him, they agreed they'd better keep their liaison away from the office. They arranged to meet at the top of the steps of the Marble Arch tube station, to finish off their Christmas shopping together. She'd swapped shifts with a colleague, Jane Arbuthnot, so she'd have the day clear to spend with her boss.

But as Ryan's train pulled into Marble Arch, he shivered. All morning, he'd had an uneasy feeling that something was wrong. As he walked up the stairs to meet his date, he pulled his thick wool coat tighter around him to keep out the blast of icy air. The feeling was growing stronger. It had started out as a faint edginess; now he felt it grow into a definite conviction that there was something seriously awry. At points throughout his career, he'd had the same instinct that trouble was about to happen. He'd learnt to ignore it at his peril.

Adrienne Butterworth was standing waiting for him at the top of the steps. He walked up towards her, smiled and kissed her lightly on the cheek. 'Adrienne . . . I'm sorry,' he said. She smiled back at him, uncertainly. 'Look, I've just got this feeling that something's wrong,' he continued. 'I don't know why, but I've got to get back to the station. I'll call you later and explain.' With that, he turned on his heel, dived back down the steps and was instantly lost in the crowds pouring into the West End on the busiest shopping day of the year.

The journey back to Chelsea seemed interminable. Ryan's mind was racing as he changed at Victoria for the district line. What could be wrong? Why this terrible feeling of doom? He had no idea where it had come from. Finally arriving at Sloane Square, he came out of the station and started walking briskly, urgently, towards the police station. After a minute, he broke into a jog.

And then it happened. At 1.21 p.m., there was a deafening bang, he felt the air around him shudder and a huge black cloud billowed up in the distance.

Ryan immediately started running as fast as he could towards the station. He flew up the stairs leading to his office, and pulled on his uniform. At that moment, his phone began ringing. It was the control room downstairs. 'Thank God, we found you!' the young officer was yelling. 'There's been a bomb! A bomb's just gone off in Harrods!' The journey there took only a few minutes. As his car pulled into the smart, moneyed suburb of Knightsbridge, Ryan was rocked by the sight that met his eyes.

The scene was devastating, terrible. A lot of the people were being carried away, but cars were on fire and glass was still falling from tall buildings all around. I think the tallest was six storeys. There were bodies, blood everywhere, people lying there. Harrods' shop windows had been blown out and mannequins that were in the window were on fire and half in and half out. People had been blown from the road into the window and the dummies had been sucked out of the windows on to the street. So among the bodies in the street, you couldn't tell which were real and which were dummies.

Eighteen years on from that dreadful day, Ryan's eyes still fill with tears at the memory. 'In amongst all these injured were my police officers, helping people despite the trauma of seeing so many of their colleagues killed and seriously injured,' he whispers. 'Their bodies were there. There was no mistaking the injury that they'd suffered. But I remember one of my officers, she was kneeling down beside a man and she had got her jacket off which she'd propped under his head. It was freezing cold, but she's tearing her shirt to make bandages for this man.'

Five people had been killed, including a policeman and policewoman, and ninety-one wounded in the blast from fifteen kilograms of explosives left in a blue Austin 1300, registration number KFP 252K, parked just around the corner from Harrods, on Hans Crescent. A man with an Irish accent had phoned the Samaritans just thirty-seven minutes before, warning of a bomb outside the Queen's favourite store, two more inside, and a fourth in nearby Oxford Street. Police searched frantically for the devices, trying to clear the streets and the store at the same time. But it had been a mission doomed to failure. Details in the call had been too vague to pinpoint the likely locations of bombs, and there had been too many people swarming through Harrods, the streets and nearby shops to evacuate the whole area quickly. The call had come simply too late to prevent a massacre and the biggest death toll from a single bomb since 1974 when twelve people were killed in a coach carrying servicemen and their families from London to Aldershot. Even worse, it marked a terrifying shift in IRA tactics away from concentrating on military and political targets, to aiming for civilians.

Sergeant Noel Lane, 26, a newly married and freshly promoted police officer, had noticed the parked car pointing the wrong way down a one-way side-street. He pulled up in his patrol car, and got out to have a closer look. His suspicions aroused, he took out his radio and reported in to the control room with his call sign. He never finished his next sentence. 'I've just . . .' he began, and then all the room could hear was the roar of the explosion. He was killed instantly. Close by was Constable Jane Arbuthnot, 21, the friend Adrienne Butterworth had swapped shifts with to keep her date with Ryan. She had been with the force for two and a half years and was looking forward to her wedding planned for a few weeks later. She had been issuing parking tickets in the streets around Harrods as part of an anti-terrorist tactic aimed at keeping the area clear. She too was killed immediately.

When the bomb exploded, it devastated the first four floors of Harrods, sending slivers of glass and metal slicing through the Christmas crowd. Many people were blown off their feet by the force of the blast, and cars on the street outside toppled over. The twisted remains of the bomb car's bonnet were found later on the roof of offices opposite Harrods. The manager of a nearby shop said, 'People were screaming and jumping out of their cars. A lot of people just stood on the pavement crying. It was chaos. It was pandemonium.' French photographer Jean Claude Gheno described it as 'a boom and blast wave that compressed my chest. Many were hurt. One girl was blown through a plate-glass window and had all her clothes ripped off. I saw wounded children blown on to a traffic island by the zebra crossing.' Flames leapt from the wreck of the car and a huge pall of smoke billowed into the sky.

Among the ninety-one injured were thirteen police officers, all ferried to hospital by a fleet of seventy-five ambulances. Eleven civilians and four policemen were in a serious condition. A third officer, Inspector Stephen Dodd, died later. The civilian dead were journalist Philip Geddes, 24, American management consultant Kenneth Salvesen, 31, and Caroline Cochrane-Patrick, 25. Many of the injured were maimed for life, including dog-handler PC John Gordon, who lost one leg in the blast, and then later had to have the other amputated. His dog, Queenie, was so seriously hurt she had to be put down.

Some of the injured officers had raced over the moment they heard of the bomb warning from their refreshment building close to the station at Chelsea where they'd been having a break, 'It was those officers who took the brunt of the explosion,' says Ryan. 'They could have stayed behind to have a meal, but they didn't, they volunteered. It cost them so dearly.'

Police had already been dealing with twelve or thirteen calls of suspect packages when the warning came in. While they all raced to the scene, it was difficult to know what to do for the best. There were 5000 staff and tens of thousands of shoppers in Harrods and on the streets outside. Indeed, if the store had been completely evacuated, the carnage would have been unthinkable. A Salvation Army band that had been playing on the corner of Hans Crescent the previous Saturday had, luckily, been moved over to Brompton Road that day to avoid causing a bottleneck. That single action had saved the lives of countless more among their own ranks and the crowds that would have been standing around them.

As it was, the aftermath was still terrible. Ryan, as the senior officer, took charge of the scene immediately, arranging for roads to be blocked, uninjured people to be cleared away, casualties evacuated, and police officers marshalled to command posts. He set up his own incident post at the back of Harrods and asked the anti-terrorist bomb disposal and investigations unit for scenes of crime to meet him there.

I can't forget the calm that I felt in dealing with it. I didn't panic. At first, my mind went numb. Then I switched into calm decision-making. I was thinking it through. I had this incredible clarity of thought. But it was extremely hard; the stress was absolutely enormous. One of the hardest things to do was prevent police officers coming to the scene because, once the news had broken, the reserves all flooded in to help. There were just dozens and dozens of police available for duty, but I wanted just to marshal all my troops and find out who was injured, who was there. We already knew who was dead. A senior manager from Harrods kept wanting to go in and secure the place because everybody had run out leaving all the tills full of money. But we were completely surrounding the store, so there couldn't be any looters. Even so, goodness knows what people ran out of the store with.

The Prime Minister then rang in on the radio-phone to ask Ryan what had happened. She listened in silence, then said she'd be there as soon as she could. She arrived a few hours later, dressed all in black, with husband Denis in tow, and was taken on a tour of the scene. Everyone was tense. The warning had included other bombs, and there were fears there was still one yet to go off inside the gigantic store. The police detection equipment kept registering an electronic signal, taken to be another explosive device, so everything halted every time the signal came. Later that evening, it was discovered to be a burst of digital information being transmitted through a media centre nearby.

Mrs Thatcher then asked to be taken to the police station. She wanted to visit everyone who'd been on duty that day, and who'd rushed in to help with the rescue effort. She'd always felt a special bond with that station in any case, she told Ryan. Her home in Flood Street was less than a kilometre away, so it was actually her local station. Once there, she was clearly moved by both the atmosphere of highly charged emotion, and the stories of selfless courage. She walked through the station slowly, speaking to every officer there. Many were still in shock. Others were openly weeping. Ryan saw tears glint in her own eyes and gently suggested she come to his office for a cup of tea. They sat quietly as the tea was made. There seemed nothing to say. Tears began to roll down Mrs Thatcher's face. 'That touched everyone,' says Ryan, 'to see the so-called "Iron Lady" so upset by what she'd seen. Everyone cracked and started weeping.'

Once she'd finally regained her composure, the Prime Minister called a press conference. There was no trace of tears then, just simple anger as she described the terrorist act as 'a wicked crime against humanity – and against Christmas'. Home Secretary Leon Brittan later declared, 'No words can adequately express my feelings of outrage and horror at this cold-blooded, ruthless and cowardly act.' At 5 p.m. Ryan was interviewed for the TV news bulletin. Mike Jukes, sitting at home, unaware of what had happened, switched on to see him talking about the tragedy. 'He came across exceptionally well,' he says. 'He was very calm and obviously holding things together.'

Halfway through the afternoon, Sergeant Noel Lane's wife phoned in, almost hysterical with worry. By 2.30 p.m. Ryan had known Lane was dead. But because the body hadn't been found – it was thought still to be lying under the bomb car – he was forbidden by the commander of the anti-terrorism squad to tell his wife anything. 'But who else *could* it be?' pleaded Ryan. They'd found the torn uniform epaulette with C51 on it, Sergeant Lane's own ID. 'No one else would have been wearing his uniform! We've *got* to tell his wife.' The commander, however, refused, and the wife rang and rang and rang. By the end, towards nightfall, she'd started calling everyone liars. '*Why* aren't you telling me?' she'd sobbed. At 7.30 p.m. Ryan finally told her.

A briefing centre was set up at the newly evacuated Holiday Inn on Sloane Street for meetings between the anti-terrorist group, Ryan, his senior commanders, the area commanders, and advisors from Scotland Yard. The immediate concerns were to work out casualty clearance and housing evacuations, how to get London back to normal, and the progress of the investigation. At 9 p.m. the group dispersed, and Ryan trudged towards the door ready to go back to the scene. The hotel manager grabbed his arm just as he was about leave. 'Where do you have to get back to tonight, Peter?' he asked. Ryan told him he was going back on duty and would then head off back to North London, to his flat in Hendon to catch a few hours sleep before reporting back on duty the next morning at 6 a.m. 'Oh, you can't do that,' said the manager, 'Stay here overnight and then go straight back on duty tomorrow.' Ryan, nearly dead on his feet, nodded wearily. 'That'd be great,' he said, his voice thick with tiredness. 'Thanks. I'll be back about 10.30 p.m., as soon as I've handed over to the night shift.'

The next morning, Ryan called for a sergeant and the two walked slowly back through the scene to check they hadn't missed anything the night before. Apart from the crash of the earth-moving equipment and the continuing steady thin drizzle of rain on the pavement, there was an eerie silence. The air was filled with the acrid stench of burnt rubber. Scarlet pools of blood still lay on the road. There was the brass glint of a battered trumpet left by the Salvation Army band, and streamers fluttering from a smashed drum. A couple of brightly coloured balloons were tangled round a lamppost. Ripped awnings slapped in the cold breeze. After ten minutes, Ryan suddenly stopped dead. He could swear he'd heard a faint whimpering. They retraced their steps back to a bank just around the corner from Harrods. The doorway was completely blown in, and covered with broken glass, billboards and car parts. The pair started tearing it away with their bare hands. The pleas for help grew steadily louder, as they started to make out the inside of the bank, with banknotes strewn all over the floor. Pulling away the last piece of hoarding, they uncovered a tiny old lady, dressed all in black, with black lace gloves and a long black skirt, looking for all the world like a character straight from a novel by Dickens. The sergeant picked up the woman like a child. She'd been trapped in the bank since the lunchtime before, she explained. She was uninjured but confused. As the volunteers poured her tea, she gradually started making more sense. 'I just wanted to get some money out to buy Christmas presents for my family,' she said. 'I haven't been out of the house for weeks.'

It took nearly a week to clear the scene, only a few days for the IRA to claim the bombing was an 'unauthorised' attack on civilians by a rebel active service unit, and months to effectively rebuild morale among the shattered officers at Chelsea division. Everyone there was in deep shock at having a shift of officers hospitalised or killed. 'The hardest thing was to bring the station round, to hold it together so it didn't fall apart,' says Ryan.

> I kept them on their feet by encouraging them to express their feelings, to talk to each other, to talk to me. Everybody looked at you, and you'd put your arm around them or just held a shoulder or shook their hand, and said, 'It will be okay, it will be fine, just keep going.' I remember straight after the incident and all that day, people came in off duty and wanted to put their uniforms on and work. Of course I had to send them home again, because then they wouldn't have been any use on their own shift. Scotland Yard thought they were being helpful by sending me some sergeants and two busloads of police to work with us in the police station to take the place of those who'd been injured, but as soon as they arrived, they realised they were outsiders. They hadn't shared the experience, they weren't one of us, and they found it very difficult.

Because now, Ryan was most definitely one of the team at Chelsea. The way he had dealt with the tragedy, his traumatised officers and the demands of the press brought praise from all sides. 'He played a blinder,' says Barry Greenhalgh, who recently retired from the police. 'I've seen a lot of headless chickens in my time when things go wrong, but he was never one of them. He worked everything out in a logical sequence, and disseminated information and organised things without ever going off at a tangent. He did exceptionally well. He's a very able man.'

Adds Jukes, now an inspector working in counter-terrorism in Hampshire, 'He was very calm; I never saw him flap.' Roger Lashbrook, these days working in the Divisional Intelligence Unit at London's Notting Hill, agrees. 'The Harrods bomb was a terrible disaster,' he says. 'Police and civilians alike were blown away, but he came in like a knight on a white charger, leading from the front. That won the respect of everybody. He was so new, but he took us all on board.'

Ryan was, however, feeling the strain. The days following the attack proved draining. Officers were off visiting the injured, some of whom came back to work on crutches or in wheelchairs, and usually heavily bandaged, invariably to a hero's welcome. In the car park, the Fiat Panda WPC Jane Arbuthnot had bought the week before the bomb, sat gathering dust. Everyone saw it, but no one moved it until five months into the new year. Ryan struggled to keep the station functioning as close to normally as possible. He organised extra cars to transport the dead and injured officers' families around. 'He set up the welfare system,' says Bell, who was seconded into that section. 'We didn't have any problems as a result of that. He was thrown in at the deep end, but he never stayed aloof. He mucked in with everyone else.' Ryan's deputy Mick Haimes worked tirelessly beside him to make sure the officers' families didn't suffer any more than they were already. Since, in those days, there was no police welfare structure, Haimes battled to make sure everyone was supported.

Ryan also greeted the tide of well-wishers dropping into the station to offer their support. Some were locals, deeply touched by the bravery of their local bobbies, and forever grateful. Some were politicians, from both the Government and the Opposition. Other visitors were from further afield – police officers from New York, Chicago, and all over Europe. All came to pay their respects. The station was inundated with gifts: champagne, whisky, chocolates and cash.

Ryan set up a trust fund for the money for the dead and injured, and organised a raffle of the gifts to raise money for the fund. Often, visitors would move the entire station to tears. Lashbrook recalls the morning a woman walked in with her 7-year-old son. He was carefully carrying a cake aloft. 'My son said he wanted to donate his birthday cake,' whispered the woman, as the little boy tried to lift it on to the counter. There wasn't a dry eye in the place.

'There were so many letters that came in in sympathy,' says Lashbrook. 'I remember seeing Peter Ryan sitting there and answering every single letter by hand. Some letters were very tearful. But Peter wrote to each and every one of them, saying thanks.'

Throughout the misery of the funerals too, the police station bonded closer and closer together. Police came from all over the country, and the world, to attend, with crowds huddled outside St Luke's Church to listen to the services being broadcast, and traffic stopping on the road by the church as a mark of respect. After each funeral, everyone would pour into the pub next door, The Bricklayer's Arms, for beer and sandwiches, and vent their grief. Not one uninjured officer took any time off for sick leave or stress during all that time. Everyone just wanted to be together. 'Those days changed my life,' says Ryan. 'It was the trauma of the deaths and injuries, and the effort of trying to keep the station going and officers together on their feet. It was an extraordinary period.'

They were also among the toughest days he would ever have to experience. Alone in London, with his family, friends and steady girlfriend Gillian far away up north, he had little personal support of his own. He hadn't had enough time to make any close friends in London and, having known Adrienne for only little more than a week, this hardly seemed the right time to start a new relationship. On the outside, he was the cheerful, upbeat, tower of strength of the station. On the inside, he was struggling. One night when a group of his men saw him huddled late in his office yet again, they knocked and went straight in. 'We're taking you out on the piss tonight, Sir,' Lashbrook told him. Peter sighed and eventually agreed to go out with them.

But it was even harder when the families of the dead came into the station. The father of the American, Kenneth Salvesen, kept dropping by, wanting to talk about his son. Ryan listened sympathetically. One day, desperate for mementoes, he asked him if they'd found his engraved Rolex watch. Ryan phoned forensics, who went back to the body and found the crumpled watch still on his wrist. He then organised for it to be restored by a jeweller before handing it over to the tearful family. Jane Arbuthnot's parents' visits were draining too. They were always very emotional, and Ryan would find himself weeping with them in his office. 'It didn't take much to upset me,' he says. 'It was a very, very hard time. In those days, there was no such thing as stress counselling.' Her brother made an application to become a special constable, but he was turned down, in case he wouldn't be doing the job for the right reasons.

Things were trickier with Noel Lane's wife. Despite the tradition that every police officer who dies on duty be given a police funeral, she was determined that he was going to have a private send-off. His colleagues begged her to reconsider, but she was adamant: she wanted something very, very quiet, with only a few senior officers permitted to attend. It was probably because she'd felt so betrayed that she hadn't been given the news of her husband's death until six hours afterwards.

On Christmas Eve, Ryan went to the hospital with Haimes to visit Inspector Stephen Dodd for the last time. His wife was sitting by the bed, gazing sadly at the terribly injured shell of the man she'd loved. Ryan put his arm around her, and agreed to stay for a conference with the doctor. The prognosis was without hope. Nothing was registering on the instruments except a heartbeat. As Ryan held her, she agreed to turn off the life support. He then returned to the station and, together with Haimes and the others on duty in the communications room, sat and rang every officer from the station, wherever they were in the country, to tell them that Stephen had died.

The publicity over the attack continued unabated for the next three months, fuelled by outrage, fear that other parts of the mainland would be targeted, continuing debate over whether the Sinn Fein should be outlawed and the hunt for the bombers. Ryan was pictured regularly on TV talking about the bombing and its aftermath. At first, the suggestion was that the IRA unit responsible had been acting independently and the bombing was never authorised.

Much later, it turned out the unit was on an official mission to attack Harrods, 'to let the Brits know we could still strike at their hearts' said the Army Council, although the intent was never to kill civilians. Eventually, the man thought to have been in charge of the unit responsible, Paul Kavanagh, was sent to jail for thirty-five years. Ryan was blunt on the subject. 'No, I don't forgive those bastards,' he'd say, when asked. 'How could anyone? Look at what they've done. I've no forgiveness. They're murdering, evil bastards.' Later, he moved on to thanking the efforts of those all around the country who'd launched sponsored walks and marathons, and even a cycle ride the length of Britain to raise money for their trust fund. Gradually, it all turned him into a well-known national figure.

Finally, in a bid to close the chapter on the tragedy, Ryan suggested the police hold a ball, together with the nurses and doctors from the trauma units who'd treated the bomb victims, and invite anyone along who wanted to buy a ticket. All the gifts brought into the station could also be raffled on the night to add to the coffers. His area commander poured scorn on the idea. He urged Ryan to move on, and argued it would be an embarrassing flop, with no one wanting to buy tickets or wear black tie. He couldn't have been more wrong. The tickets sold out within days and the only person not to have a good time was Ryan himself. It was held the night of his 40th birthday and, with Adrienne off attending a sister's wedding, he sat at his table at the Carlton Hotel in the middle of a crowd of nurses, and had never felt more alone in his life.

CHAPTER 7

Out of
the ashes

IT HADN'T BEEN the most promising start to their relationship, but
Peter Ryan and Adrienne Butterworth grew close very quickly in
those dark months after the Harrods bomb. Under incredible strain
at work, and without friends or family locally, he came to look forward more and more to their evenings out, and their nights in her
flat in Twickenham, West London, or at his place in Pimlico. She, in
turn, was flattered by the attentions of the boss, a man who was
obviously going places, and touched by the vulnerability he occasionally allowed her to glimpse.

There were obvious hurdles. For a start, there was the problem of
Ryan being the head of the station and she being one of his staff, particularly in such a conservative organisation where demarcations
were strictly observed. Both knew their liaison would be frowned
upon, and did their best to keep it secret. Adrienne confided only in
her closest friends; Ryan told no one. They met well away from the
station, and at work tried to preserve a pleasant, professional distance. They felt they were being incredibly discreet, but it's hard to
keep secrets in the police force. Colleague Roger Lashbrook was
amused. 'One day, I came straight out and asked her, are you having
an affair with Peter?' he says. 'She denied it. I told her to stop telling
porkies [lies]. In the end, she admitted it and asked, "Does anyone
know?" I had to smile. "Yes," I said. "Everyone does."'

Then, of course, there was the age difference. Ryan was 39 when
they went out on that first date, while she was just 23. And finally

there was the unsettling fact that he was still seeing Gillian back in Lancashire.

Adrienne knew all that, but she was determined, in any case, that she wouldn't allow herself to get too involved. When Ryan had asked her out that afternoon in his office, she'd had to take a moment alone to reflect. It hadn't been exactly a surprise; she'd often seen him studying her during meetings he had with the Policy and Planning Group of which she was the only female member, and had checked the book at the front desk which contained everyone's personal details to see whether he was married. When they were alone, he'd even been a little flirtatious, in a formal sort of way. That evening, she went to visit her father, Michael, who lived around the corner from Chelsea. An ex-military man, separated from her mother, he'd warned her of the difficulties of dating across the ranks. 'Look, I'm only going to go out with him this once,' she'd replied. 'I'm just curious to see what he's like.'

The age difference wasn't much of a consideration. Her father Michael had been ten years older than Adrienne's mother Margaret when they'd married and after their divorce, twenty-two years later, had married an even younger woman when Adrienne was 17. In turn, Adrienne's mother had gone on to take a second husband, Gerald, who was twelve years older. Besides, Adrienne had always been attracted to older men. 'They do say you tend to marry people like your father,' she admits. 'In some ways, he was. He was very traditional in his values, but then I'm quite traditional and conservative too.' As for Gillian, whom Ryan visited regularly one weekend out of every three, Adrienne wasn't particularly bothered. After all, she was still dazzled by the boss's attentions, and wasn't terribly experienced with men. She didn't really feel in a position to object and, if they were only to go out once or twice, what did it matter?

The bomb may have caused a false start in their relationship, but the aftermath changed everything. Her heart went out to Ryan as she watched him on TV, putting a brave face on a tragedy she knew had shattered him. She worried over the way he lost six kilos in just five days. She fretted that he was so lonely, 'He doesn't like to be alone,' she says. And, gradually, she fell in love.

The intensity of Ryan's feelings for her took him by surprise too. He'd been attracted to her from the first day he saw her.

She was very good-looking, tall, slim and with this beautiful long hair like you see on advertisements for shampoo. It was shiny and wavy as she walked, and she also had a little bit of a wiggle, and the combination was more than I could resist. She was highly intelligent, very articulate, spoke very nice English and was obviously very cultured. I think she was shocked when I asked her out, and quite rightly, because a commanding officer with a young woman . . .

Appearances always mattered to Ryan, and Adrienne, always immaculately turned out and well spoken, fitted in neatly with his own aspirations. Indeed, she stood out in a profession that still tended to be dominated by working-class men. She'd even been nicknamed 'The Duchess' at the police training college because of her cut-glass accent, and teased that she probably always farted into a Tupperware box.

Adrienne had ended up in his office quite by chance. Born in Zambia as the youngest of three daughters, and nicknamed 'Tiny' by her excited sisters on her birth, she'd continually moved schools and countries as her father was posted around the world by the British army. Studying for her A Levels when her parents split up, she left school shortly afterwards at 17, halfway through the course, and found a job in a money-broker's office in London. One of only three women out of 500 men, she loathed the macho environment and became disillusioned when told by her boss that it would be almost impossible for a woman to become a fully-fledged broker. Visiting her mother at her office opposite Scotland Yard one day, on a whim she called into the police careers office. She'd never considered a career in the police before, but had always found TV dramas about the police vaguely exciting. Her first day as a 19-year-old probationer in the Metropolitan Police was on 19 May 1980 – exactly seventeen years, to the day, after Ryan graduated from the cadets to join the force.

Adrienne, still called 'Tiny' – despite standing at 1.77 metres tall – didn't enjoy the first few years. In those days, you went out on the beat alone and, while men had a hard hat and truncheon for protection, women had only a soft hat and the handbag that the regulations stated they had to carry. 'I hated going on the beat,' she says. 'It was always cold, miserable and lonely. You'd get into fights and get kicked and shoved. The men resented us because we got £1 0s 17d more than them, for our tights [pantihose] allowance, and they treated us like second-class citizens. I made a close friend, Melanie, and we spent most of our time in the station toilets, eating chocolate cake and playing cards.' When forced out on to the beat at night, a boyfriend would bring her pizza and keep her company. Constable Mike Jukes, then a constable, remembers her as not the most enthusiastic of officers. 'She'd come in and then spend the first half-hour brushing her hair,' he says. 'But I liked her. She could really hold her own with anyone. She and Peter were a good match.'

She was stationed at Kensington at first, but had problems with her supervising inspector. He was universally loathed by his crew for telling them to falsify arrest records for prostitutes and for his entrapment tactics with gay men. He also had a thing for Adrienne. He forbade the men to let her join their traditional drinks at the end of the night shift and, when she started going out with a constable colleague, started appearing in the driveway of her police section house, or parking at the end of her mother's mews. Finally, the station bosses acted by transferring her away from trouble to Chelsea station. Once there, she jumped at the chance of an office job with the newly formed Policy and Planning group, being trialled at Chelsea to examine a new set of ideas called 'Policing by Objectives'.

It was a group warmly endorsed by Ryan. For the first time, business management techniques were being applied to the running of the force, and he was eager to see his Met division being run smarter and more efficiently. Officers there at the time say he introduced better briefings, in place of the old system of only issuing information on a need-to-know basis, and focussed on cutting down burglaries and motor-vehicle crime, rather than merely responding to emergencies. 'The only time the old boss spoke to you was to lay into you, tell you off,' says his old inspector, Mike Jukes.

Peter Ryan always played his cards close to his chest, but told us to tell him when things went wrong, so they could work out how to make it better next time. We used to just report crime, not investigate it. But he continued the work of using crime analysis to look at where crime was happening and when, so he could put more manpower on at those times, rather than just dividing us all into three shifts. The reality is that bobbies on the beat make the public feel good, but it doesn't prevent crime. People just commit crime round the corner. Resources are better used investigating crime and catching people. If you put police on street corners, the crime figures go through the roof.

That was a policing debate going on to the very last day of Peter Ryan's time in Australia. Politicians love the idea of putting police on the streets where people can see them; Ryan along with many international experts in the field, believes they often work more effectively when they can't be seen.

Back in Chelsea, Adrienne wasn't the only one growing fonder of him. Lashbrook appreciated the way he was so positive in his outlook, spoke well and always looked good, although he wasn't above taking the micky out of him for it. 'He could be a little bit of a poser,' he says. 'I remember catching him one day in his office doing his hair and trying to work out if he looked better in his mac with its collar up or down.'

Yet as Ryan's popularity with his troops increased, particularly as a result of his handling of the bombing, he was becoming a thorn in the side of some of the command above him. They didn't like the fact that his station had been selected as a 'model division' by the Met Commissioner Sir Kenneth Newman, and given the 'Policing by Objectives' initiative to trial. The publicity he was receiving as a result of the bomb was also resented. 'It irritated the hell out of certain metropolitan commanders, senior officers who thought that I was an upstart,' says Ryan. Things grew worse when he put in a report saying the police officers, nurses and doctors who ran to the scene when everyone else was running away should be given medals, or at least a Commissioner's Commendation. The Area Command refused point-blank: there couldn't possibly be any medals given out when the culprits hadn't been caught. Ryan was incensed, and started a campaign within the station to win his officers recognition. Three years later, they were finally given Commissioner's Commendations but, at the time, it did nothing to help his standing with his senior officers.

The prickly relationship came to a head one day at one of the regular district commanders' meetings at Earls Court. On Ryan's way there, a report came over the radio of an armed robbery in progress at a jeweller's shop 100 metres away on Kensington High Street. He immediately said he'd attend, called for back-up and jumped from the car. He raced into the shop, sized up the gunman, and crash-tackled him just as he raised his revolver to shoot. The shop-owner's son leapt over the counter and dived in to help. A young constable on foot patrol peeped around the door as they wrestled, and Ryan asked if he had any handcuffs, so the villain could be arrested and taken away. At that moment, the armed robbery squad and armed diplomatic squad screeched up, and reeled back in surprise at the scene.

Ryan dusted himself off and continued on to the meeting. At the front door, the Commanding Officer's staff officer was pacing backwards and forwards. 'Where have you been?' he barked. 'You're late! They're furious with you.' Ryan went into the office and was immediately assailed with a stream of invective. 'I want a word with you, how dare you insult us by being late!' shouted the Commander. 'You think you're bigger and better than us, do you?' Ryan tried to stay calm. 'I've just arrested an armed robber down the street,' he said. 'If you look out of the window, you'll just see him arriving in the charge room.' The Commander was unimpressed. 'Bloody typical!' he muttered. 'Ryan upstages us all again!' Ryan shrugged. He was later to get a similarly hostile reception when he took over as Commissioner in New South Wales. 'That was the type of treatment I received in London,' he says. 'So coming to New South Wales, I felt I'd already been there, done that and worn the T-shirt.'

The strain of anxiety about further IRA activity continued unabated too. Among the sackloads of mail from well-wishers were death threats to both those in the station and Ryan personally, as well as two hoax parcel bombs and one real one. One Sunday evening, when he returned to his apartment in Pimlico from a weekend in Lancashire, he put his key in the front-door lock and the door fell in. It had been taken completely off its hinges. Fearing a booby trap, Ryan dived to the side and lay there, waiting for the explosion.

It never came. Eventually, he crawled, on his hands and knees, along the hallway, and called the local police. A young constable arrived a couple of hours later, took a cursory look around the flat, and offered the suggestion that maybe vandals had been at work. Then the Special Branch called round, fingerprinted the entire place and ordered that the door be reinforced with a fitted-iron frame and bars.

Much of the time in London, however, was spent policing the various massive demonstrations that were marching through the capital: against apartheid, racism, the Chilean dictator Augustus Pinochet, and for gay rights, abortion on demand and animal liberation. With so many marches starting in the Chelsea area, the other commanders took great delight in constantly nominating him to look after the entire routes of the demonstrations. Ryan's tactics were always to try and keep a march moving and peaceful, with minimal arrests, although others were often eager to call in the riot police and clamp down hard on the slightest infraction. One 15 000-strong anti-vivisection march threatened to descend into chaos when a truck carrying a giant teddy bear speared with syringes wouldn't move off. Battling his way through the crowd to reach it, Ryan was amused to hear his deputy threaten to arrest the drivers for torturing teddies if they didn't get a move on. A gay rights march nearly descended into a riot when three participants were arrested for becoming involved in an altercation with a couple of drunks shouting obscenities on the steps of the National Gallery. The entire march sat down in the road by Trafalgar Square in protest, threatening to bring the city to a grinding halt. Ryan demanded that the men be set free with a caution, in the interests of getting the march going again, against the determined opposition of those who felt officers in riot gear should be called in to clear the crowds.

Exhausted at the end of that day, Ryan still then had to go into the station for the late shift. That night, there were three murders and since so many people were on annual leave, he had to set up the incident rooms, launch investigations into each one, organise for witnesses to be interviewed and make the arrests of suspects. After working the Monday and Tuesday afterwards, he was shattered, and took the Wednesday off. When he returned to work, however, he was paraded before the Commander for taking time off without permission.

I was in no way a rebel, but I didn't fit in with the useless way they managed the place. I was never a mason, which was a problem. The first time I set foot in a masonic lodge was in Sydney where we use the Masonic Centre for conferences. But there was obvious corruption, too. It wasn't so much people taking backhanders – although I'm sure that did happen in some areas – it was mate-ism, and covering-up. It was all about long, wet lunches in very, very smart hotels for which people would pay a huge amount of money and travel from all over London. That was networking, that was how you got on. They often ended up almost secondary Lodge meetings. It was very difficult.

In March 1984, Britain's second big miner's strike had begun and fast developed into one of the country's longest and most acrimonious industrial disputes of the century. The Thatcher Government had announced plans to close twenty of the country's 174 State-owned coal pits with the loss of 20 000 jobs. National Union of Mineworker's president Arthur Scargill called his members out and refused Government dictates to hold a national ballot on the strike action. A few days later, forty-four pits went back into production, run by miners mostly in Nottinghamshire, who refused to obey the strike call. It was a bitter division that caused a massive rift not only between miners and the mining communities at the old industrial heart of Britain, but in the country as a whole. On the one side stood Mrs Thatcher, determined to break what she considered to be a trade-union stranglehold on the nation to restructure the economy along free-market principles. On the other were those who saw the confrontation as a watershed for organised labour, determined to protect jobs in areas of Britain hardest hit by industrial decline. The struggle was marked by the almost daily clashes between striking miners picketing the working pits, and those miners crossing their picket lines to keep them going.

Police from around the country were bussed to the pits. Ryan was sent up with a large contingent of Met officers on two-week secondments to the picket lines in Nottinghamshire. He'd already had plenty of experience policing picket lines in Lancashire, standing grimly outside factories as the traditional industries slowly died out and the workers vainly tried to defend their evaporating rights. These picket lines were different, however. No one in Britain had ever seen such ferocity in an industrial dispute before. The police were determined to take a hard line with the strikers. Their training had included the example of the disastrous battle of Saltley Gates, where miners on their 1972 strike had formed a mass picket that successfully closed the Saltley coke depot in the Midlands – the first-ever defeat for the police – which led directly to the miners' eventual triumph.

But this time around mostly it was simply cold, miserable, boring work for the police. The striking miners would stand around braziers trying to keep warm, chatting to the police, until a shift of non-striking miners would arrive and the scene would explode into pushing and shoving, chants of 'Scab! Scab!', thrown bricks and attempts to dive in front of the buses bringing in the workers. Often people would be injured in the clashes. Then everything would quieten down again until the shift ended and the working miners came back out through the picket lines.

The relationship between the police and the pickets was a volatile one. There were some who saw themselves as natural enemies. Some officers would openly taunt the striking miners, with boasts about the kind of huge sums in overtime pay and away-from-home allowances they were earning. Others, however, were more circumspect. Ryan, from a northern industrial area himself, often felt sorry for the miners, who were having to eke out a living without wages, any State benefits and even their traditional coal allowance. 'As the strike went on, they obviously ran out of money and they were absolutely poverty-stricken,' he says. 'At the picket lines, the police were always fed. A truck would arrive in the back of which was plenty of hot food and we had things like chocolate bars, fruit and sandwiches. There was always plenty to eat. Of course we shared it with the miners because they didn't have anything. Often the relationship between the police and the miners developed, instead of into enmity, into one of tolerance.'

Between trips to Nottinghamshire and back to Lancashire to see his family and girlfriend Gillian, and amidst all the trauma of the Harrods bombing and its aftermath, Ryan's relationship with Adrienne back in London was becoming more and more intense. 'I'd never been out with another police officer before, so I think there was an understanding there of the problems,' says Ryan. 'I also think we got very close more quickly because we understood the trauma of the bomb, and the pain of it all. We were able to help each other. It was shared experience.' One evening, tired of the secrecy and fed up with going alone to the various evening functions he was obliged to attend as Chelsea's Chief Superintendent, he decided to take her along to a soiree at the Irish Embassy. She looked gorgeous and, as all eyes in the room swivelled onto her, Ryan thought how wonderful it was to be out with her publicly at last – until the head of the Diplomatic Protection group came over and asked who she was. The very next day, Ryan received a summons to the office of the District Deputy Assistant Commissioner. He'd been told about the relationship and plainly didn't approve. 'It's not done for a Chief Super to be taking out a constable,' he said. Ryan argued back, saying the force was so huge, it was all pretty inconsequential. His boss was unmoved. 'If you were married, though, it would be different,' he said. Ryan arranged for Adrienne to be moved away from Chelsea, to a posting at Earls Court, and, from that point on, the relationship became more serious.

The pair of them got on extremely well. When Adrienne brought Ryan back to her mother's place, Margaret liked him instantly. 'He was good looking and a very dapper man, which I felt was tied up with his ambition,' she says. 'I liked him from the beginning. I felt I could trust him totally. I could talk to him. It was a bit of a concern about the age gap, but I don't think it matters.' Indeed, when Ryan and Adrienne came to spend the weekend at her and husband Gerald's home, she even let the pair share a bedroom, something she'd never allowed her two older daughters to do with their boyfriends. 'Well, I didn't feel as if I could object,' she said. After all, she was only five years older than him.

The shadow of Gillian still fell over their relationship, however. Adrienne gradually began to resent the fact he was still seeing her, even though he kept promising that the end was imminent. In truth, he was still wavering between the two. One weekend, Gillian came down to London for a visit, and Ryan told Adrienne apologetically that he wouldn't be able to see her that week. She couldn't resist phoning him, but put down the phone sharply when Gillian answered. In a fit of pique, she took up with the constable she'd originally dropped for Ryan. 'I was pissed off with Peter, so I started seeing Phil again,' she says. 'But, to be honest, by that stage, I was in love with Peter.'

In August 1984, eight months after that first abortive date, the couple had their first big row. Adrienne had invited Ryan to the wedding of her best friend in the Met, Melanie Lockhart, but, when they arrived at the reception, she disappeared to socialise with all the other friends she had there. Ryan was left alone and livid. If his car hadn't been blocked in by others on the road outside, he would have walked out, right there and then, on both the wedding and the relationship. As it was, he was forced to stay and they had a blistering argument: about Phil, about Gillian, and about where they wanted their relationship to go. Ryan was torn between the two women in his life, both so different. Gillian, he felt, was always happy and smiling and they never had an argument all the time they were together. Adrienne was a different prospect entirely. They couldn't even agree on the outcome of their row: Ryan says Adrienne proposed to him; she says he proposed to her.

Their friends were taken by surprise. 'I liked him, but at first I thought he was too serious and staid for her,' says Melanie. 'She was always so bolshie and lively. I warned her about the age difference between them too. I don't think it was true love in the beginning. It was more of a partnership. I think his rank was attractive to her, and obviously she found him attractive. And when you compared him to her previous boyfriend, that boyfriend seemed like a little boy.' Maybe it wasn't true love, at first, for Ryan, either. David Renwick has his own theory. 'They seemed to marry fairly quickly and perhaps it might be cynical of me to say he felt he was in a position where he needed to have a wife,' he says carefully.

A few weeks later, however, their decision to marry assumed a new urgency. Ryan received three headhunting phone calls, one asking him if he'd be interested in applying for a job coming up with the Thames Valley Police, another with the West Midlands Police, and a third with the police in North Yorkshire. When North Yorkshire heard they were in competition for his services, they immediately pushed their interview forward, and made it clear they were eager to take him on board as Assistant Chief Constable, to start in November. Ryan was delighted; he had always been on the fast track to success, but this was even faster than he'd ever dared imagine. His Met bosses were annoyed; they'd planned to send him on a six-month advancement program at the Royal Naval Academy in Greenwich and then promote him within London. He couldn't forget or forgive, however, the resentment he'd had to endure there for not being a southerner, and couldn't help but be seduced by the idea of being headhunted and promoted outside London. He arranged to meet Adrienne for a drink in a pub in Sloane Square and broke the news to her there, knowing this was also going to be make-or-break time for their relationship. 'It was almost an ultimatum,' he says. 'But from that time, we agreed that we'd work towards the wedding.' Adrienne was quick to congratulate him, but said she couldn't go with him to Yorkshire at such short notice. She was preparing for her sergeant's exams in February 1985, and knew she wouldn't be able to move until after those. They agreed, therefore, to marry on 16 February, the day after her exams, and that she'd then come and join him.

Many of Ryan's friends were still startled at the haste of the wedding plans. To David Holt, it seemed one weekend he was visiting Ryan in London and his mate casually mentioned his girlfriend might be dropping round. The next, he was receiving the wedding invitation. 'I was surprised how quickly it happened,' he said. 'They'd got involved very quickly.'

At Chelsea police station, his farewell party was packed. Some officers were even tearful to be losing the man who'd built them into such a strong team after the Harrods disaster. 'He was so popular and the speeches showed how everyone had come to love him,' says Lashbrook. 'We saw him as a real copper's copper. He was quite overcome by it all. I remember standing with him at the bar and saying, "Look around, Peter. This is what we think of you." He gulped.' Barry Greenhalgh, too, was very sad the boss was off. 'He was a man's man, forthright and competent,' he says. 'He called a spade a spade, and didn't suffer fools. With him, you got what you saw. He knew exactly what he was doing. He consolidated his team, and things improved one million per cent under him. He built a good unit.'

Even then, the Met weren't going to make his leaving easy. They nominated him for duty on a demonstration that took place on the Saturday he was meant to be leaving and heading up to Yorkshire. Later that day, to top it off, he received a call saying a raid on a suspected arms dealer was being planned on his patch on the Sunday night, and he would have to attend. He didn't finish until 12.30 on the Monday morning and had to change out of his Met uniform, and start the long drive up to Yorkshire to get to his first day at work there on time. As well as having to adapt to another completely new culture, this time he also had to cope with the separation from Adrienne.

Finally, the day of the wedding dawned cold and bright. Ryan, dressed in top hat and tails, breakfasted alone at the London club where he'd stayed the night, and then set out for the historic old church of St Luke's in Chelsea, in Sydney Street, the same church where Charles Dickens had married – and the funeral services for the Harrods bombing victims had been held. Adrienne arrived, fashionably late, in a full-skirted, high-necked cream gown, its front panel made of antique lace, and her hair caught in a soft bun with long wisps framing her face. She carried a bouquet of yellow and white roses in baby's breath. Her bridesmaids were Vicky, the daughter of Ryan's brother Geoffrey, and Jessica, his god-daughter (the daughter of his friends David and Brenda Holt back in Lancashire). James, the son of Adrienne's older sister Nikki, was her attendant.

The congregation of eighty friends and family shivered through the wedding. There'd been a heavy frost that morning, and the heating pipes in the church had frozen. Adrienne started coughing halfway through the vows and had to stop while the vicar went off to find her a drink, returning with undiluted orange cordial since the water-pipes were frozen too. Despite that, Ryan's sister Maureen looked on approvingly. 'Adrienne was a lot better match for him than Gillian,' she says. 'I've never actually said that to him. But I felt she could go with him. She's the woman behind every man. I'm sure she's good for him.'

That, say Ryan's friends, quite possibly figured too, even if subconsciously, in his decision to choose Adrienne. 'His relationship with Gillian was quite physical,' says Malcolm Bowry. 'But she wouldn't have been right for his career because as you go up the ladder, your partner has to be able to mix comfortably with other people. Adrienne has the great attribute that she understands the business, having been in the police, knows what's required, and isn't fazed by anything.'

The reception, with cocktails and finger food, was held at the Duke of York's Barracks officers mess nearby. From there, they left in the early evening to stay in an old manor-house hotel near Heathrow Airport, with its own four-poster bed. Ryan had booked a cruise in the Carribbean for their honeymoon, but at the last minute the booking fell through, so he managed to find a trip to Sri Lanka, instead.

It wasn't an unqualified success. The setting was idyllic – on a vast silver beach, fringed with palm trees, lapped by a sapphire sea – yet the hotel was deserted but for a few other couples. Naturally, they gravitated towards each other at the swimming pool bar until the man told Adrienne he was a police officer in Yorkshire, on holiday on the bonuses he'd received from the miners' strike, and was planning to tell his employers that he'd hurt his back and would have to go on an ill-health pension until he retired. His initial friendliness, unsurprisingly, turned to ice the moment she told him her husband was his new boss.

On one of their first days at the beach, Ryan went over to investigate a commotion by the water's edge, and ended up helping the locals drag the drowned body of a German backpacker from the sea. Since the village was so remote, and there were no officials within miles, he took charge of the scene, ordering them to take the body to the shade and cover it, while he waited for, first, a doctor, and then the police, to attend, and finally issued instructions for getting in touch with the German consul. By the time he'd arrived back to the hotel, he was terribly burned from the sun. Another night, he was bitten by an insect and his arm and hand swelled up like a balloon. On the way to the airport for the return journey home, the minibus in front of them hit a herd of cows and overturned, leaving its injured passengers lying in the road. Despite Ryan's entreaties, the driver of his vehicle refused point-blank to stop and sped off straight past the accident. Arriving eventually at the airport, they discovered their fellow passengers were a huge crowd of Dutch couples who'd been in Sri Lanka to adopt babies, which, predictably, cried all the way to London.

Finally, gratefully, touching down, the newlyweds went to the house of Adrienne's father Michael for the night, then drove up to Yorkshire the next morning. There, Ryan had rented a cottage that was part of a farmhouse just outside Harrogate. As they started to unpack the car, the couple who owned the farm came over to tell Ryan that there'd been a phone call from a couple who needed to speak to him urgently. Ryan and Adrienne exchanged a look. It was Gillian's parents.

As they went into the house, they agreed he should phone them back. Maybe something had happened to Gillian, or to her grandfather to whom Ryan was particularly close. Ryan picked up the phone and dialled her number. Her mother answered. She'd just heard about the wedding and was absolutely furious. 'How could you do this to our daughter?' she raged. 'She loved you; we all loved you. You led her on and now you've married someone else and ruined her life. How could you have done this to her? It was only recently that I was still doing your washing!' Ryan tried to explain, but she would not listen. Eventually, he put down the phone, shakily, but not before he heard the click of the extension. Adrienne had heard every word.

CHAPTER 8

Family heartbreak

ADRIENNE RYAN WAS devastated by what she'd heard on the phone. Her new husband was adamant that he'd finished with his other girlfriend Gillian in October, but it was obvious that, at the very least, Gillian had not seen it the same way. Tearfully, Adrienne phoned her mother.

'I was shocked and really upset,' she says. 'I remember, though, my mother saying, "He married you, not her." I thought, well, she's right really. After that, it wasn't really an issue. If anything, we laughed about it afterwards.' Adrienne was nothing if not a realist, and her mother Margaret Milner was genuinely fond of Peter Ryan and felt he'd offer her daughter a very happy future. Ryan was nonplussed. Yes, he'd certainly played the field while he was single, often hedging his bets with more than one girlfriend at once but, as the wedding grew close, he'd been sleeping only with Adrienne.

Gillian, however, had a tougher time. Even today, she's brokenhearted about the end of her relationship with Ryan. Working for a small company in the Lake District, she has never married. When asked to talk about Ryan, she burst into tears at merely the mention of his name. 'He hurt me very much,' she says. 'Nobody was more surprised than me that we didn't marry. I thought we would. I was shocked when he married someone else. It's still a scar that runs deep.' She says she wants time to think about whether she's prepared to talk about him. When I phone her as arranged, a few nights later, she says she's decided not to. She finds it all too painful to talk about their relationship and its sudden unexpected end. Even the previous brief conversation had churned up again all that raw hurt. Ryan still feels guilty. 'She loved me desperately,' he says. 'Looking back, I obviously treated her very badly. That's the worst thing with relationships, particularly when one person moves on leaving the other with a broken heart. After that, I missed her friendship so much.'

As for Adrienne, married life had a miserable start that March 1985. She'd caught some kind of bug on the honeymoon (they thought at the beginning it might be mumps) and spent the first month back in the UK in bed. When she was finally well enough, the couple started house-hunting. They'd wanted to live in Harrogate, but the Chief Constable, much to Ryan's irritation, said that was too far from the Northallerton HQ. Once again, Ryan felt he was butting his head against authority, but he had little choice in the end but to obey. They finally settled for an old-fashioned-looking new house built in the middle of an orchard in the picturesque village of Bishop Monkton, further north, near Ripon. Adrienne had quit the police force, knowing it would be too tricky working in a relatively small force of just 4000 people under her husband. Instead, she found a job as a security officer for the department store Debenham's in Harrogate.

Meanwhile, Peter Ryan was discovering that life as Assistant Chief Constable of the North Yorkshire police force was a world away from the Met. On his arrival on that first day at 7 a.m. after driving all night from London, still thinking about the previous night's raid on the arms dealer, he'd parked his car outside the big country manor, Newby Wiske Hall, which served as the North Yorkshire Police HQ. It was frosty, but bright. He wound down the window and sniffed the fresh air, watching the pheasants and rabbits scurry across the lawns. There was nothing but the sound of birdsong. He smiled, wound the window back up and closed his eyes for a quick snooze. At 8 a.m. he woke, climbed stiffly out of the car and, seeing someone stroll past the front of the building, walked up and asked for the canteen. It was the caretaker, who told him the canteen was closed on Mondays. Moreover, he didn't know what accommodation had been allocated for Ryan. And none of the bosses usually arrived until much later. Apologetically, he showed him into the building, made him a cup of instant coffee, with powdered milk, and the pair sat there in his caretaker's cupboard, waiting for the North Yorkshire force to file in. The contrast with London was a body blow. By 7 a.m. he'd always been at his desk with all hell breaking loose around him, arrests to be processed from the night before, and schedules to be drawn up for the day ahead. Here, it was nearly 9 a.m. and there was only the faint voice of an occasional arrival trickling in.

Ryan found his office and his secretary, and then asked to see the Chief Constable. He was told to wait until he was sent for. He was incredulous. Brought up with a strong sense of protocol, and a healthy estimation of his own self-worth, he was appalled at being treated so off-handedly. He waited and waited. It was 9.45 a.m. before he was told that the Chief Constable was finally ready to see him. If he was annoyed by the time he entered his office, he became more furious by the minute inside. The Chief Constable, instead of warmly welcoming his new executive, simply listed the rules, ordered that he not buy a house any more than 25 kilometres away from HQ, inquired about his marital status, and then announced that he'd have to pay his own removal expenses. Ryan wondered if he'd been right to quit the Met.

It took him about three months to settle down. After the sheer speed and pace of London, the terrorism, the embassies, the High Commissions and the bustle of the city, the pace of his new job felt deathly slow. 'I craved the excitement of city policing,' he says. 'I was a pretty unhappy person. I felt I should have held out for that Assistant Chief job with the West Midlands.'

The county of North Yorkshire, while including the ancient cathedral city of York and the towns of Scarborough, Harrogate, Selby, Richmond and Northallerton, is mostly rural, full of beautiful scenery and historic sites, with large iron, steel, coal, textile and clothing industries. When Ryan was posted there, there were just ten murders a year in the whole of the county, compared to, say, a city like Sydney where there are more than ten a month. The only other excitement was the miner's strike, which dragged on until March 1985 when the trickle of men returning to work turned into a flood.

The police were determined to learn whatever lessons they could on industrial-action tactics, logistics and planning from Britain's last mass trade-union strike, but it was the aftermath that presented the most difficult problems. Many officers, used to hefty overtime pay packets, continued to spend at the same rate on their normal wages, ending up heavily in debt. Others found it hard, after all the aggression and confrontation of the dispute, to go back to serving as local bobbies in small towns and villages. There were many reports of stress and complaints about behaviour and attitude. Ryan spent a great deal of his time smoothing out trouble, as well as helping put together the case for the Government to fund the policing of the miners' strike, rather than the entire cost coming out of the police budget. The money that was finally forthcoming was used to re-equip the force, buy new vehicles and refurbish stations. Much of the rest of his time, Ryan spent completely rebuilding the police's administrative system, personnel system and the way that new methods and technology were introduced to support prosecutions.

His main satisfaction came from the easy, leisurely lifestyle afforded by North Yorkshire, giving him time with Adrienne and the chance to complete an Open University MSc on research methods applicable to advanced education and social science. They'd talked about children before they'd got married, but neither had been terribly keen. 'He had been single for ten years, with no responsibilities, and I think the idea of children frightened him,' says Adrienne. 'At that point, we decided we didn't want children. I was only 24; I was happy to say we won't have them. Peter even asked the vicar to remove the prayer in the wedding service asking God to bless the marriage with children.'

As a smoker, Adrienne had gone off the contraceptive pill, and moved on to the cap. In 1986, however, a year and a half into the marriage, she discovered she was pregnant. They were both surprised to find themselves delighted. But eight weeks into the pregnancy, she started bleeding and was prescribed hospital bed-rest in a ward with two other women also desperately trying to hold onto their babies, and, in an incredibly insensitive bed allocation, four more who had just undergone abortions. After nurses explained that morning sickness was the best indication that the baby was alive and well, Adrienne spent each morning turning away the cooked breakfast for a plain biscuit, trying to tell herself she was too nauseous. Yet in her heart, she knew it was a charade; the queasiness was more a product of her mental desperation. Ryan was away on a secret exercise with the Special Air Service (SAS) and, by the time he could be contacted to make it to her bedside, they both knew she had lost the baby.

Adrienne was devastated and consumed by the desire to become pregnant again. 'I was desperate,' she says. 'I suppose it's typical to want what you can't have.' Two months later, she was, this time with twins. 'It didn't make up for the child we'd lost, but it did feel a little like we were being blessed with winning the lottery and the bonus prize.' Ryan was similarly thrilled. 'We were excited, amazed and overjoyed,' he says. 'Twins seemed to be a huge bonus.' The pair went about in a state of bliss, buying cots and a double pram, mulling over colour schemes for a nursery, and swapping their two-seater sports car for a station wagon.

The pregnancy, however, was fraught with worry for Adrienne. She couldn't rid herself of the feeling that things weren't right. She felt her womb tightening and, routinely, she'd weep down the phone to her mother, and then sob in front of her obstetrician, only to be told she had absolutely nothing to worry about. But an internal examination at twenty-five weeks found she was dilating. She was sent home from the hospital and told to return the next day. Lying there, wide awake all night, she knew something was wrong. At 4.30 a.m. she asked Ryan to take her to the hospital. He drove as fast as he could through the fog on the icy April roads, with Adrienne, white-faced with pain, pleading for him to hurry. When they arrived, the obstetrician examined her again and said there was nothing he could do for her: she was in labour and her babies were going to be born so prematurely that they would die. The twin delivery suite at the hospital in Harrogate was full, so Adrienne was bundled into an ambulance on a stretcher to take her to the hospital at Leeds. The driver became lost halfway there, and the local police raced out to give them an escort and stop the other traffic. Then they turned off the road towards Bradford; the Leeds' delivery suite was also full.

Ryan, following along behind, was sick with worry. The fog had got worse and they often had to crawl along at a snail's pace. 'Please hurry up,' he pleaded. 'Please God, take away the fog; help my wife, save my children.' He had no idea what was going on in the ambulance or how she was feeling. When he was stopped by a young police officer, concerned he might be tailing the ambulance to get to work faster, it required a superhuman effort to remain civil.

When they finally arrived, they realised there was no hope the minute Adrienne was examined and the young doctor walked into the delivery suite and asked the nurse, 'They do know they're going to die, don't they?'

Seven hours later, on Good Friday 1987, Adrienne gave birth to a little boy and a little girl, who were christened Simon and Clare by the attending priest giving them the last rites. Immediately, they were put in incubators and moved to another room to die. Adrienne was told to return to her own room. Her regret at doing as she was told and not sitting with them as they died, has haunted her forever. Ryan found the experience similarly traumatic. 'I watched as my first child was born and when I looked at him he was so perfectly formed,' he says. 'I was surprised that he was so big: I had expected a premature baby to be so small. I remember thinking he looked just like me. The nurse took him away and hurried off with the tiny bundle, small arms and legs moving and little mewing sounds coming from inside the blue blanket he was wrapped in.' Clare was born and was also taken away. The couple just sat and hugged and held each other, sobbing. 'We wept for their lost lives and for all the things they would never see or know,' says Ryan. 'I often find myself wondering how the twins would have grown up and . . . I will never know or understand the love a father has for his son.'

Ryan was then sent home, while Adrienne was transferred to the maternity ward, where she lay and wept as mothers nursed their newborns all around her. 'I cannot begin to put into words the pain I experienced sitting there with them as their babies cried and they each, in turn asked me what I'd had,' she says. 'I left that hospital within hours of having given birth and I returned to my home with a shattering sense of loss and hopelessness.'

On Easter Sunday, the couple went to church, but Adrienne fled a few minutes into the service, her faith shaken by the tragedy. Later, the twins were placed together in a small white coffin to be cremated, and their ashes were scattered in a garden of remembrance in the grounds of Bradford Crematorium. Ryan's brother Geoffrey, his wife Christine and their daughter Vicky, Adrienne's bridesmaid, came to their house to bring them flowers and sympathy. A hassock was embroidered – with a picture of a little boy and girl holding hands and the names Simon and Clare – and placed in the 12th-century church of Saint Mary de Haura in New Shoreham, Sussex, next door to Adrienne's mother's house. Gerald planted a tulip tree in memory of the twins in the church grounds, which can be seen from the window of the house.

Still grief-stricken, Adrienne returned to work. Ryan went back to his office, also feeling numb, yet trying desperately to be strong for his wife. Even today, Adrienne weeps whenever she talks about her lost children.

> The experience does change you profoundly. You're never the same person afterwards but, because it's still a taboo subject, people aren't encouraged to talk about it. They don't realise there are other people out there for support, while people who haven't gone through it don't understand why we feel the way we do. They don't realise it's not something you get over quickly and move on to the next pregnancy. For me, it's something that will always be part of me and part of my family.

Much later, when in Sydney, Adrienne wrote a book about the experience, *A Silent Love* (published in 2000), talking of her heartbreak and speaking to many other Australians who'd also been through miscarriage.

For some, the unresolved grief can destroy relationships; for others it serves to make the tie between partners stronger. While Adrienne says Ryan tends to internalise his emotions and thus finds it easier to compartmentalise his life, and move on, it did draw the couple closer. 'We weren't good at talking about it with each other, but I think it brought a real strength to our relationship, as tragedies can,' she says. 'It added an extra bond between us.'

A few months later, in August 1987, Adrienne became pregnant again. This time, she stayed in hospital for the last four months of the pregnancy, her cervix was stitched and she took four-hourly doses of a muscle-relaxant drug. On 29 March 1988, four weeks early, she gave birth to Elizabeth. Within minutes, the baby was rushed to the Special Care Unit and attached to medical monitoring equipment because she seemed to have trouble breathing. Adrienne and Peter felt the same sick dread, all over again. Finally, three weeks later, she was cleared to go home.

Ryan had now been in Yorkshire for over three years, and he felt it was time to move on and up. He was highly regarded within the force, and applied for the vacant Deputy Chief Constable position in the county of Durham, near Newcastle in the north of England. He went up for the interviews and got the job, to start in June 1988. The day he was appointed, he had a phone call from the Met. They had a position for a Deputy Assistant Commissioner and, if he'd like to apply for that, they'd guarantee the job would be his. He told them, with bitter regret, it was a day too late.

With a small baby and a house to pack up, Adrienne wasn't ready to travel with Ryan at such short notice. He moved up to Durham alone, and travelled back to visit his little family at weekends. It wasn't easy. 'Elizabeth screamed every time she saw him,' says Adrienne, 'because she didn't know who he was.' The job always involved sacrifices but, now they had their first child, they were beginning to see how hard those sacrifices sometimes were. Ryan missed them. Adrienne missed him. 'But at the same time, I encouraged him always to go for these promotions,' she says. 'I knew he was ambitious when I married him. I knew we'd end up having to move around a lot. Moving to Durham would be that step closer to becoming a Chief Constable. It was exciting for both of us. He could sense he was getting closer to the top.'

CHAPTER 9

Always
moving on

WHEN PETER RYAN was with the Lancashire county police, he'd become good friends with an officer in the Manchester City force, which covered an area in those days completely surrounded by the county. Every morning, there'd be a trading between the two forces of offenders arrested in the county for committing crimes in the city, and vice versa. If someone had transgressed on both patches, they'd be taken by the officer on whose turf they'd committed the most serious offence. Ryan's new boss, Frank Taylor, the Durham Chief Constable, was that officer from Manchester.

Their friendship eased Ryan through the task of adapting to yet another culture – and Durham was certainly different. Set between the Pennines and the North Sea, it was a county of lonely moors and rivers, of stunning Pennine valleys and pretty little towns. Economically, however, it faced tough times. Once, it had 250 thriving coalmines, a massive steel works at Consett and the great shipyards of Sunderland. All had since closed down, leaving the area with a chronically high rate of unemployment. Ryan could never get over the way, when anyone was arrested and asked their occupation, they'd always name the job they *would* have been doing if any of those industries had survived, rather than admitting they were on the dole. It was also an extremely parochial society. Many people moved only one or two streets away from their parents when they left home to marry. Persuading someone to accept a promotion within the force if it entailed a change of area was always a struggle – even if it was only

118

to a station thirty kilometres away. As a result, over 95 per cent of the force was made up of locals, which meant it had a community strength, spirit and resilience extremely unusual among British police.

All that was in stark contrast to the city of Durham at the centre of the county. With its fabulous 12th-century cathedral, widely regarded as one of the most perfect examples of Romanesque architecture still in existence, its Norman castle, built by William the Conqueror in 1072, and its cobbled streets, it was a magnet for well-heeled tourists, and was over-run by students from the prestigious, wealthy university which, in 1837, had taken over the castle for a college. Indeed, just two years before Ryan arrived in Durham, the castle and cathedral were designated a UNESCO world-heritage site.

Yet it wasn't so much the divisions between rich and poor that concerned the police as past divisions between the police and locals. Certainly, memories of the miners' strike of 1984 and 1985 were still raw, but it was more a long, long history of police being used to intervene in industrial action that rankled. Just before Christmas, Ryan, as a member of Durham's Rotary Club, had been working to raise money to put on a lunch for the widows of the city, and went along to help serve the meal. As he was putting down a plate in front of one elderly woman, she turned to him and her eyes narrowed with hate. 'I know you!' she spat. 'You're that policeman! I don't want anything to do with you. I remember during the strikes, you gave my husband a really hard time.' Ryan was rocked, wondering if there was any truth in her allegation, until someone pointed out she'd been talking about strikes at the county's mines in the 1950s when he was just a boy.

Civil litigation was still being taken out against the police by miners who'd been on strike in 1984 and 1985. Ryan was shown photographs and a video of one particular battle that had taken place in the area. He'd watched, horrified, as miners were beaten with police truncheons, then watched as miners beat the police right back. Working out who had started the fight was impossible; besides it was hard to pinpoint which contingent of police posted to the area had been involved. The anger and bitterness in those old mining communities was palpable. Even in areas where the mines were still working, the populations lived barely above the poverty line, with wages desperately low, and their old back-to-back terrace houses exactly the same as they had been half a century ago when they were first built. Sitting in the middle of one of those areas was one of the few police stations in mainland Britain surrounded by a high fence, topped with barbed wire. Officers attending incidents always travelled in twos and threes, and police cars were never left unguarded on the streets. If they were, they'd be turned over and set on fire.

Ryan took a house on a new estate close to the city and Adrienne and Elizabeth soon moved up to join him. Lonely and feeling isolated with a new baby, Adrienne was driven to desperate measures. One morning, she went out and knocked on all the doors of the houses nearby, inviting everyone to a coffee morning. It was her role, she felt, to find friends in each new posting, and then to nurture those friendships with dinner parties, even though she wasn't much of a chef – she could still only cook two dishes. Besides, she didn't see too much of her husband. Ryan was working ever-longer hours, and was eager to make a good impression in this job, his last before the hoped-for step of becoming a Chief Constable. One night, they went to a function where Frank Taylor was receiving his Queen's Police Medal. 'My only regret,' he told the assembled audience 'is that I was never there for my daughters when they needed me.' Adrienne stole a glance at Ryan. She feared the same thing would be true of him. 'The hardest thing with a police career is that you always feel you come second,' she says. 'Peter loved us, of course, but he also loved his job.'

In January 1989, six months after Ryan had started in Durham, Adrienne fell pregnant again. Their second daughter, Georgina Clare (named after the baby they lost) was born on 1 September.

At this time, frictions were arising within Ryan's own family. The terms of his father's will had left the parental house to Geoffrey, but with the caveat that their mother would be able to live there until her death. Geoffrey had thus moved his wife Christine and their baby daughter Vicky into the house with their mother, Margaret. It wasn't an arrangement that seemed to be working very well. Whenever Margaret came to stay for a couple of weeks with Ryan and Adrienne, she complained that she wasn't being treated well back home. Ryan, naturally fiercely protective of his mother and perhaps feeling guilty that his career didn't give him much time out for her, took her complaints to heart and frequently rang Geoffrey to demand to know what was happening. Adrienne, however, suspected that as soon as Margaret returned home, she'd say exactly the same about them. She could be a difficult woman at the best of times and, since her husband Lawrence's death, had become less and less active.

There had always been frictions between Ryan and his brother Geoffrey, in any case. The six-year age gap meant they weren't close in childhood. 'By the time I was 16, I'd found girls and football and he was still playing with trains,' says Ryan. 'I was out on my motor scooter with friends, and he was still a little boy.' From Geoffrey's perspective, Ryan couldn't really be bothered with his little brother. They grew into quite different people, too, with completely divergent values. Geoffrey, a diesel mechanic, says, 'Peter only got involved if he wanted something doing to his vehicle. Before he went to London, he was on his 46th car. He was always into BMWs and Mercs. Even today, you know them by the car they drive. I would say he's very materialistic. I used to be a little bit like that, I wanted the best car I could afford, but never over the top.'

Ryan didn't like Christine, either. He felt Geoffrey had not married well. In turn, Christine wasn't fond of Ryan or Adrienne. As their mother grew older, the discord grew worse between the brothers. Margaret adored her eldest son, and was incredibly proud of what he'd achieved. It seemed to Geoffrey that every time Peter visited, it was as if he didn't exist. He resented the pedestal on which his mother had put Peter, when he was the one spending so much time looking after her. Peter, on the other hand, didn't seem to put much effort into seeing her at all.

The terms of the will had only aggravated an already tense relationship. Doubtless, Geoffrey and his family hadn't exactly relished the prospect of moving in with Margaret, but they may not have had the financial freedom to refuse. Also, there was a sense of duty there. From Peter's point of view, Adrienne suggests there may have been a niggling feeling that he'd been cheated out of his inheritance as the eldest son. Maureen believes the will was as fair as it could be. Neither she nor Peter were in a position to look after their mother since they both lived some distance away, and they didn't need the money from the sale of the house. It seemed the best solution all round for Geoffrey to take the burden – and the spoils.

Yet when Margaret seemed so unhappy and was obviously growing frailer, Peter suggested she move into a sheltered-housing scheme. He drew up an agreement whereby Geoffrey would buy her out of her half-share of the house. To him it seemed fair; Geoffrey was getting a house for half its cost. To Geoffrey's daughter Vicky, now 23 and working in a building society, it certainly didn't. That whole episode, for her, profoundly coloured her attitude to her uncle.

> Peter would step on everyone and everybody to get where he wanted. He and dad were like JR and Bobby in 'Dallas'. He pretends he was the devoted son, but Nanna only used to see him a couple of times a year. She worshipped him. It was like God when he walked in. Dad rang her three times a day. He got all that thrown back in his face for Peter. She said, 'He's busy, he doesn't get the time to see me.' Basically, my dad didn't exist in Nanna's eyes. Peter didn't give a toss about his family. Mum can't stand him.

Jealousy? Rivalry? Greed? Who knows? Maureen believes that by the end, Margaret had cut Geoffrey out of her life. Geoffrey, however, is sanguine about the experience. He hasn't spoken to his brother for eight years now, since their mother's funeral in 1994, but is thoughtful about their relationship.

> Sometimes, I look at him and what he's achieved and I think: 'Why didn't I get there?' But we're completely different personalities. I'm quite content with what I am. He never has been. He's always looking ahead. [Our sister] Maureen is still down-to-earth. We're still on the same wavelength. She hasn't let anything overtake or override her; she hasn't changed her attitudes. But he's not down-to-earth. He moves on a different plane. You follow them like a [TV] soap.

For Maureen, the scenes at the funeral said it all. 'Peter and Geoffrey didn't speak,' she says. 'Peter was being a bit pompous and unapproachable. He and Adrienne were there in nice clothes, looking fabulous with their little girls, and there was Geoffrey in his anorak.'

Back in Durham, Ryan was growing impatient again for his next move up the ladder. Deputy Chief Constables had to serve a minimum of two years and then were permitted to apply for a Chief Constable's job, usually in another county. Ryan thought a system that always kept you on the move between forces for promotion was a good one: 'It prevents familiarity and complacency, tends to not allow corruption to creep in, and spreads best practice and knowledge.' Yet, it did have a high cost. Every time, the family had to be completely uprooted, the house sold, another bought and yet again refurbished, and a whole set of friends abandoned for a place in which you often knew not a soul.

But Ryan was ambitious, and always had been. Gerald Milner, Adrienne's stepfather, remembers Ryan taking his own son David aside just before he was leaving home to join the Navy. 'He told him to think through his career,' says Gerald. 'He told him he'd mapped his own career out when he'd begun. He'd decided that, every two years, he'd move up to the next stage and, generally, given a month or two each time, he'd succeeded in doing that. By 28 he was determined to be a sergeant, by 31 an inspector. He had his whole career worked out in his mind from a very early age. He suggested David do the same.'

This time, Ryan applied for three jobs, and was short-listed for each. Inevitably, all the interviews clashed, and it was quite possible he'd be offered all three chances to be a Chief Constable in Norfolk, Nottinghamshire, and Cleveland.

Norfolk came up first, so Ryan was forced to make a quick decision. He took it. He'd been selected out of a field of six by local councillors, who in Britain choose their own police chiefs, with the approval of the Home Office. John Alston, in the middle of his ten-year term as the Conservative leader of the county council, sat on the selection panel. 'He was outstanding amongst the people we interviewed,' he says. 'So many Chief Constables appear to be a little bit Sergeant Plod-dish, very dull. He was quite inspirational, well above average intelligence and with a great integrity and a sense of humour. He was also a very blunt and forthright person, so you felt as if you knew what you were going to get.' He was also the only candidate who didn't utter the fateful words: 'Norfolk seems a nice place to retire to.' The recruitment process hit a last-minute hitch, however, when the Home Office refused to approve his appointment. 'He's never known about that,' says Robert Chase, the former chairman of the police authority. 'But they didn't want to endorse him. It seemed as though they had something bigger in mind for him. They didn't want him to go to Norfolk. But we insisted, and in the end they agreed. He'd moved through the ranks so quickly, we knew he must be someone confident in their own ability, and special. He was a clearly a man going places.' Indeed, he'd moved up so fast, there was all-round surprise when it was discovered he'd never been given the Queen's Police Medal. 'He'd never stayed anywhere long enough,' says Gerald Milner.

From Ryan's point of view, the Norfolk police force was known to be in a state of disarray, and he felt that would be a good challenge. In addition, it wouldn't be so far from Adrienne's mother, which would be nice both for them and their children. What they didn't really realise at that point is that Norfolk is on the road to nowhere. On the far east coast rump of Britain, it's a predominantly rural area of rolling green fields, tranquil countryside, meandering broads and picturesque market towns, but is also a fairly isolated part of the country. 'The only people who go to Norfolk are those who are going to Norfolk,' says Ryan. 'And the only people leaving are those leaving Norfolk to go somewhere else. It isn't through anywhere, or on the way to anywhere.' In addition, the roads from Norfolk to London weren't particularly good. Many locals would have been quite happy too to see that situation continue. At one of the first meetings Ryan attended of the police authority, one member actually said that. 'If it was up to me, I would dig a moat around Norfolk and pull up the drawbridges to stop foreigners coming in,' he harrumphed. 'They're the people responsible for all the crime and the problems.'

The family moved down to Norfolk and Ryan started his new job in June 1990; aged 46 years, he was one of the youngest Chief Constables ever appointed in Britain. He knew the job was going to be a test. The joke doing the rounds was that all the interviews for senior staff would run exactly the same way. They'd be asked if they played golf, and if they didn't, they'd be asked if they fished.

If they said no, they'd be asked if they liked to hunt. And if they said no again, the interviewer would reply, astonished, 'So what on earth do you do in the afternoons?'

The crime rate in the county was extremely low, but that had allowed the force to grow slack over the years. There was little quality control over the way officers would be deployed, or even operations such as murder investigations. Instead, everything seemed to happen on an ad hoc basis. It was almost as if the chequebook would simply be flipped open and anyone who wanted to be involved could work all the hours they liked, with overtime paid automatically. In charge was a huge phalanx of senior officers, far out of proportion to the number of members of staff they presided over. In addition, there'd been very uneven investment, over the years, in facilities and equipment. While the police HQ in Norwich was small and cramped, with a 1950s folding card-filing system and no computers at all, they also possessed one of the first automated fingerprint systems in the country, albeit bought second-hand from the Dutch. The organisation was constantly overspending its budget.

Ryan immediately cut back on the number of divisions and senior officers, and launched into the construction of a new administrative framework, an up-to-date technological base with computers in every station linked to a central database, a fresh command structure, a different training regime and a new operational focus. Some of his senior colleagues bristled at the changes and threatened to resign or take early retirement. He was happy to let them go. Some members of the police authority were alarmed at how quickly he was forging ahead. Chase went into HQ one day soon after Ryan's arrival and was shocked to find the place looking as if a bomb had hit it. All the ceilings had been torn down for cabling to be put in to allow all the computers to be networked with each other. He asked whether it was absolutely necessary. If a computer had been needed in the past, the force borrowed one from the Suffolk police at Ipswich. Ryan looked at him with one eyebrow raised. A good computer system would speed up the collection of evidence in cases enormously. 'I've always found the best deterrent to crime,' he replied evenly, 'is to catch people.' Morale shot up as working conditions improved. By the end of his first year in the job, he'd turned around a £3 million deficit to break even. By the end of his second year, the force was underspending for the first time anyone could ever remember.

'He was the first Chief Constable I've ever known who could argue hard and fast for money, then set a budget and come in within it,' says Alston, now the chairman of the local health authority.

> He organised everything extremely well and was very, very popular with everyone. With the council, he wasn't above using his charm to get his own way – he was a good-looking man – but, if there was a disagreement, he'd always make a joke afterwards. He came across very well with the media, looking confident and in charge, which was important for the public, whereas his predecessor was a very shy man.

The family moved into a beautiful big house, Woodford Lodge, which the County Council had bought because it was in the middle of the planned route for a new motorway, just outside Norwich in the village of Wroxham. Ryan was grateful to rent the place, as it took him a year to sell their house in Durham due to the depressed local economy. After that sale had finally gone through, they bought a magnificent 16th-century beamed and thatched manor house, Lacey Farm, sitting in four acres of land in Worstead. It was perhaps the happiest time of the family's life. Friends and family alike admitted that Ryan and Adrienne were a very good match. 'He was a very steadying influence on her, and she needed that,' says Adrienne's mother Margaret. 'She has quite a volatile nature, and he's always been very patient with her. Of course, there were a few difficulties. She was quite headstrong and he was used to being in charge, so they'd have rows about what they should be doing. But as you get older, I think the age gap lessens. He was also a wonderful father. I remember him saying to me that he couldn't believe the depth of feeling he has for his children.'

Sceptics like Ryan's close friend Brenda Holt and Adrienne's best friend Melanie Lockhart were both gradually won over. 'While they are different, I think they complement each other,' says Holt. 'She's the right type of woman for Peter and the job that he's doing.'

Lockhart echoes her. 'Now, I see them as perfect for each other in the fact that she's grown along with him,' she says. 'She's blossomed with him as the years have gone on; he's been the rock behind her. In return, she's been good for him and has always pushed him. He might not have got to where he is without her. He's always been restless and wanted to get to the top, and she's always encouraged him to have a go, to explore every avenue.'

In Norfolk, however, there were some minor irritations. When, for instance, Ryan brought up the question of the car they should give him to drive, they quibbled over the money. Whereas most Chief Constables drove Jaguars, Norfolk gave him just a standard Vauxhall Senator, which had served as an unmarked police car. Ryan, always very particular about what he drove, was annoyed. At conferences with other area's chiefs, they would all turn up in a selection of Jaguars, both with and without chauffeurs, and even, sometimes, in helicopters. There, amongst the row of thirteen to fourteen Jaguars, would be his lone Senator. Every time, his face would burn with anger and shame. At the police authority – the body of elected councillors, magistrates and Home Office appointees which oversee the individual British forces – chairman Robert Chase, a Bentley-driving millionaire who also owned Norwich City Football Club, was embarrassed for him. 'I'm paying better wages and giving more perks to my 19-year-old players than I'm able to give you as Chief Constable,' he told Ryan. That did nothing to ease the niggling feeling of dissatisfaction that had proved to be such a driving force in Ryan's career.

Today, Chase believes Ryan's greatest contribution was to fast-track Norfolk's move into the 20th century. 'He was responsible for us changing direction,' he says. 'He put us onto modern technology. He got us value for money. And he was a great politician. He'd put his case crisply in a couple of sentences that people in Norfolk before had taken three pages to do, and then argue it. If he couldn't get it through, he'd just move on.' His masterstroke at police authority meetings was to bring along half a dozen officers who'd committed courageous acts (like leaping into rivers to save small children, or tackling robbers without a thought for their own safety) to introduce them to the members and praise them before the real business of the afternoon began. 'It always set a very positive tone for the meeting,' says Chase. 'And often then he'd just get his way on things. As a tactic, it was brilliant.' It was also Ryan's first real experience of learning to anticipate press reaction to his actions, and weighing up how significant it might prove. He'd wanted the police service to buy some Mercedes cars instead of standard British models, and a flash police launch for the waterways. Chase pointed out that the newspapers would have a field day. In the end, Ryan backed down, they bought Vauxhalls or Fords, and a rubber dinghy with an outboard motor, and the press knew nothing of what might have been.

Ryan was finding that life in Norfolk was beginning to open up too. Dual carriageways and motorways were slowly taking the place of the single-lane roads wandering through the county, so transport to the outside world was much quicker. Planes from Norwich Airport also flew direct to Amsterdam, one of the key air-travel hubs for the rest of the world, which was particularly handy since Ryan was travelling more and more to eastern Europe to lead training missions. He could arrive at the airport fifteen minutes before take-off and be in Amsterdam thirty-five minutes later. Heathrow would always entail a four-and-a-half hour journey, an overnight stay and long delays before going anywhere. The couple had made good friends too in the area, though once again it was Adrienne making all the running. Ryan tended to remain enigmatic. Chase, one of his closest confidants, felt even he was never considered a real friend.

He had a lot of acquaintances who enjoyed working with him, but not really friends. You always got the feeling he was moving on. He was difficult to get to know. His ascent had been so fast, we were surprised, one day, to discover he'd never been given the Queen's Police Medal – he hadn't been anywhere long enough. [Ryan was eventually presented with the medal in 1992.] We never thought we'd keep him here; it was obvious the Home Office wouldn't let go of him that easily. Most of our Chief Constables before have stayed ten years, and then retired here. We knew he wouldn't be like that; he was still on his way up. But we thought better a short time, than not at all, although it surprised us just how quickly he moved on.

Adds Alston, 'We were disappointed that he left so quickly.'

Even with the force sorted out, there were still parts of the job, however, that were absorbing. As chief, Ryan had responsibility for the broad security of the gas rigs in the North Sea off the county. Two years before, the Piper Alpha rig off Aberdeen was the scene of the worst-ever offshore petroleum accident, during which 167 people died and 10 per cent of Britain's oil production capacity was lost. Indeed, on his way down to start the job, the news came over the radio that an oil-rig accommodation platform had broken adrift and was out of control. His heart in his mouth, he pushed his foot harder on the accelerator, until hearing the platform had drifted out into the Dutch sector, where Holland would have to organise the rescue. Routinely after that, Ryan flew out to the rigs by helicopter for inspections. He enjoyed the trips. The helicopter would seem to skim the waves – with the James Bond theme music 'Live and Let Die' blaring into everyone's headphones – and then, as the green waves smashed against the legs of the oil rig, would rise up just in time to smack down on the platform.

Security was another big issue. Salman Rushdie – the author who'd been in hiding since 1989 after a *fatwa* (a death sentence) was declared against him by the Iranian leader, the Ayatollah Khomeini – wanted, at one point, to use a cottage in Norfolk as a base. Ryan refused. The costs of guaranteeing his safety would be far too high, he said. No one had the power to overturn his decision. The Queen's security at Sandringham, the royal family's sixty-acre country retreat north-west of Norwich, was a completely different issue. While the Metropolitan Police has responsibility for the monarch's safety wherever else she travels through the UK, the Norfolk force has sole charge at Sandringham. Ryan and Adrienne were invited for lunch with the Queen there soon after they arrived, the first time she'd ever entertained the Norfolk Chief Constable.

It was an eventful afternoon. While Adrienne was dragged off by Prince Edward to help him with a jigsaw puzzle, Ryan chatted with the Queen, the Queen Mother and Prince Charles about the area. When they sat down at the table, however, Ryan was annoyed that the butler serving the meal held his platter high above Ryan's head and still expected him to help himself to lamb. When no one was looking, Ryan elbowed him in the groin, and gave him a long, hard stare until the butler lowered the platter to a decent height. 'It was an obvious attempt to embarrass me,' says Ryan. 'It was as though he was saying, "You're just a peasant." I don't think the Queen saw the exchange because she was following the conversation around the table. The whole family were all incredibly warm and gracious.' There was also a minor stir when one of the Queen's corgis was sick under the dining table.

Ryan and Adrienne saw members of the royal family frequently after that. They'd often attend functions together and, naturally, Ryan would be involved every time they went anywhere in Norfolk. King's Lynn subdivisional commander David Reeve was the head of royal protection and soon built up an easy relationship with Ryan. 'He was very relaxed about it, which tended to relieve the tension, as often those visits could be very stressful,' says Reeve. Indeed, one time they were so relaxed, they even left Adrienne behind by mistake when the Queen decided to cut short a royal visit to move on early. Reeve sent a car back for her immediately they realised the Queen's table was going to be one short for lunch. He even made jokes about her warm relationship with Prince Charles, who was charmed at having such a lively woman around, with long hair and short skirts, roughly half the age of any other of the dignitaries. 'He obviously had a soft spot for her,' says Ryan's friend Malcolm Bowry. Reeve was impressed with Ryan.

> He was a very affable socialite, but was also obviously a man to be reckoned with. You got the feeling that if you decided to take him on, you'd have to be sure you were right. He had a very straightforward approach, but he was also forceful and would take the responsibility for firing bullets if he had to. On top of that, he was one of the smartest men I ever worked with. He took great pride in his appearance, and he was a good 'shop-window' for the force.

For the next three Christmases the Ryans were in Norfolk, the Queen would make sure to send them a brace of pheasants.

His profile was rising in other areas, too. Producers from Anglia TV approached him a year after he'd started in Norfolk to ask if he'd be the model for a new TV series they were planning about the politics of policing. Ryan agreed, more out of curiosity than anything else, and talked to them about life as a British Chief Constable, then read through their scripts, taking a consulting role on the show, 'The Chief'. In the first series, the fictional star, based on Ryan, was played by Tim Piggot-Smith, later to be replaced in the second by 'The Professionals' star Martin Shaw. The show first went to air in the UK in 1993, and has been repeated on pay TV in Australia.

The job itself also still gave Ryan enough time to play a major role in national police activities, with the influential Association of Chief Police Officers. He'd joined in 1984 in Yorkshire, become secretary of its personnel and training committee in Durham, and now worked his way up to becoming committee chairman. It was a very powerful force within the force: whenever chief officers wanted assistance on training or personnel issues, or the Government of the day wanted advice, it was always to that committee they turned.

Ryan enjoyed the work, and the way it gave him a national focus on the force away from Norfolk. One of his research papers was on the chaotic way police training was conducted throughout the country: by the national staff college at Bramshill, Hampshire; by individual forces; and by six disparate recruit training centres – all duplicating the work of the others. Indeed, the whole system was costing a staggering £150 million a year. Even so, it was still a surprise when he received a call from the Home Office, saying Home Secretary Kenneth Clarke wanted to see him.

Ryan drove down to London, mystified. The offer came straight out of the blue. Clarke, a man determined to modernise the police service, reduce bureaucracy and raise efficiency, wanted him to become Britain's first national director of police training, pulling together a single comprehensive system of police training across Britain, and devising new practices and procedures. He'd be promoted to the highest grade of Chief Constable and would have free rein over the entire British police force. 'It's got to be more cost-effective and efficient than it is now,' Clarke told him. 'I'll be behind you and with you all the way. Make it happen!'

Ryan went back to Norfolk that day, his mind racing. It sounded like a huge job, with enormous responsibilities, yet it would be a wonderful challenge too. As he considered his options, Robert Chase and the leader of the County Council, John Alston called him in. They'd both been assessing what a great job he'd been doing for them in the past three years, and wanted him to swap his modest car for a top-of-the-range Range Rover, and to cut back on his work a little. He should take more time off to relax, play golf, and enjoy what the county had to offer. Ryan smiled back his gratitude, but inside he was in a state of flux.

The choice was clear-cut. Should he stay in Norfolk, kick back, play golf and spend more time with his young family, or should he strike out once again for yet another unknown territory, in a job he knew would bring him into dramatic conflict with every Chief Constable in the land? Norfolk was pretty, it was easy, Adrienne and the children were settled, and they'd made some great friends. Bramshill would be like starting out all over again. He could comfortably imagine staying in Norfolk up until his retirement ten years later, picking up a knighthood and then spending the rest of his days there in luxury. But Bramshill . . . he had no idea.

Two days later, he called Chase and Alston together and gave them his verdict. He was off. It was a move he was to regret to this day.

He might only have been 18 months old, but the young Peter Ryan was already revealing his love of uniforms, pictured in September 1945 in his favourite cowboy outfit.

At three years old, Peter's love of mischief already shone through in this studio portrait.
Photograph: J.H. Anderton, Ashton Studio, Lancaster, 1947.

Peter, aged 10, was an enthusiastic member of the St John Ambulance Brigade, and enjoyed the regular inspections.

Peter, 13, on holiday with his parents, Lawrence and Margaret, at one of the northern seaside resorts around twenty-five kilometres from home.

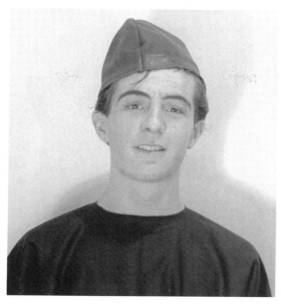

Peter was often ordered by his English teacher to take part in school plays, particularly as he turned out, at 16, to be a promising young actor.

Peter, 17, played the drum during parades as a part-time member of the band while he served with the Territorial Army Reserve.

At 18, Ryan was already a smart dresser, pictured here in his suit outside the backyard of his home all set for a date.

As Superintendent of the Leyland district in 1980, Ryan's duties included commanding all major events.

The Harrods bombing sent shockwaves throughout the world. 'I think yesterday was the worst day not only of my career, but of my personal life,' Ryan told ITN news in Britain on 18 December 1983.

Photo: Courtesy of ITN, London.

In the first of many personal sacrifices Ryan was to make for his career, he endured a three-and-a-half-month separation from Adrienne to take up the post of Assistant Chief Constable of North Yorkshire in November 1984.

Ryan and Adrienne, pictured on their wedding day on 16 February 1985.

Photograph: Malcolm Morgan Photographers, Hatchend, Middlesex

Ryan inspects a passing-out parade of new recruits as Deputy Chief Constable of Durham in 1989.

Ryan was appointed Chief Constable of Norfolk in June 1990, one of the youngest chief constables Britain had ever seen.

It became a family celebration the day Ryan was awarded his Queen's Police Medal in Norfolk in 1992. He holds Elizabeth, four, while Adrienne has Georgina, three.

As head of British police training at Bramshill, Ryan went over to Ghana in 1994 to help restructure their police force. While there, he was made an honorary tribal chief.

Ryan loved flying and took his pilot's licence as soon as he could. While at Norfolk, in 1992, he even flew a fighter jet with the Gulf War's Desert Rats at RAF Coltishall.

Prime Minister Margaret Thatcher visited Bramshill regularly, having met Ryan first during the aftermath of the Harrods bombing. She is pictured at a formal dinner at the college in 1995.

CHAPTER 10

Old guard, new broom

WHEN HOME SECRETARY Kenneth Clarke wooed Peter Ryan to become the butt-kicking national director of police training at the Bramshill police staff college, he'd pledged to be 'behind you and with you all the way'. But, in May 1993, a few weeks before Ryan took up the job, Clarke was appointed Chancellor of the Exchequer.

His successor, Michael Howard, was a tough law-and-order politician, but didn't take much interest at all in reforming police training. So when Ryan arrived at Bramshill, a picturesque 300-acre country estate surrounding a 17th-century mansion in Hook, Hampshire, he found himself left to fight his battles alone. Howard's top civil servants doubted whether Ryan would be able to bring a whole Home Office department into one single line of management – and that was even before the entrenched line of opposition that emerged from the ranks of the police forces of England.

At the time, there was a great deal of debate in the country about reducing the number of individual police forces from forty-three to a far smaller number of large regional groups. Successive Home Secretaries had, at various times, tried to standardise the forces, each with completely different police uniforms, vehicles, methods and priorities, all to no avail. Now, there was a gathering momentum to aggregate the various forces and govern them via a single board of chiefs each overseeing a certain area of the service, rather than the map. The country's forty-three Chief Constables were outraged. They viewed that push towards centralisation as a direct assault on their own positions of power, influence and autonomy. Ryan's mandate – to bring together all training and impose, for the first time, a broad set of regulations on teaching officers – was seen as the start of an insidious process to undermine them and a vision to be resisted at all costs.

Ryan's first move at Bramshill was to conduct a review of all the training offered by the various police establishments, and to draw up a strategy document outlining a much more streamlined vision. He wrote to everyone involved with training to ask for their input. His Bramshill staff officer Jo Hampson says not a single person replied. Clearly, the individual forces had managed to agree on one thing: Ryan must be stopped. A concerted campaign of passive resistance in not supplying him with the information he needed was the first shot in that battle.

But Ryan knew what he wanted and, faced with the lack of cooperation stunned everyone in his office, especially the sceptics, by dictating a twelve-page document, straight off the top of his head. The fact that, in revision, it needed only six amendments was a testament to his clarity of vision as much as to his obvious intelligence.

Finally, he presented his report, 'The Future of Police Training'. The Home Office was delighted; the Chief Constables were predictably furious and, from that moment on, most seemed to oppose every suggestion Ryan made. To add to his difficulties, the Home Office had decided to keep Ryan on the highest rank of Chief Constable rather than make him a member of Her Majesty's Inspectorate, as it had with previous Bramshill Commanders, believing that it would make it easier for him to operate within the circle of Chief Constables. Instead, the other chiefs merely regarded him as the enemy within. Hampson witnessed it all firsthand. 'It was a brilliant paper, with many of its conclusions still appropriate today,' she says. 'But all forty-three Chief Constables turned their backs on him. In England, they're like Chinese warlords – no one can make them do anything they don't want to do – and here was someone trying to tell them how they should train officers and where they could send them.' For Ryan, it was a bitter struggle. 'They gave me a pretty torrid time,' he says. 'The ostracism made the job extremely difficult. They saw me as almost a Home Office figure instead of one of them.'

One outsider with a very clear view of what was happening was Barry Newton, a high-level management consultant with the global business advisory group KPMG. He'd been seconded to the Home Office and spent a great deal of time over in Bramshill, shadowing Ryan, seeing how the program of change was being managed. He emerged with the opinion that no other Chief Constable in the country would have been prepared to take on the task that Ryan had agreed to.

I never understood why Peter moved from a very good job in Norfolk, with a great police authority, a nice house, and good schools, to take on a poisoned chalice like that. It was a no-win job. It was a hornet's nest. One of my specialisms is managing change, but, if we'd been asked as an organisation to manage the change at Bramshill, I would have declined because I don't think we could have achieved it, no matter what the Home Secretary would have paid us. It was just too damned hard.

One of the main problems was that Ryan was never quite sure who his boss was. Was it the Home Office, the Home Secretary, the Chief Constables, the various police authorities or even the officers he was training? 'Even if it were the Chief Constables, there's an old saying that if you have forty-three different Chief Constables in England, then you'll have forty-four different opinions – because there'll always be one who can't make up his mind,' says Newton. 'As well, they'll have each gone through about a year's training at Bramshill at various times before reaching that rank, and it can be like a kind of indoctrination. So then there's this guy coming in trying to change the gospel according to Bramshill.' Also, how do you work out a comprehensive training program for a group of people whose very function is constantly being philosophically debated?

Add to that the innate conservatism of an organisation like the police, and the traditionalism of Bramshill, a college that had always been run rather like Sandhurst Military Academy, where things are done in certain ways merely because they always have been, and you have a puzzle of Byzantine complexity masquerading as a political minefield. Even a number of Ryan's own staff may not have been particularly enthusiastic about change, says Newton.

Some may well have moved there from the police force outside for an easier life, and had fond memories of their own training that their boss was now trying to change. Plus, when Ryan went in, many of the officers working at Bramshill had at least thirteen weeks of holiday a year, free accommodation, first-class travel entitlements and no end of perks, says Hampson. 'There was huge abuse, they led very privileged lives and Bramshill offered no value for money. Peter was trying to change that. He closed one of the training estates and tried to hold the other six to account for the first time ever, and it made him hugely unpopular.'

Even today there's still no consensus on police training, says Newton.

> There was recently a paper came out from the Home Secretary on how to change training again, the Chief Constables wrote back and said, 'That won't work!' so he said, 'OK' and out it went. That job's too hard. But in Peter's time, he shook it all up quite dramatically and got change through, and survived, which was a real credit to him. He had all these novel ideas and wanted to move on them very quickly, and had a genuine passion for what he wanted to do. And all the time he was walking a tightrope between his career aspirations and job satisfaction.

There was a constant demand for better and longer training, and Ryan proposed to extend the sixteen-week recruit modules into twenty-six or thirty-two-week courses. He felt more thorough training would help police cope with some of the newer challenges of the job, like ridding the force of old racist attitudes and increasing the representation of ethnic minorities, but all his schemes were rejected. There was also a clear need for better management training for senior officers who were in charge of an organisation with an annual budget of £7.2 billion (A$18 billion), yet who had rarely worked in any other job but the police. He felt too there needed to be a switch of emphasis to more training in operational skills and tactics in basic police areas such as managing murder investigations. He introduced a common approach to detective training rather than have each force follow its own favourite codes and methods.

Ryan's main ambition, however, was to establish a national crime faculty, an operational group designed to bring together the computer databases scattered around the country on child and serial sexual offenders, child murderers, those with a history of serious assaults on women, and rapists. It was a passion he later brought to Sydney, with the establishment of CrimTrac in New South Wales. If all such cases could be brought into one central database, they could be far better analysed, and experiences pooled to train others on best practice and investigation. The findings could also be combined with the records of forensic scientists, researchers, profilers, psychologists and prison workers in order to come up with better ways to support officers who are dealing with a serious offence for the first time in their careers, like a complex murder with no obvious suspect.

The strength of the opposition to the idea took Ryan by surprise. To him, it seemed obvious it would be a valuable addition to the police armoury. To others, it looked like yet another attempt to usurp their individual authority. Finally, after a series of protracted battles, he managed to push the vision through. Today, it's a world-renowned institution, regularly tapped into by other countries' police services, seeking help on everything from how to investigate serial killings to tracking down suspects on the run. The Home Office has stationed its own research unit there, and the USA's FBI has even acknowledged it to be better than their own profiling unit, with one of their officers working from the base. 'It's become a fantastic and unique organisation,' says Ryan, 'but trying to get it going was just unbelievable. We faced an incredible amount of opposition and a lack of vision by so many people. Later, [Kent Chief Constable] Dave Phillips and [West Midlands Chief Constable] Ted Crew joined me to help push the concept through. But it was such a fight.'

The battles even followed through into Ryan's personal life. After uprooting themselves yet again, Adrienne and the two children came down from Norfolk, and, rather than base himself at the Home Office in London, the four settled into one wing of the 500-year-old manor house at the centre of the Bramshill estate. It was a stunning Jacobean mansion, under the supervision of two ghosts, set among the manicured lawns, lakes, gardens and wildlife, including a rare herd of white deer. The reception and security for the entire college was based in the hallway of the house, but Ryan moved them out into a separate, purpose-built building in the grounds. He saw that as one small part of his master plan to modernise the college; some of his officers viewed it as a way purely to claim the whole house for himself.

'Living in the mansion, people expected him to play the role of the country squire, knowing everyone and knowing who was having babies, and wandering around with a swagger stick and a spaniel at his heels,' says Hampson.

> But he didn't. He kicked arse. He wanted to run the place as a business to make money. People then resented his enjoyment of Bramshill. They came out fighting some of the time, and Peter retreated. So one of the things we used to do as staff officers was to make sure he'd go down and have a lunch once a week, so he could be seen and talk to people. But actually you'd get there and nobody would talk to him, and he wouldn't talk to them. So he'd end up keeping himself to himself, which wasn't the best strategy.

The family, however, made the most of living at Bramshill. The girls had a ball playing hide-'n'-seek in the great drawing rooms and morning rooms of the mansion, and Ryan himself found respite from the politics of the job in restoring most of the rooms to their former glory. He had the intricate ceilings repainted, the tapestries repaired and rehung, and installed furniture from the correct period to the main public rooms. Some of the areas of the house that had been closed and neglected for years, he opened up again for public use and began restyling the gardens with the help of the Hampshire Garden Trust. He started a tradition of power dinners there too, with a few Chief Constables or the Metropolitan Commissioner Paul Condon and a couple of executives of big companies like ICI and B Sky B's Australian boss Sam Chisholm all getting together to discuss the state of the nation.

But the mansion's facelift was short-lived. When Ryan left, his successor decided not to take over the house, instead living in a small apartment on the estate and going back to his family home outside at weekends. The college's administrative staff then moved into the building. 'When I returned a year later, I was horrified to find the quarters I'd lived in had been turned over to offices,' says Ryan. 'All the furniture that I'd carefully collected and scattered around the house to reflect its glory had been moved somewhere else. The whole place had an air of despair and shabbiness that was upsetting.'

The one great positive of the job itself was all the travel it entailed. Ryan represented Britain at police conferences throughout the world, and even ended up chairman of the Interpol conference on global police training. He also worked closely with the John Jay College of Criminal Justice in New York, and went once a month to Brussels to meet his opposite numbers in Europe to discuss police cooperation, training, public-order issues, traffic, forensics, staff exchanges, and programs for further developing communications. Gradually, the idea grew out of those meetings for an Association of European Police Colleges. That association was eventually launched in Brussels, with Ryan as its founding president. The dream was one day to have an actual police college in Europe, and today there are plans being drawn up to build such an institution.

Ryan also visited Prague and Budapest to work with the governments and their police forces, emerging from the militaristic models of the old communist system. It was a struggle, however, to build police forces that reflected the new democratic orders, and often the senior police figures selected to train at Bramshill were called back halfway through their term when their governments changed.

In February 1994, Ryan attended an executive course at the FBI Academy at the United States Marine Corps Base at Quantico, Virginia. Principally for chiefs of police of major cities, it is the most advanced course the FBI holds, with a huge variety of participants, from the head of US Marshals and the chief of police in Washington, to one Tony Lauer, the Australian New South Wales Police Commissioner. The pair fell into an easy camaraderie. 'He seemed a pleasant enough fellow, but he always gave the impression of being preoccupied,' says Ryan. 'Whilst he took part in the activities, he always seemed a bit reserved and stood back a bit from what was going on. He was always on the telephone, one assumes to back home. He did say they had some quite severe political problems, and that potentially they could get worse.' The reason for all those calls became patently obvious the next month when ICAC recommended a series of charges against serving and former police officers. In May, the Royal Commission into the New South Wales police force was announced.

Further afield, Ryan was invited to China by the Chinese Ministry of Public Order who trained officers at the university in Beijing. He visited parts of the Ministry that no one from the west had been allowed to see before, and met with the Minister in charge of public order to discuss methods and means of cooperation, particularly with reference to the handing back of Hong Kong to China. The trip started off with his vehicle, on the way to the training academy out of Beijing, careering off the road and into a ditch when the driver was confronted by a truck on the wrong side of the road, coming straight for them. Ryan was bounced out of his seat, hit his head on the roof and ended up in a heap on the floor, injuring his back badly: it still gives him trouble today. On arrival, he sat at a long red table, in the biting cold wind, watching hundreds of officers – some in bare feet, others in sandals of string and hay, some in socks, others in sports shoes, a few in boots – perform a display of marching and self-defence, all in perfect unison with neither commands nor music. Then came the tour of the academy, through which every one of the one million-plus public-order police for the country pass at some time. As well as enforcing the law, some also dispense the law like magistrates. At lunchtime, there was a banquet with delicacies such as sliced ducks' tongues, fried scorpion, snake and ducks' brains that were spooned from a head cracked down the middle, which Ryan politely declined.

The toasts were many and often, each finishing with everyone downing a drink. Ryan switched from wine to beer, realising otherwise he'd never be able to continue. The General in charge of the academy at one point asked Ryan for permission to take his jacket off. Looking over at him, Ryan was touched to see his shirt was threadbare, with most of the buttons missing and frayed cuffs, his jumper dotted with holes and he had on two odd socks in worn, old shoes. 'I felt really sorry for him,' says Ryan. 'I wanted to give him clothes out of my suitcase because he was obviously so poor. He chatted away, through an interpreter, with me nodding and smiling, until eventually someone asked me if I like karaoke – because he did. I thought it would be impolite not to say yes, so immediately everyone beamed, leapt up and wheeled in a huge karaoke machine.' Ryan was glad of the alcohol when it came to his turn to sing 'New York, New York'. He wasn't so glad the next day when he was violently ill from something he'd eaten, and doubled up in pain from his back.

While in Hong Kong receiving treatment for his back, he made another of those spur-of-the-moment decisions that have repercussions for the rest of one's life: he decided to return to Britain via Sydney. He put in a call to Lauer, asking if he could come by and say hello and have a look at the New South Wales Police Service. Lauer said he'd be happy to show him around. Ryan caught the next flight over.

Ryan flew into Sydney and drove up to Charles Sturt University's Wagga Wagga campus, which was handing out certificates to the first group to take the new course on policing for recruits. He then went over to inspect the Police Academy at Goulburn where there had been work done with Norfolk's University of East Anglia, where Ryan was a fellow of The Centre for Applied Research in Education, and spent a couple of days talking to staff about police training and practices, and comparing them to how things were done in the UK. Finally, he returned to Sydney, and arrived at the New South Wales Police Service HQ at College Street, Sydney, on 26 March 1995, four months after the start of the Royal Commission hearing. It was the very day a new Labor Government under Bob Carr was elected to replace John Fahey's Liberals, and Paul Whelan was appointed Police Minister. Ryan recalls:

Tony Lauer was finding it quite stressful, trying to bed in a new minister. He was up and down like a yoyo, going between his office and Paul Whelan's. He was furious that he was having to keep going to see him about every issue Whelan wanted to discuss when, as he pointed out, the telephone would have been quite adequate. But to compound it all, a Royal Commission into the police had just begun its work, asking questions, seeking out papers, files and people, and I don't think at the time that the full impact of that had actually struck home. The police were in a state of denial that anything was wrong, saying that it was just a political ploy – a payback on the service, and corruption wasn't as bad as people were making out. Yes, there were problems, but weren't there problems everywhere? The thinking seemed to be that it would all blow over quite soon, as there wouldn't be too much to find.

Ryan was given a tour of HQ, of the service generally, of the harbour on a police launch, and of the Easter Show. He was impressed. He liked Sydney immediately, and he was intrigued by the police service and its problems.

From my observations it seemed like a typical police service, it worked reasonably well, but the portents were obvious. A number of individuals came up to me while I was there and said, 'This is going to be worse than we think, things are worse than they're accepting and it looks like the Police Commissioner is on his way out.' That was the general gossip around town and among the police. It was at that stage that it first occurred to me that I wouldn't mind working here. I enjoyed the place, and I could see that perhaps I could make a difference. That's when the first seeds were sown.

When Ryan arrived back home, he spoke to Adrienne about the possibility. He'd never been particularly interested in Australia before, and she was taken aback by his enthusiasm. Over the next few months, he stayed in contact with some of the people he'd met in Australia, who all talked of the likelihood of a big shake-up for the police, and predicted that Lauer, and some of his most senior officers, wouldn't survive it. In June, the Royal Commission watched videotape of Inspector Graham 'Chook' Fowler, who had headed Kings Cross detectives, apparently receiving money from another corrupt officer, and calls for Lauer's head grew ever louder. Clearly, the end was in sight, and very soon they were going to need someone new, with wide experience, quite possibly a cleanskin from outside.

When Ryan received a phone call at the beginning of January

1996 telling him that Lauer was set to announce his retirement, he wrote to the New South Wales Government and expressed an interest in the job, should they decide to look beyond Australia. Even though Lauer eventually resigned on 15 January, Ryan's letter wasn't even acknowledged; he heard absolutely nothing back.

A couple of months on, in February 1996, Ryan received a request from the New South Wales Government for Whelan to come and look at what he was doing at Bramshill. His mind raced on to the Commissioner job, but Whelan didn't mention it once during his entire visit. 'It sort of sat there between us like an unopened parcel, which neither of us touched,' says Ryan.

Three weeks later, however, a firm of headhunters in London, working in conjunction with the executive recruitment agency Russell Reynolds Associates in Sydney, called Ryan to ask, ironically, who he thought might be suitable for the vacant Commissioner job. He gave them a few names of good English Chief Constables, and then casually brought up the subject of his own interest. They made a few notes, and rang back a short time later to ask him down to London to meet with both the British and Australian recruitment consultants to discuss the job. Ryan knew they were interviewing at least ten others, but gradually many of them dropped out. Some didn't want to move their families, and said the problems of tackling a huge organisation with such entrenched levels of corruption would be too hard. Others were more blunt: they wouldn't touch it with a bargepole, they declared. It would be too difficult, too dangerous and too uncertain a career move.

I had a more optimistic view. A number of things attracted me. First of all, it was a challenge. Yes, it was difficult, it would be awful; it was a huge organisation in need of root-and-branch reform. But that excited me as that's what I like to do, and could do. I was also attracted to the idea of being in charge of security for the 2000 Olympic Games. In terms of a professional police officer's career, that would be a very exciting thing to do. Not that it could advance you any further in terms of your career, however, because once you become Commissioner of somewhere like New South Wales, there's nowhere else to go. You're

it. But in England, I'd got as high as I could go – with the exception of becoming Commissioner of the Met or moving sideways
at the same grading level to another police service. I thought
this could be a new, fresh challenge.

Ryan felt more than ready to leave Bramshill. He'd given it his best
shot, and forced some change through, yet still regretted having left
Norfolk so early to take on what had turned out to be such a thank-
less task. In the meantime, he'd applied for the post of Chief Constable
of Lancashire, with the chance to be chief in his own home county
being one Ryan longed for. Sadly, it was the one job in his career he
wasn't offered. Instead, it went to Pauline Clare, the first woman to be
appointed Chief Constable in Britain. His old mentor Tommy Watkinson was philosophical, 'They wanted the kudos of having the first
woman in the country.' Another colleague, Barry Newton, who was to
work later with Ryan, agrees. 'Everybody knew they wanted a woman.
I tried to tell him, but he wanted to go back home.' Still, Ryan was bitterly disappointed. Pauline Clare declined to comment for this book.

Shortly afterwards, he applied, and was shortlisted, to take over
the West Midlands force, Britain's second biggest after the Met. This
Australian job, however, offered another, intriguing, option. A date in
May was earmarked for an interview via teleconferencing with the
New South Wales Police Board. Ryan happened to be at a meeting in
Scotland at the time, so had to race to Edinburgh for an 8 a.m. link-
up with Australia. Every member of the board had obviously read the
headhunter's report, and took turns to ask questions. One issue not
raised was why it had taken them so long to find someone who had
put his hand up for the job months before. It wasn't until Ryan was
firmly installed in the position that the Auditor General reported to
Parliament that the subsequent executive search had cost $267 340.

Anyway, after an hour and a half of grilling Ryan from the other
side of the world, the board adjourned for a few minutes into
another room, then the figure of the board chairman Don Mackay
loomed back onto the screen.

'Could you come out to Australia for an interview immediately?'
he asked. Startled, Ryan replied, 'What do you mean by "immediately"?' Mackay responded blithely: 'How about . . . tomorrow?'

CHAPTER 11

The best police force money can buy

THE NEW SOUTH WALES police service: 'the best police force money can buy'. It was a popular joke among those in Australia's murky underworld in the 1960s and 1970s, and now it was being used once again to describe a force in absolute crisis. The former head of Kings Cross Police detectives, Graham 'Chook' Fowler had been seen on national TV apparently accepting a wad of cash as a bribe – he was later jailed for two years – and fresh evidence was being produced daily before the Wood Royal Commission of police either being directly involved in crime, selling heroin or being bribed to turn a blind eye. Notorious criminal Louie Bayeh had claimed he'd paid off up to 100 officers to protect his strip clubs, and a detective sergeant was filmed actually ordering child pornographic videos, having sex with a one-time prostitute and pocketing drugs.

As the stack of cases against the police mounted, and more than twenty-five officers were sacked and nearly 500 more resigned, New South Wales Police Commissioner Tony Lauer's position had begun to look more and more untenable. At the start of the Royal Commission, he'd insisted, 'There is no entrenched corruption in the police service today,' and that claims to the contrary were 'figments of the political imagination'. On 15 January 1996, with his acting chief of staff Bob Lysaught sacked for misbehaviour revealed at the Royal Commission, and his Assistant Commissioner, Ray Donaldson, resigning protesting his innocence after being also named, he announced he'd be taking early retirement.

Confidence in the police service plunged to an all-time low, with the New South Wales force now being described as one of the most rotten in the world. Sydney was dubbed the 'Chicago' of the region, with the police playing Al Capone. Even though the vast majority hadn't committed crimes, many had stood by and allowed their colleagues to do so in a culture of corruption that had apparently remained unchanged despite numerous inquiries, commissions, operations and Commissioners dedicated to cleaning up the force. Now the public was increasingly cynical that the corrupt cycle could ever be broken. The British-born publisher of the media company Fairfax, Alan Revell, remembers the time his house was burgled while he was away on holiday. 'Did you tell the police you were going away?' asked a neighbour. 'No, I didn't,' said Revell, regretting that he hadn't had the foresight to ask his local station to keep an eye on the house. 'Oh well,' responded the neighbour, 'it wouldn't have been them, then.'

The Royal Commission, under the stewardship of Justice James Wood, had been rumbling on for seventeen months by the time Peter Ryan arrived back in Sydney in May 1996 for his interview for the job of New South Wales Police Commissioner, in charge of the 4th largest police service in the English-speaking world, behind the Metropolitan Police in London, the New York Police and the Royal Canadian Mounted Police. With still no end in sight to the series of stunning revelations about corrupt cops, and little hope for the future, morale in the service was at rock bottom. All major promotions were on hold pending the outcome of the Commission, while those in senior executive posts were on month-to-month contracts. Neil Taylor, Lauer's former deputy, who had been planning to retire in April, had agreed to stay on until a replacement Commissioner had been appointed, to oversee the State's 13 000 officers and 3000 public servants. Many were drawn to the previously anathemic idea of appointing an outsider, if for no other reason than the public perception that no officer could have made their way through the ranks without having either been tainted by corruption or, at the very least, having failed to notice it was going on – hardly a great recommendation for a top police officer.

So Ryan arrived in Sydney to face three days of intensive interviews with everyone from Justice Wood to each of the five individual members of the New South Wales Police Board. Then Ryan was called before the Board chairman Don Mackay. They passed a few pleasantries before Mackay dropped his bombshell. 'You've got the job,' he said, bluntly. 'What do you say? When can you start?'

Ryan was taken aback. Up until that moment on 31 May 1996, the position of New South Wales Police Commissioner had been little more than an idle daydream. He'd thought the job sounded intriguing, he liked Australia, and he was eager to move on from Bramshill, but he hadn't really given the possibility a great deal of thought. He hadn't even had the chance to discuss it seriously with Adrienne. She'd fallen pregnant again with twins, and had lost one of the babies just two days before he'd flown out to Sydney. They'd have to work out the likely impact on their two girls, too. Besides, none of the details like length of contract, salary, terms and moving arrangements had been raised. 'I can't give you my answer right now,' said Ryan, 52. 'I need time to consider it.' Mackay seemed annoyed. He'd wanted an answer immediately. They'd interviewed people from all over Australia, New Zealand, the UK, Canada and the USA for the job, he insisted, and they needed to know right now whether Ryan wanted to take up the offer. He felt sure he wouldn't be able to prevent the Police Board's decision being leaked to the media.

Still, Ryan stalled. He called Adrienne. She listened silently while he told her what they'd said. 'So, how would you fancy going to live in Australia?' he asked her. There was a pause, then he could hear her taking a deep breath. 'No,' she said. 'We can't make a decision like that over the phone. We can't just say yes like that.' Ryan was surprised by the vehemence of her tone. 'But, Tiny, this could be a great job for me, and Australia really is a lovely place,' he coaxed. 'The kids'd love it.' 'Maybe,' she replied. 'But this is such a big decision, we need to talk it over, face-to-face.' He could understand her lack of enthusiasm. The offer couldn't really have come at a more awkward time. She was now 35 and had given up so much for him. In return, he'd encouraged her to fulfil her dream of studying for a university degree. She was now in the final year of a BA in Politics and International Relations at University of Reading and was devastated by the loss of one of her babies, and desperately worried about the health of the other so early in her pregnancy.

But over in Sydney, Ryan was being pressured to give his answer. 'They said about seventy-five people were seen by the headhunters about the job, but most had either been turned down as unsuitable, or had turned it down on the grounds that it would be too danger-ous or difficult a job,' he says. 'But then I was expected to say there and then, "Yes, thank you, I'll take it." But there was so much to be considered and discussed, so I said, "Sorry, I can't make that decision right now."' Instead, they hammered out a compromise: they agreed to let Ryan go back home to talk it through with Adrienne – but insisted he be back within three days. It would give him twenty-four hours in England to reach a decision. A few hours later, he received a call in his hotel room while he was feverishly packing to leave. There had been another miscarriage – Adrienne had lost the other twin she'd been carrying. Ryan flew home with a heavy heart.

He arrived back in Bramshill on the Wednesday morning to find Adrienne pale and emotional – devastated by this, her fifth miscar-riage. The couple clung to each other. Ryan stroked her hair, and wept those familiar tears of loss, once more, with her. It felt almost as if one part of their life was over and maybe, Ryan mused, this was a sign that they should move on swiftly to a new beginning. He was exhausted from tossing the offer over and over in his mind all the way from Sydney, and was looking for a sign of what to do. On the one hand, it sounded a marvellous challenge: to head a police force tainted by a long history of corruption and battered by a continuing flood of revelations from the Royal Commission, yet one now deter-mined to chart a fresh course for the future. He'd had first-hand experience of the long-term consequences of corruption of the UK police, and had even helped put a number of bent coppers behind bars. Through all his postings, he'd learnt the most effective ways of restructuring services, and overhauling practices to introduce checks and measures to guarantee accountability. And, at Bramshill, he'd trialled all his ideas about how to train police into becoming the best officers possible. In addition, he was undoubtedly the kind of cleanskin outsider the New South Wales service badly needed. A local, he felt, couldn't possibly do the job.

On the other hand, however, he was under no illusion: this could be one of the toughest assignments he would ever face. His three

THE BEST POLICE FORCE MONEY CAN BUY

days in Sydney had already shown him that. There, he'd been interviewed by the complete Police Board, then by each individual member in turn. In addition, there'd been Justice Wood; his senior counsel Gary Crooke; the former Wran Police Minister and Police Board member Peter Anderson; and head of the Cabinet Department Roger Wilkins among the dizzying array of people to troop in and grill him about everything from the minutiae of his past to his opinions on the future. Most of the members of the Police Board were interested, professional and polite. One, however, was aggressive to the point of rudeness, and was warned by the rest of the Board to moderate the tone of his questioning.

Ryan made a mental note to be wary of Gary Sturgess. Yet when the time came for their one-on-one interview, he was shocked at the level of hostility from Sturgess – a lawyer, anti-corruption campaigner and one-time powerful head of the New South Wales Cabinet Office under Liberal Premier Nick Greiner.

> He made it quite clear that under no circumstances would he ever support the appointment of an Englishman to the job. He even went so far to say he'd have anyone in the job *but* an Englishman. In any event, he already had a candidate he thought would be far more worthy of the job, a man called Peter Lamb, senior investigator with the National Crime Authority. I didn't enjoy his interview. I found him an aggressive, bombastic, shallow man. His questions were extremely ill-informed. He surrounded himself with a sort of veil of secrecy, as if he knew things that were happening and no one else had anything like the same handle on corruption. It was as if it was his prerogative, therefore, to ask the questions about how I'd fight corruption. He even asked me if I subscribed to the Internet. When I asked why, he explained that pornographers subscribe to it and therefore they wanted to know people who did.

The rest of the Board, however, had made their decision: they wanted Ryan, and they wanted the choice to be unanimous. Sturgess, adamant that only an insider could do the job effectively, reluctantly agreed to abstain, but very soon the fact that the Board was not wholly behind the choice was leaked to the press. Ryan was under no illusions that Sturgess wouldn't prove a formidable foe.

Now back at Bramshill, he talked the offer through with Adrienne for agonising hour upon hour. They brought the subject up with Elizabeth, aged 8, and Georgina, 6. They were excited at first, but then wary. 'Daddy said it was always sunny and warm, and it never rained, and it sounded kind of cool,' says Elizabeth, now 14. 'But when I realised I'd have to leave all my friends, that's when I didn't want to go. And at that point, I'd lived in nine different houses, so I didn't want to move again.' They talked it through with Adrienne's mother Margaret Milner, her stepfather Gerald, her father Mike Butterworth and her stepmother Patricia. Ryan discussed it with his closest friends and examined it from every possible angle. He knew it could be one of the most important decisions of his life.

On the plus side, the family had few permanent ties in Britain; his own parents were dead and, after eleven years of marriage, he and Adrienne had still never lived anywhere longer than two and a half years. On the other side, it would be hard, after working in Sydney, to return to the British police service at anything like the same level he'd left it. Yet what was left for him to achieve there? The only job that excited him was the Commissioner of the Metropolitan Police, but no one knew when Paul Condon might be vacating the post. Still, there were Britain's closer ties to Europe to consider, which would make his role as President of the Association of European Police Colleges even more important; there was his short-listing for the West Midlands Chief Constable job; and there was still plenty to be done at Bramshill, with the dream of successfully revamping the British police's training structures only partly realised.

Then there was Sydney, the thrill of the professional challenge, and the excitement of a whole new lifestyle. By the time Ryan's twenty-four hours were up, he'd finally decided to take the job. He and Adrienne kissed the children goodbye, leaving them with Jo Hampson, and went to board the plane for Australia, nervous, but happy that they'd made the right decision.

Back in Sydney, however, the New South Wales Government was coming under increasing pressure to rescind their offer to Ryan, and reconsider local candidates who had a close working knowledge of the local police service. Outgoing Police Commissioner Tony Lauer had urged on his retirement that a successor be appointed from within New South Wales, after reports that he'd also been lobbying hard in favour of Australian Federal Police Commissioner Mick Palmer; and Premier Bob Carr sounded suddenly unsure of the wisdom of bringing someone in from overseas when he was interviewed on Radio 2UE. 'We would need strong arguments to reach the position that someone from outside Australia could be able to quickly assume all these responsibilities,' he said. 'The question we would have to ask . . . is whether an outsider, somebody from outside Australia, would be able to quickly familiarise himself with all aspects of police regulation and police culture in Australia.' The Liberal Shadow Police Minister Andrew Tink immediately seized on this to claim there was a clear division between Carr and Whelan. 'Mr Carr has now . . . cast serious doubt over whether a foreigner can, or should, be appointed Police Commissioner in New South Wales,' he declared.

Ryan, on his arrival, took the whole controversy with a pinch of salt. 'I knew that just before I arrived, [Carr] had been pushed into a corner on the issue,' he says. 'I think his statement was really out of political expediency. He sort of played a little bit to what he thought was public opinion.' The offer still stood, and the details of the contract were hammered out. It would be a five-year contract, on $315 000 per annum, much more than Ryan's salary at Bramshill, and $60 000 more than his predecessor Tony Lauer, a sum that would make him one of Australia's highest-paid public servants. Ryan met up once more with Police Minister Paul Whelan, was introduced to Carr and formally accepted the job. He was asked to start the next day. He'd love to, he said diplomatically, but he happened to have a job back home. He'd return as soon as he was able, when his notice had been delivered and worked through. He then walked into a press conference with Carr and Whelan on 11 June, for the announcement to be made. He reeled back in surprise to see the rows of photographers, reporters and TV cameras waiting. In Britain, few people would even recognise their Chief Constable on the street. Here, his appointment seemed to be the most keenly awaited, and debated, event of the year. He smiled at the assembled gathering uncertainly.

Carr took the microphone. 'We see this as an historic opportunity to deliver to the people of this State a clean and effective police service to make all our lives safer,' he said. Ryan followed. 'I am looking forward very much to putting on the uniform of the New South Wales Police and becoming a New South Wales police officer and identifying myself with the men and women in the police service,' he said. 'I'm going to lead that organisation, I'm going to command it, and I'm going to give you a good, effective police service. It is going to be a blow to some people to think we've brought an outsider in, but we're all professionals here. I will appeal to their professionalism to see it through together.' Hands went up in the sea of journalists before them. Everything was going well until a question came from the sidelines about how he imagined he'd deal with a rogue policeman like disgraced detective Roger Rogerson, the 'Blue Murder' anti-hero who shot and killed heroin dealer Warren Lanfranchi and later served three years in jail for conspiring to pervert the course of justice. Ryan paused. 'Who's Roger Rogerson?' he asked, in an artless admission that was immediately seized upon by the press and those opposing his appointment then, and forever more, as evidence that an outsider, with no experience of the New South Wales criminal culture, just wasn't equipped to do the job. Afterwards, Ryan says he bitterly regretted the remark.

I'd been given a tape of 'Blue Murder', but I didn't watch it until I'd come here to live. I remembered reading about Rogerson, but for some reason I remembered it as the Mick Drury case. It was a question that caught me out. I don't want to excuse myself, but in the situation – a big room, all that media – I was taken aback by the question. I hadn't yet had a briefing, hadn't been sat down by anyone to learn all the local issues. The play that was made of it was unfair. Who the hell was he to people outside New South Wales? Absolutely nobody.

Ryan returned to England to finish up his old job, under the constant assault of phone calls, faxes, emails and visits from those he'd be working with in Australia, including Gary Sturgess. He'd declined to go to Atlanta after the bomb blast at a live site during the Olympic Games, and was plagued by last-minute doubts after being approached by the British Home Office with vague intimations about a glowing future for him in Britain. There were also his fears about uprooting his family all over again, and settling for life in a country, and a culture, he barely knew. Finally, the Atlanta bomb proved the turning point. The challenges of Sydney 2000 loomed vividly before him. He was confident he was up to them. 'I felt I could do a good job in Australia. It was a gamble, but I wanted to try.' He had no idea how high the stakes really were.

Part II

AUSTRALIA

CHAPTER 12

'See what you've let yourself in for?'

BY THE END of the first day in his new job as New South Wales Commissioner of Police, Peter Ryan was left in no doubt about the open hostility among senior police to his appointment. When he'd accepted the invitation to the annual Commissioned Police Officers Association Dinner for the evening of Friday, 30 August 1996, at Sydney's Rosehill Racecourse, he'd thought it would be the perfect date to get to know a few people. But he was ignored by outgoing Commissioner Tony Lauer at the top table, and then snubbed by the officers' lukewarm reaction to his own speech. To make matters worse, when Lauer spoke, the room, to a man, rose to their feet, stamping on the floor and giving him a rapturous standing ovation. Police Minister Paul Whelan whispered to Ryan, 'See what you've let yourself in for?' And Ryan felt he was beginning, finally, to understand.

As soon as Lauer finished, Whelan made a beeline for the door. A few minutes later, Ryan mumbled his apologies about still suffering from jetlag and beat a hasty retreat too. 'I didn't want to stay in that company that night because it was obviously hostile,' he says. 'I thought I'd be leaving myself open to a hiding to nothing if I stayed on.' He didn't attend another of those dinners for the next two years. It was one of the last times he saw Lauer. 'He'd been friendly to me before I got the job, but not after,' says Ryan. 'He probably thought I should not have got it. Maybe he thought I should have gone to him for advice as to who's who, and so on. But I purposely chose not to do that. I had to be seen to be, if nothing else, neutral of everybody.'

Certainly, that may have irritated Lauer, and he may even have felt slurred by implication. In the next few months, while his predecessor John Avery spoke out a number of times on Ryan's behalf, Lauer himself remained stoically silent. As a former head of the police union, the Police Association, his public failure to endorse Ryan and his reforms may well have, however unintentionally, spurred on rebellious officers throughout the ranks who so obviously felt enormously fond of their old boss.

Indeed, Ryan was fast realising just how many enemies he had. Before he'd even flown into Sydney on Tuesday, 27 August 1996 to take up the job, he'd had people phone him and write to him in England with warnings to beware. His first night in Australia he noticed an old car parked across the road from the North Shore house he'd been taken to by Special Branch for his temporary accommodation and, when he saw it again a couple of days later, he called the local police station to report it. It turned out to be an officer on protection duty, assigned obviously because it was felt to be necessary. The former Independent MP John Hatton, who was instrumental in establishing the Royal Commission, warned him not to trust the advice being given by some of his senior officers. Whelan offered the same opinion. When death threats began arriving at the office, both written and on the phone, his chief of staff Grahame Smith suggested he get a bodyguard. His daily diary was made available only to a few colleagues in the office.

The enormous media attention that had followed him from the moment he stepped from the plane caught him unawares too. He wondered how anyone could operate in such conditions, under the constant scrutiny of so many journalists. 'Moving around in England, everyone knows you've got what it takes,' he says. 'But coming here, I was an unknown. I could see the media interest wasn't going to go away. I knew I'd have to be better than anyone else.' Three days later, by the Friday, he'd started to adjust to the attention as he addressed police across the State via a satellite link-up, pledging to restructure management, expose corruption and lead the service into a bright new future. A couple of hours on, however, he was overwhelmed by the number of people who turned up to witness his swearing-in as New South Wales's 18th Commissioner at Parliament

House in Macquarie Street. There he saw everyone from a collection of judges to the Royal Commissioner Justice James Wood himself, MPs, members of the New South Wales Crime Commission, the Ombudsman, and senior police officers. He couldn't help smiling at the pomp of the proceedings, curiously far more elaborate than anything back in the UK. He was similarly taken aback the next week by the incredible degree of anachronistic pageantry at another official engagement, the police debutantes' ball. Here, the adolescent daughters of senior police officers would 'come out', in the old social sense, before the Commissioner and his wife. Their dance partners for the evening would be the male cadets from the police college. It was organised by the Commander of Professional Responsibility, at that time Assistant Commissioner Geoff Schuberg, who was about to be one of the new regime's first victims. After Schuberg's departure, Ryan was relieved when no one volunteered to continue such a passé tradition, particularly since new recruits were being taken out of training school for what seemed to him an inordinate amount of time to be taught a skill he saw as quite unnecessary in a modern, forward-looking police service: how to waltz.

Back on the afternoon of his swearing-in, he went to police HQ to meet his staff properly for the first time. They'd been shaken earlier that day by the sackings of two senior officers as a result of Royal Commission hearings: Superintendent John Garvey, who'd been set to oversee security for the Olympics, and Detective Superintendent Brian Harding. Both officers had been named in connection with the 1985 arrest of a cat burglar, after which the man had allegedly been sprayed in the face with mace. Garvey and Harding were later charged with assault and attempting to pervert the course of justice after claims they fabricated evidence to convict him. They were, in March 2001, finally cleared in the magistrates court, and in February the next year asked to be reinstated.

The atmosphere in Police Headquarters was icy as Ryan walked in. He made a snap decision to be short, and get straight to the point. 'Look, here I am,' he told them. 'Some of you don't want me to be here; some of you hopefully might be pleased I'm here. But whatever your feelings, we're going to have to work together because I'm now the Commissioner and I'm going to make it work. You either work with me, or you work against me. You make the choice, and I'll be the judge.' When he finished, there was a cool silence. 'They all sat there glaring at me,' he says now, 'trying to work out who I was and how I ticked, and how I would respond. I think it took quite a few of them aback that someone should be so brazen and upfront, even aggressive. But I wanted to make it clear that I was the new boss and I was going to behave like one.'

Adrienne and the children had arranged to stay on in England until the new Australian school year started in January, so Ryan, freed of any distractions, was able to throw himself totally into his new job. He told Justice Wood that he intended to give him a report on reform after the first ninety days, and started sizing up the problems, the structure of the organisation, and the people around him, trying to decide whom he'd be able to trust.

The immensity of the task ahead was daunting. His priorities were to get rid of those officers adversely named by the Royal Commission, to open up the hierarchy of the service, to streamline the structure from top to bottom, to release more police from administrative duties and get them out on the beat, and to modernise methods of investigating crime. Of course, that would also mean introducing safeguards against corruption for the future, as well as restoring the morale of those left, and inspiring the confidence of an extremely cynical public. It was hard to know just where to start. Travelling around the State to meet as many officers as he could on the ground, he was regularly shocked by the way some operated. In some commands, there were detectives who hadn't arrested anyone for two years, yet who were still claiming they were ace investigators. Many senior detectives had left during the term of the Commission, and there was a long list of outstanding, unsolved murders. Squads often weren't supervised particularly effectively, and weren't being held at all accountable for their results. In addition, the senior officers around him were all quite old, a reflection, he felt, of a service that seemed to promote on length of service rather than merit. Most of those had been through only the usual six-weeks of recruit training, and hadn't done any training since. Even among those who'd studied Masters of Business Administration, there was little in the outcomes of the work to suggest what they'd learnt had ever been applied to the way they did their job.

Command and control wasn't anywhere near as professional as in the British police force. Nobody seemed to do what was expected of them; at the end of the day they just did what they wanted to do. There was a complete lack of supervision and the belief, which still lingers today, that good policing is sitting around, hiding out, in your police station. You'd hardly ever see anyone out on the beat; they were always busy doing something else. One of the excuses that kept coming up was that the computer systems were quite complex, and files require a lot of maintenance by officers, few of whom are touch typists. So they were constantly back at the police station making their entries on the computers. We had lots of IT, but it was all piecemeal, and there was no strategic plan to make it work *for* us.

When four unrelated murders occurred within a single twenty-four-hour period in late October, some of the issues materialised in stark relief. Firstly, one of the dead was 17-year-old student Michael Hegedus, shot during a petrol station robbery at the town of Inverell, 600 kilometres north of Sydney. Ryan found that often there wasn't the expertise in the service, particularly in country areas, to deal with such serious crimes. A local senior detective constable might have twenty years' service yet never have dealt with a murder in all their career. Eventually, Ryan brought in senior investigators from the city to deal with the case. 'But it showed me how much work I had to do in reforming crime investigation, particularly in serious crime,' he says.

Secondly, the murders sparked political panic, with Premier Bob Carr defending his Government's record in making the community safer, and Whelan informing the press he'd called Ryan – twice.

I began to realise at that stage how quickly the Government responded to any troublesome newspaper headline and looked for immediate solutions as if they were being blamed for the murders, so they had to look for someone else to blame. They were all saying, 'Let's have crisis talks with the Commissioner,' which was a silly response. But it was a lesson to me that I would have to watch very carefully how we needed to be on the front foot whenever unusual incidents occurred because you could expect very little help politically to deal with such things.

His first set of reforms, however, were enthusiastically received: putting 500 desk-bound police back out on the streets, detectives back in uniform, more officers at railway stations and extra beat-patrols in tourist areas like Bondi Beach, where British tourist Brian Hagland had just been beaten up and killed. Trying to come to grips with internal corruption was a great deal more difficult.

Back in the UK, Ryan had been visited by Gary Sturgess from the Police Board who, while making it clear he didn't want a Pommie in the job, claimed a certain degree of knowledge in this field.

He persisted, both in England and later when I'd arrived in Australia, in saying that only *he* knew the depth and breadth of corruption in New South Wales. I kept asking him to tell me who and where the corrupt officers were, so I could do something about it. But, instead, he simply proved obstructive. He used to ring me and say, 'By the way, there's a file on so-and-so or a complaint hidden away in a cupboard in a particular police station. I suggest you go and take it into your custody before it disappears.' And, sure enough, I'd send the people out I felt I could trust, and they'd find something – but it would relate to nothing in particular.

He was obviously being fed information by people within the service, but he was also, in my view, laying traps for me to fall into by suggesting that things were there to be found and if I didn't find them then I was obviously going to be exposed as being incompetent. But if he did know anything, why on earth wouldn't he give it to the cleanskin who'd been brought in with no history or baggage, and in a position to do something about it? At the end of the day, I was forced to conclude that he knew nothing. When one looks at his contacts in the service – who are now no longer there – it was all based on speculation and innuendo, and one might even say he bore grudges against certain individuals.

These days, Sturgess is based in London, and says his antagonism towards Ryan was a result of not believing he should have been appointed, because there wasn't enough known about him at the time. In addition, he felt an Australian should get the job. 'It was next to impossible for an outsider to come in and understand Australian culture, Australian policing culture and New South Wales policing culture,' he says. 'I quite like the English . . . but felt it was dumb to fly someone in, pay them a huge salary and dump everything on their shoulders.' Even those from interstate, like Perth-born ICAC Commissioner Ian Temby, claims Sturgess, never really grasped the peculiar nature of corruption in New South Wales.

Yet the Police Board, the civilian watchdog that made all the recommendations for transfers and promotions in the service, was cooling towards Sturgess. At that stage it was chaired by NRMA president and law-firm partner Don Mackay, and made up of former KPMG Asia–Pacific chairman George Bennett, University of New South Wales Law School lecturer Dr Sandra Egger, former Wran Police Minister Peter Anderson and Sturgess. For each monthly meeting, board members would struggle in with suitcases full of papers, containing every single detail anyone could ever wish to know about candidates for jobs or moves under discussion, including every kind of allegation or innuendo ever made about them. Ryan's set of papers would sometimes be half a metre high.

According to Ryan, Sturgess's contribution was always, 'Well, I know something about this person, so we shouldn't promote them.' When everyone asked what he knew, he'd clam up. 'I can't tell you,' he'd say. 'It's confidential, and if I tell you what I know, I'll expose my informants.'

The chairman of the board would then say, 'For goodness sake Gary, if you know something you must tell us within the confines of this room.' But Sturgess would refuse. It was stupid, ineffectual and a useless waste of time, and we were getting absolutely nowhere. I couldn't believe it. No wonder the police service was in such a mess. And as Police Commissioner, I didn't even have a vote on the board; I was just there as an observer. How on earth can you run an organisation and be held accountable when you're just there as an observer on the board, with no status whatsoever? The whole thing was crazy.

Sturgess's role was soon to end, however. One by one, the other Police Board members refused to work with him, angered by his allegations in the media that nothing was ever done when he raised allegations of corruption at board meetings and that he appeared so steadfastly opposed to Ryan. In September 1996, after six months on the Board, he tendered his resignation to Whelan and, in a decision that surprised some, it was accepted. Ryan was relieved; Sturgess was outraged. 'I believe it was Peter Ryan's decision to do away with the Police Board and in that, he lost what could have been a very important tool,' says Sturgess today. 'It could have been a good sounding board for him, a source of excellent advice, and something that would back him in some of the big decisions.' Ryan had no idea how dangerous an enemy Sturgess would continue to prove operating on the outside.

Ryan's problems with the Police Board itself were far from over. He wanted more control over promotions of staff, but the Board had its own ideas. In its submission to the Royal Commission, it asked for many more powers allowing it to give orders to a Police Commissioner, with Ryan's role downgraded, more or less, to merely implementing the decisions of the Board on running the service. Ryan was outraged. Wood and Whelan backed him. Whelan then went further and threw his weight behind a Commissioner's right to appoint his own senior staff. Six weeks later, Premier Bob Carr agreed to abolish the Board.

'I used to feel sorry for the individuals because I'm sure they were really frustrated by the process,' says Ryan.

I enjoyed a good working relationship with some members but, with the demise of Sturgess and the increasing revelations by the Royal Commission plus the changes I was already beginning to implement in terms of selection procedures, administration, and the removal of people who were found to be, or who were suspected of being, corrupt, the role of the Board became increasingly redundant. It was obvious to all of us, including the Royal Commissioner, that the Police Board was a hindrance rather than a help. But I thought it was a brave decision to dispense with the Board and, of course, I was blamed for it, even though I did no more than contribute to a debate about it.

With that decision, Ryan, suddenly unfettered by civilian overseers, had become possibly the most powerful Police Commissioner in history. The backlash, when it came, however, was ferocious. Mackay, the man who'd appointed Ryan to the job, accused him of being behind the move and said, 'He has bitten the hand that fed him. We are all familiar with the adage of how power corrupts, but absolute power corrupts absolutely.' Sturgess, predictably, warned darkly of trouble ahead. Journalist and author Evan Whitton, who covered the Fitzgerald corruption proceedings in Queensland and who was a consistent critic of Ryan from the very beginning, invoked the ghost of Fred Hanson 'with the power to dismiss honest cops and to promote crooks'. Hanson, Police Commissioner from 1972 to 1976, was said to have knowledge of, and possibly encouraged, criminal activity in the force and later committed suicide. And lawyer John Marsden, a former member of the Police Board who was himself investigated by the Royal Commission and cleared, and who had pushed the cases of Ryan's rivals for the job, Christine Nixon and Clive Small, wrote a letter to a newspaper, saying 'Peter Ryan has only been here a day . . . I suggest . . . that the failure of the Police Board relates to other matters, including the lack of respect given to it by various Commissioners of Police rather than the principle of a civilian Police Board.' He too would re-emerge as a bitter critic of Ryan.

But the biggest battle of all was fast approaching. As well as the axing of the Board, Justice Wood also proposed that Ryan be entitled to sack any officer deemed to have lost his confidence. They, in turn, would lose their right of appeal against their sacking to the Industrial Relations Commission, and only be allowed to contest it on the grounds of natural justice at Supreme Court level. This was a daring proposal aimed at allowing Ryan to get rid of those officers who'd been named as corrupt, lazy, ineffective or inept by the Royal Commission, without having to go through the extremely difficult and time-consuming procedure of having to prove beyond reasonable doubt that they deserved the boot. Already, 70 per cent of officers sacked for criminal convictions had managed to win reinstatement at industrial tribunals; this highly controversial move would give Ryan the chance to sweep a new broom throughout the entire service.

'I wanted to support honest cops and the only way to do it was to have an effective discipline system,' says Ryan.

> I had this huge backlog of discipline cases from previous years and many people who had been named in the Royal Commission as being implicated in some corrupt deed or other. The expectation was that these people would disappear overnight. But under the existing legislation, that was impossible. Often, individuals were mentioned for being a friend of somebody, or going to a particular pub where it was alleged they got free beer and free meals, but unless you had proof of it, however are you going to investigate all of that? Goddamn it, that's what the Royal Commission was for. They should have done all of that. They would deny it, of course. They'd say all they had to do was expose the thing so it could be dealt with elsewhere.
>
> But the Commission lasted nearly four years in total, at enormous cost, and if all they could do in that time was expose it as being a problem, how on earth could I ever be expected to investigate individual cases to the point of beyond all reasonable doubt? It just couldn't be done. Not only was it physically impossible for me, but who would I trust to actually do the investigating so I knew it would be done properly? The whole thing was madness – a point consistently lost on the Ombudsman and media too.

Ryan knew he would need clear-cut powers of effective dismissal to act instantly, and decisively, on those people he felt should be out of the force. After all, 300 officers had been named at the Commission, and a staggering 200 serving officers had been revealed to have criminal records. Such powers would be an essential component of the reform process, and Ryan gave his assurances to the Commission that they would only be used in proven cases of serious misconduct or ineptitude. But the police union, the New South Wales Police Association, was unconvinced. Rumours immediately began circulating that Ryan had drawn up a list of officers he was preparing to sack, and the Association leapt into action. All other workers, officials argued, were entitled to a hearing at the Industrial Relations

Commission; it wasn't fair that police officers be singled out for exclusion. In addition, such wide-ranging dismissal powers were open to manipulation, whereby honest police could be subjected to campaigns to have them removed.

On 18 November 1996, war was officially declared. The Association took out a series of newspaper advertisements arguing its case against the 'loss of confidence' proposals. Ryan was furious. So was Justice Wood. 'I think the message is clear,' said Wood. 'The police associations are either with this process or they are not – and they should stand up and be counted.' But two days later, the argument turned ugly. Between 1500 and 2000 banner-waving police and trade-union sympathisers marched through the city in protest at the changes, then stood before the gates of Parliament, chanting, 'Send the Pommie back!'

Ryan, who'd been buoyed by the grassroots support voiced by officers he'd met across the State in his first eleven weeks in the job, and burning with the passion to make a difference, spoke out angrily about their bullyboy tactics and claimed the campaign had been orchestrated by corrupt cops. In truth, however, he felt absolutely crushed. Coming from a culture in which police would not dare cross the line from being keepers of the peace to turning up in public like a lynch mob, their hatred and rage had shocked him to his very core.

CHAPTER 13

Who can
I trust?

The ferocity of the police demonstration led to chaos throughout the service, the Government and the reform process. Looking on from the Royal Commission, Justice James Wood branded it the 'saddest day in the history of New South Wales policing'. Taken aback by the strength of feeling, a meeting of the State Labor caucus voted by a narrow majority that evening to give the police what they wanted, and allow appeals to the Industrial Relations Commission. This put New South Wales Premier Bob Carr in an awkward position, torn between a Party traditionally expected to uphold workers' rights, and the needs of his new Police Commissioner eager to purge the service. But Carr rode straight into battle. He delivered a stirring plea to politicians to support the reform process, and all the measures thought necessary to put it into practice – and had the caucus decision overturned the next day.

Peter Ryan, however, couldn't get rid of the crushing sense of having been betrayed by his officers, the very people he felt he'd come over from the UK to help. In particular, he was stung by the sight of officers waving banners daubed with the slogan, 'Support Honest Cops.' 'That was exactly what I wanted to do,' he says, angrily.

But by denying me the right to remove the dishonest ones, that was in no way supporting the honest ones. In all organisations, particularly the police or military where it's a disciplined group,

you are subject to peer pressure where quite often the dishonest ones put fear into the honest ones. Then the honest ones are
too scared to stand up and speak out because they believe corruption is so rife, they'll be crushed, they'll lose their careers
and they'll be ostracised. So the bad ones always come to the
surface, and the good are suppressed. But, later, the Government lost its nerve. They allowed the proposed legislation to be
weakened so horribly, we might as well not have bothered with
it. Instead, it has developed into a nightmare of legal debate,
which, in essence, means I have got to be able to be convinced,
beyond all reasonable doubt, that the things alleged against the
officers are true, and only then am I able to exercise my judgement that they should be removed. We have had nothing but
hugely expensive hearings in the Industrial Relations Commission and working parties on it ever since. Instead of giving me
a disciplinary system which was quick and fast and effective for
officers, it's taking months, even years to get rid of corrupt ones.
It's made the whole thing totally ineffective.

In the end, I had all these officers who'd been named by the
Royal Commission but, because of the weakness in the framing
of the new legislation, I was denied, legally, the ability even to
draw on much of the evidence of the Royal Commission to support my disciplinary action. This put me in a hell of a bind. The
Ombudsman's office, ever anxious to go public and show they
are doing a job, were constantly saying, 'Ryan hasn't done anything about those people named,' as if I could go out personally
and arrest them, in addition to the million other things I had to
do to pick up this police force from its knees and rebuild this
ruined house. Still, I did what I could.

His most potent weapon turned out to be a smart confidence trick
of his own. 'I found my greatest strength lay in talking tough, and
saying I was going to get rid of all these people,' he says. 'People
didn't understand the legislation and so, when the spotlight fell on
them, they simply resigned.'

There were some who felt the resignations of the guilty should
not be accepted, saying they'd be getting away without any of the

stigma of being publicly labelled corrupt, but Ryan argued that they should be simply let go. First, whether they resigned or were sacked, it made no difference to their pension – they collected it in any case. Secondly, there was nothing in law that would allow Ryan to deny them a resignation. And, finally, they could always be denied references, and their files marked, 'Not to be re-employed.' Many would also go off on sick leave and then claim an ill-health pension.

Yet the confusion over the dismissals caused the first chink in Ryan's public image as the omnipotent police chief, backed unconditionally by the Government, and prepared to act decisively whenever the occasion warranted it. The public, fired up by the media, were outraged that police officers suspected of corruption weren't being put behind bars. The very idea of them sailing off into early retirement, largely unsullied, did nothing to sate their hunger for revenge for having had their trust so badly abused. Ryan could say little. To admit that his ability to trick bent cops into leaving the force was the strongest weapon he had at his disposal would have seen even that avenue closed off.

The controversy over that power to dismiss also cast a shadow over his first major speech at the end of his first ninety days in office, delivered at the last of the two-year Wood Royal Commission hearings, outlining his vision for the future of the police. He'd been preparing for it for weeks: visiting police stations, speaking to officers at every level of the service, going over the paperwork, examining minutely the structure of the service and working out how everything could be done better.

Two days before he was due to appear came the bombshell: a New South Wales Government report recommending the closure of nearly a quarter of the State's 469 police stations. Ryan was livid. He'd had no idea the issue was being examined, let alone a report prepared.

I'd already decided then that we had too many police stations in the wrong places, and felt that we could brigade them together to save enormous costs and free up large numbers of police for frontline duties. We also had many allegations during the Royal Commission – and I came across this myself too – that officers on patrol, where there was a station, would go in, shut the door, never answer either the door or the phone, and just sit there watching sport on TV, and sending out for pizza. It wasn't common, but it was common enough. So to have more police stations for people to go and hide in, where there wasn't someone truly in charge and accountable . . . well, you might as well not have them at all because they weren't providing anything to the community. The biggest number of complaints we were getting at that time was from the public saying they'd rung the police and no one answered, or they said they were too busy to assist.

So part of my first plan was to increase the number of police on the streets by saying we need to be more effective in the way we use our resources. My views in those early days were pretty well known, but then suddenly the Government releases a report saying 107 stations could close because they weren't effective. No one had spoken to me about it, no one had shared their analysis and recommendations with me, and, of course, we were caught on the hop. I was going to say something similar, but then I was put on the defensive. It was bizarre.

Ryan suspected the Government's Council on the Cost of Government had been working with people in the organisation who had deliberately kept him in the dark.

There was no doubt a lot of that going on, I was being given selected and selective information on what people thought I ought to know. I was becoming increasingly convinced I was being denied information so that it would look like I didn't know what was going on. It was being deliberately obscured, hidden away and not discussed in my presence or reported to me by people who were either creating mischief or who wanted, or supported those who wanted, the job themselves. It really was a tough time. People deny that now of course, but it was too obvious to be anything else. You can't expect one individual to come into an organisation from outside, completely outside with not one friend within the organisation and be able to get into the knowledge stream and find out what the hell is going

on. You've got to hope that there are some who want you to succeed and who are prepared to provide you with the knowledge
and protect you from those who would deny you it. Of course,
that took a little longer than two months to generate.

Ryan hastily rewrote his speech in the light of the station closure recommendations and finally took the stand. He spoke with an authority
and a confidence he did not truly feel. But his appearance was a triumph, as he slowly, deliberately, outlined his plans to assess the files
of ninety-six police thought to be either corrupt or inept, to move
sergeants back on to street patrols, to cut down on administration by
using more civilians, to flatten the command of the service with
eleven regions replacing the region-to-district-to-station command,
to introduce a Code of Conduct, and to press for pay increases. It was
greeted as the most wide-ranging reform of the service in 134 years,
and a milestone in New South Wales's history. That done, Ryan felt
the next step was to start assessing the people around him, and working out exactly whom he could trust, and whom he could not. He
decided to start right at the top.

In this, the chief of staff he brought over from England with him,
Jo Hampson, was an invaluable help. She fed gossip back to him,
arranged introductions, gave him rundowns on people, generally
watched his back and warned him, continually, against one officer in
particular. 'I used to watch his senior officers and who they went to
talk to and who was meeting whom in whose office,' she says. 'Sometimes, though, he wouldn't listen which I found very frustrating.
I think eventually he stopped listening to me and felt he had to let
go and trust others.'

The New South Wales State Commander at the time oversaw operations, while the Deputy Commissioner headed the service's administrative side: the finance, personnel, training, and all the softer sides
of policing. This seemed a ridiculous waste of an experienced officer
to Ryan, and instead he decided that a civilian director of corporate
services should take on the administration, and a proper finance
director look after the figures. From that point, he could rebuild the
rest of the force into his new local area commands, and the other
specialist units (like detectives, boats, aircraft, forensic scientists, the

Special State Protection Unit and specialist technicians) could be brought under the umbrella of another head. Ryan therefore decided he needed two deputies: one to command uniform field operations and the other to look after specialist operations.

Bev Lawson, who'd been working as an acting deputy, was someone he warmed to immediately. Senior officers said there was absolutely no doubt at all about her honesty, and that she really lived for the job, moreover she seemed well liked and respected throughout the State. Ryan himself started listening to her advice and invariably found it to be good. He was also impressed that she never said anything negative about other officers under her command. Jeff Jarratt, who'd been a candidate for Ryan's own Commissioner job, was the other obvious contender. Ryan wasn't so sure about him, though his experience, his staying power and his seniority were undeniable. He knew both Lawson and Jarratt had their eye on field operations, they wanted to be in charge of all the thousands of police out there in the stations responding to the community, but Ryan had to make a choice. He chose Lawson.

> With the support she'd given me in drawing up the plans for the new regions and new structures, I decided she would be better because she was, in my view, more in tune at that time with officers on the ground. She already had a very good idea of what was required in the new structure. Now I know Jeffrey wasn't too pleased with that, but you can't please everyone. I did promise though, that within a year or two, I'd swap them over to give them experience of each other's role and help them develop themselves for the future.

That then left two other applicants who'd unsuccessfully stood against Ryan for the top job: Clive Small and Christine Nixon. Ryan gave Small the detective side because of his experience in that area, and Nixon took the executive director of Human Resources, which became an operational unit in its own right. Des Mooney was recruited from outside to run the administration as executive director for management services.

Ryan then sat down with Lawson, Jarratt, Small and Nixon to

plan the biggest upheaval in the New South Wales police service's history. Appointing new regional commanders to each of the eleven new commands was an enormous task in itself. There were few chief superintendents left after the Royal Commission and barely any Assistant Commissioners. Most of the senior officers remaining were only superintendents, so to promote them to head up commands would entail a huge leap in rank and responsibilities. Therefore, all were appointed into the roles temporarily until they could be properly assessed. Not all passed the assessment process, designed with the help of outside experts, so they were given extra training, mentoring and guidance to help them rise to the level required for their roles. It was, by its very nature, a flawed process. There was no room for people to fail, as there was no one waiting in the wings to take their place.

The challenge of building up a strong team from a group of officers with little managerial experience was one Ryan, with his background in training and development at Bramshill, relished. Yet the difference here was that the group had to be developed with a new leadership style, one that would help the task of changing the culture and behaviour of the service itself. 'The difficulty is that it isn't something you can mandate,' says Ryan. 'It's something that has to be encouraged and fostered and will take a long time. Even Wood said it would take a generation.' Resistance to change started almost immediately.

> There was a massive weariness coming out of the Royal Commission. There were almost sighs of relief of 'Thank God, we're out of that,' then they had to go into the reform process. People were weary of being battered around the head by the media for being ignorant, ill-educated, ill-performing, corrupt and part of what was always being talked about as a rotten organisation. They were told they must change, they must reform, and we started getting resistance. So we had to get over this by introducing features which people could actually identify and want to be associated with, like crime reduction and public safety.

Ryan started building behavioural change by getting his officers to focus on definable goals. He'd talk of the need to reduce crime by

arriving at the scene more quickly, being more thorough and professional in the investigation, treating the victims with more care and
respect, and making sure the written reports were free of ambiguity
and embellishment so they'd stand up more firmly in court. All those
things would be done ethically and fairly, with no room left for corrupt behaviour of any kind. The difficulty was always persuading
officers, particularly senior ones, to embrace that approach. Often,
the longer they'd been in the job, the more experienced and older
they were, the more they resisted change. With the average age of
the New South Wales service much higher than any Ryan had ever
worked in before, because officers seemed to be promoted on length
of service rather than on merit, that posed a particular difficulty.

> They knew it was right, but how to get them to change was the
> problem, and we're still having trouble with that. A lot of them
> are jolly nice people, but they aren't always capable of accepting
> change, particularly the older they get and the longer they've
> been there. Some will embrace it and others will find difficulty
> with it. But it's no good expecting people to change merely
> because they've been told to. You have to have your managerial
> team totally behind you, so they can lead from the top, by
> example, by encouragement and by accountability. That was
> sometimes a problem.

Ryan felt he could trust Lawson, but he was never as sure about Jarratt, Small and Nixon. Each of the three had applied for his job; how
could he be certain they weren't each looking for an opportunity to
oust him and take the top job themselves? It was perhaps here that
he made one of his greatest errors. He decided to keep each at arm's
length, refusing to take any of the three into his confidence. He
cocooned himself on the 18th floor of Avery House and they started
regarding him as a more and more remote boss. 'I think, within the
service, that made him appear unapproachable,' says one former
senior officer, and a close friend of Small's.

> Even his closest colleagues had to book in time with him, for a
> window once a week, when we saw it as ludicrous they couldn't

call in to see him at any time. The perception was that he was
creating a bunker and didn't trust anyone. You could understand
that, but the fact was that there was little resistance to positive
change, most people *wanted* the service to improve. We were all
so ready for it. Yet you felt he was treating everyone as an enemy.
He had to get a team together. He could never do what he
wanted to do alone.

The plotting that was going on was usually less aimed at destabilis-
ing him, than jostling for position for after his departure, says
another well-placed observer. 'They actually wanted him to succeed
to a point, as none of them wanted to inherit a service in chaos,' he
says. 'It was in their interests that he get it right.'

But Ryan believes cutting himself off was the only way he could
function effectively among people of whom he was still forming a
judgement.

A lot of people wanted to take me under their wing and nurture
me, but I just didn't know who they were or what I would be
getting myself into. I just wanted to sit back a bit and not get
involved with friendships. All the time, I was trying to work out
whom I could trust. Jo was working away behind the scenes,
talking to people and trying to advise me on who was on my
side and who wasn't. I'd talk to James Wood and ask if he had
anything on so-and-so, and talk to the Royal Commission.
Someone from the New South Wales Crime Commission told
me I should have brought a Jumbo Jet of people from Britain
with me so I'd have *someone* I could trust. Everyone here, he
said, seemed to be implicated in one way or another, either by
activity or lack of action against those who were behaving
improperly. Those early months were very difficult.

Besides, he felt he was coming increasingly under siege in every
direction. Police officers were campaigning for a 25 per cent pay rise;
they were being offered 3 per cent by the Government. Ryan was stuck
in the middle, believing they were badly paid, but unable to openly
criticise their paymasters. A seemingly innocuous interview he'd given

to the British journal *Police Review* about his first 100 days in New South Wales had been picked up by the Australian press, which had pounced on his description of the level of crime in the State as 'horrific', and on his claim that it had strong links with Lebanese, Chinese, Vietnamese, Russian and Hong Kong criminals. Ethnic community leaders were outraged that he'd linked race and crime and accused him of ascribing criminality to different migrant groups. Premier Bob Carr then also leapt into the fray and, in what was widely seen as a public rebuke to Ryan, said crime and gangs were the issue – not race. Ryan was incensed.

> I learned a lesson from that which had been relearnt several times in those very few short months, that everything I said, everything I did, was going to be reported on, and, if it gained them some advantage, politically, economically, professionally or internally, someone would comment on it. There was no way I was going to get away with saying anything. I spent all my service in the UK being able to say pretty well what I wanted. You could attack the courts for sentencing, you could demand changes to legislation, you could defend your police force against verbal attack, and you could actually say one group or another group of people were responsible for a particular type of crime and not be regarded as some outspoken nitwit who was breaking every social taboo. All of a sudden you've got a police chief who's actually saying something that the public understand and wanted him to say, and everyone was trying to howl you down. Subsequently, even Carr came round talking about crime and race, as though it was all his idea! In Britain, you were actually considered to be the expert in the job you were paid to do, instead of everybody else thinking they are the experts and you are just the lackey that does what you're told.
>
> I think the Royal Commission had given everyone a taste for commenting on the police, and the more critical the better. The journalists who'd been covering the Commission needed something else to write, and here they had this new man they could prod and poke, and see if he would respond to it. In my view, we had an unhealthy, overlarge interest in policing.

During these dark months, there were two things that kept Ryan going. The first was the support he felt from rank-and-file officers, who'd frequently approach him shyly as he walked through Sydney or while he was on a lightning tour of the State. They'd walk up, shake his hand and welcome him to Australia, saying how they hoped the bad old days were behind them now and better times ahead, and wish him luck. Often, Ryan would feel his smile freeze as they'd add, cheerily, on the end, 'Well, you might be a Pom, but we'll still give you a fair go . . .'

The second light at the end of the tunnel was the prospect of his family coming out to join him, so they could have their first Christmas together in Australia. The strain was beginning to tell, and he was desperately lonely. He went to see a few houses and ended up buying a five-bedroom freestanding house in Westbrook Avenue, in leafy Wahroonga on Sydney's North Shore, to enable him to get right away from Police HQ. With the help of Jo, he furnished and decorated the place completely so Adrienne, Elizabeth and Georgina would have a welcoming home to come to. He went to the airport to meet them, and felt close to tears as they all flung themselves into his arms, amidst a shower of kisses.

Their happiness was short-lived, however. Just after Christmas, Adrienne left to return to the UK to finish the last two terms of her university degree at the University of Reading. Her father Mike Butterworth and his wife Patricia came out to help Ryan look after the children. It was set to be a short separation, and it was always going to be painful, but no one could have imagined just how painful it was to be.

CHAPTER 14

The days of the long knives

The rumours began about the state of the Ryans' marriage almost as soon as Adrienne had left Sydney to finish her studies. It started as whispers in police circles and grew rapidly into a loud murmur before strong hints started appearing in the newspapers that the couple had split up. Finally, on 16 February 1997, it hit the headlines. 'Marriage Wreckers' yelled the banner headline on the front page of Sydney's *Sun Herald*.

Seven-year-old Georgina was the first to show the strain. The next morning, Ryan received a call from her headmistress at Abbotsleigh School saying the little girl was in tears after her friend told her she'd heard her mummy had left and wouldn't be coming back. The little girl was inconsolable. 'I'd told Peter to talk to the girls about the rumours, in case they heard, but he didn't,' says Adrienne. 'They were really distressed and hurt. It was absolutely terrible.' Ryan, too, was devastated. He'd primed himself to deal with the steady criticism of his professional abilities and actions; he'd never seriously imagined an attack on his personal life. He took the girls aside and told them to ignore the rumours. Three days later, however, Georgina waited up for Ryan to get back from work. 'Daddy, please don't be angry at me,' she said, nervously, 'but the girls at school say mummy's divorced you and she's gone to England and married a judge. But they told me not to say anything to anyone.' Ryan was incredulous. He later realised one of the newspaper stories had said Adrienne was seeking legal advice about the claims so, somehow, that had become tangled in children's retelling.

It was disgraceful. Imagine hurting two little girls like that! They were broken-hearted and had to be counselled at school, and kept asking, 'Why has mummy run away and left us, and are you getting divorced?' I know the rumours started within police HQ and I knew I had enemies there, particularly since I was getting rid of so many people. But I was shocked to see garbage like that in the newspapers. There was never even an attempt to ask me about it, or get our side of the story. I was so extremely busy with work at the time, I guess I did ignore the family to some extent and just hoped they'd cope with it all – something I'd never do again. I can only speculate there were people who wanted me off and were feeding information to the newspapers to achieve as much damage to my family as they could.

That Monday night, the day before the couple's 12th wedding anniversary, Adrienne joined the fray. Holed up in her rented cottage just outside London, under siege from the press and with the local police threatening the surrounding journalists with stalking charges, she polished off most of a bottle of white wine and finally asked one of them to publish her message of support to her husband. 'I adore my husband for he is all that anyone could ask of a husband and a father: devoted, loving and caring without reservation and we have a strong and enduring marriage,' she wrote in her letter published on 18 February by Sydney's *Daily Telegraph*. 'Sweetheart, I love you. Don't let the bastards get you down!' 'I hadn't told Peter I was doing it, but it was something I wanted to do to show everyone that the rumours were rubbish,' says Adrienne.

The children were suffering too. At first, it was a novelty to see their dad in the newspapers. That quickly wore off as school friends insisted on telling both Georgina and 9-year-old Elizabeth whenever anything bad was said. 'I never read the stories,' says Elizabeth. 'I suppose I didn't want to know what they were saying about daddy. But I'd hear them talking about it at school. It was very hard as everyone knew who we were. I was in Year 4, but girls in Year 6 would come up to me and say, "I saw your daddy on TV last night." Maybe 40 people would say that every day.' For Georgina, two years younger, it was even harder to deal with, especially the stories about her parents' marital break-up.

'People came up and told me it was my fault,' she says. 'They said they must have got tired of me and my sister fighting.'

For the girls, life was particularly hard in a new country and schools, without their mum and with their dad usually not home till 9 o'clock every night, way after their bedtime. Their grandparents often struggled to cope. 'We were no substitute when they really wanted someone's shoulder to cry on,' says Adrienne's dad Mike Butterworth. 'There is no avoiding the fact that a certain animosity – a certain unwillingness to do what they were told to do by people whom they had always seen as being just cuddly grandparents – quite quickly arose between us and was the cause of much unhappiness during our time there.' There were the more unusual difficulties of life with a man considered to be such a target too. A blown toaster fuse one evening set off the main alarm direct to Police HQ just as the girls started a fight in the house and, with the police operator troubled that no one knew the secret password with two girls screaming in the background, sent over a full contingent of police to check out the situation. 'We all went through a very tough learning process, at different levels and in varying contexts,' says Butterworth. 'This lasted for a long time and had a particularly wearing effect on the girls, on whose small shoulders most of the burden was falling.'

Away from the misery of home, life out on the streets was no less torrid for Ryan. Touring the State's police stations had only hardened his resolve to see many of them closed down. Time after time, he had been shocked to witness the filthy, rat-infested, almost derelict state of some of the older stations, once built on main thoroughfares, now languishing, impossible to find, in the backstreets after their suburbs and towns had grown in a different direction. But he knew it would be tough to win the support of the Government to cut the number of stations. 'Everybody was elected on the usual auction for police,' he says. '"We promise you more police and more stations and that your station won't close if you vote for me." In my view, that indicates a bankruptcy of thinking in political life, as very little else ever appeared to be on the agenda.' On this issue, however, Ryan's resolve was rock hard. He felt it took a lot of officers to keep stations open, officers who could otherwise be far better engaged fighting crime and, unless they were in the right location, residents weren't even visiting them. Instead, he wanted fewer, bigger, better-located stations in which an investment of modern technology would be infinitely worthwhile. At that moment, every time he changed a computer system, he had to change everything in hundreds of stations, which became staggeringly expensive.

There was little better example of a badly placed police station than in Redfern – where problems were erupting in Eveleigh Street. Early in 1997, there had been an explosion of crime around the area, including near the railway station. Residents were being mugged, motorists carjacked, handbags snatched, drugs increasingly peddled, police assaulted, and so many taxi drivers attacked that they were refusing to drive into the district. It was fast becoming a no-go zone, something Ryan felt was absolutely unacceptable in a city like Sydney. As a result, on 14 January, he authorised a dramatic forty-strong police raid to clear up the area. Immediately after that, he called a meeting of all the appropriate agencies that serviced Redfern, including housing, education, community services, and the council, along with representatives from the Aboriginal Housing Commission and the Aboriginal and Torres Strait Islander Council. He debated with them an idea that the whole Block be bulldozed and rebuilt, complete with a community centre, and a well-placed police station to offer help to locals who needed it. He was disappointed that it never happened. Parts were knocked down, but his grand scheme foundered as politicians nervously deliberated. 'The police station itself is still a dump,' says Ryan. 'It's hard to get to; it's not easily seen down its dingy, narrow back alley, completely isolated from where the action is. Unless you absolutely knew it, you would never be able to find it – and you certainly wouldn't try to get to it on foot.' In the war over police stations, that was one battle irredeemably lost.

By January 1997, Ryan had formed an idea about who he wanted to remain in the police service, and who merited a place in the top team. The four-region, twenty-eight-district, 172-patrol structure was to be cut down into larger, better-managed groups of eleven regions and eighty local area commands that wouldn't require anything like the unwieldy tier of senior management that existed at the time. Everyone agreed: the service was horribly top-heavy, and often with managers who were too old-fashioned and lacking in management skills, too used to doing things in a certain way and without the ability to either inspire the officers below them, or come up with dynamic solutions to problems. After weekly talks at the Royal Commission, meetings with some of the members of the former Police Board, and a number of sessions sitting in on annual performance discussions with the most senior officers of the service, Ryan sent out letters to his sixty-strong senior executive asking them to choose a preferred career option – retirement or serving in his restructured team. He then decided he would call in all his officers ranked chief superintendent and above, and would face them one by one to discuss their future.

He hired a suite of rooms in the Marriott Hotel, next door to police HQ, with the idea that officers could be called in with some degree of anonymity, and that there'd be on hand any necessary support services, such as welfare officers, redeployment specialists, advisors, and even a chaplain, in case of extreme distress. And then, at 9 a.m., Tuesday, 28 January, he started calling his top people in.

One of the first officers in arrived with his shoulders already slumped. 'I know what I'm here for,' he said. 'I've already seen your broad structure for the service. I don't see myself fitting into that structure, do you?' Ryan shook his head slowly. 'No, I don't,' he replied. 'In that case,' said the man, 'I'd like to resign. I've been thinking about it anyway. Do you mind if I hang on until April then I'll catch up with my outstanding leave, and go?' Ryan nodded gravely and shook his hand.

Another case was more difficult. This man saw himself with a glowing police future; Ryan didn't. 'Look, to be quite honest, there's nowhere for you in the service,' said Ryan. 'The Royal Commission has mentioned you on a couple of occasions and, while there's nothing there that we can pin on you in terms of corruption, I don't think I can take the chance. You haven't performed particularly well anyway, so I'd like you to leave – and as soon as possible, preferably by the end of the week, or the month.' There was a tense silence before the shocked man started protesting his innocence. After a few minutes, he stopped. A few weeks later, he left the service.

One person to come in early in the process was Acting Assistant Commissioner Geoff Schuberg, Commander of Professional Responsibility, who'd run what had been the Internal Affairs Unit. This was going to be the hardest task of all. It would have been easier to keep him on in his position, Ryan knew, but the bottom line was that he felt Schuberg did not suit the plans he had for a completely revamped Internal Affairs. He was welcome to stay in the service, but as a Chief Inspector instead.

> He just wasn't performing to the level he was being paid at; he wasn't doing what was required, and internal affairs was useless. It was slow, there was no imagination, the investigations were poor, things just weren't happening. I just couldn't afford to have an internal affairs running as it was running. It needed someone else in there, and it needed changing completely. The State Government had also put an extra requirement on me to have fewer people in the State Executive. I had too many – but that's because they'd made this ridiculous arrangement years earlier to move policemen into these positions which was rather silly.
>
> In addition, Geoff was an acquaintance of Gary Sturgess, and I was trying to work out how Sturgess was always in the position of being well informed about what was going on in the service, and sniping at me in the newspapers. He was getting his information from somewhere, and the type of information he had could only have come from someone highly placed in the service. As Sturgess was not the most popular of men and some people disliked him intensely, I had my suspicions that Geoff could have been a source of his information. [Schuberg denies having ever leaked information to anyone outside the service.] Sturgess knew the journalist Evan Whitton who kept writing disgraceful pieces about me as the 'fleshy Englishman'. I knew there were some strong Liberal-Party connections there, and I was getting enough from the Liberal Party at the time without encouraging people close to me to give me more.

Schuberg, naturally, was devastated by Ryan's verdict. He protested that he was doing a very good job, that he'd always been very loyal, that he'd been a top corruption-fighter, and that he didn't deserve this treatment. He didn't want to take a lower rank either, as that would mean a loss of pay and prestige. He was shocked and horrified by what was being meted out. Eventually, he stormed out of the room and slammed the door behind him.

Ryan once again braced himself for the backlash, but even he was amazed by how quickly and ferociously it came.

Within minutes it was all over the radio that Ryan was into sacking all the senior executives, and here was Geoff Schuberg, hero of the service, the man who'd just been given the Police Medal in the Australia Day honours after thirty-four years service, being sacked, despite being diligent and hardworking and brilliant. It was ridiculous. Chief Executives in any organisation get to choose their top team. When a new head of Westpac comes along, for example, many of the old guys don't survive, they move on, as he brings in new top people. But here people were saying I had no right to do my job – and as if they were in a better position to judge! Besides, I wasn't operating unilaterally on this. The Minister had agreed beforehand and advice had been taken from the other executives.

But Ryan had made yet another enemy. And, at the time, he had no idea just how powerful this enemy was to become. Opposition police spokesman Andrew Tink immediately took up Schuberg's case as evidence Ryan had no idea what he was doing. With so much crime, he said, how could we afford to lose such experienced officers? Corruption-fighter Bob Bottom, who'd campaigned with Sturgess on police corruption before the establishment of the ICAC, wrote a piece in a newspaper the next day, bemoaning the fact that Ryan had become Commissioner instead of Schuberg, with the portentous headline: 'Beware the ghost of an honest cop.' Six weeks later, Schuberg was publicly criticised by State Ombudsman Irene Moss. She ruled that during his time as head of Internal Affairs, he had not seen any conflict of interest in the case he was investigating of a senior officer giving character evidence for a drug-trafficking neighbour, from whom the officer had accepted favours. Even so, the wounded Schuberg later went on to be championed by lawyer John Marsden, radio host Alan Jones, a whole crowd of disaffected officers, and, ironically, the new Police Minister Michael Costa, who was appointed in November 2001. With that kind of support, he would prove one of the most dangerous foes Ryan had ever made.

No sooner had Schuberg's story hit the radio waves than the Marriott came under siege from the press, eager to see who might be arriving for their interviews from HQ next door. Reluctantly, Ryan closed down the operation, realising he could no longer shield officers' dignity, and set up again in his own office. They all shuffled in one by one, some nervously, some belligerently, some simply stunned by what was happening. Ryan, however, was determined to speak to each personally, believing that was the role of a good manager. As the hours rolled by, some officers started phoning in and asking if they could retire without seeing their boss. He agreed, as long as they could come up with a retirement date that would fit in with his requirements.

More difficult were those feisty characters Ryan desperately wanted to stay on for the next two to three months until the new organisation had been put into place, but who wouldn't have a job at the end of it. Gingerly, he asked each one to stay on to help him. To their credit, nearly all of them agreed. At the end of the week, Ryan checked with the Royal Commission and Whelan, and then announced his new team.

> Sometimes, I wonder whether I should have gone into it a bit deeper, and taken out more people and given others a chance. In some respects with one person, I think I should have done, but I really didn't have anyone to put in their place. There was simply no one that had the experience to operate at the levels I was wanting them to operate at. It really was very, very difficult because I didn't know anybody and since everyone had been promoted on their years of seniority rather than merit, there was no one further down that had any experience that we could have taken a risk on. On some people, I was taking a huge chance as I had literally elevated them from relatively small jobs with not a great deal of experience into very big jobs with thousands of people under their command, in circumstances that can only be described as extraordinarily difficult.
>
> It was also a huge risk-taking venture on my part, to remove people who were quite popular, some of whom have never forgiven me to this day. A few of the people I removed because I and others thought they were incompetent were suddenly being branded as some sort of hero, and I was this stupid Pommie

chucking them out, even though that's what I was brought in to do in the first place. Two were still acting and working away within the police to undermine what I was doing, and me personally. Two are definitely doing that now from outside the police service. They've got friends here, but I neutralised some of those friends by moving them on and making sure their power-base was disrupted. Others, I confronted and told them I knew who their friends were, and that I had made my decision and they had to accept it – and if they didn't, they might be next. I had to be ruthless; I couldn't be soft here.

Observers were still divided on the efficacy of Ryan's purge. Former Commissioner John Avery praised him for 'having the guts' to be so brutal. Former Police Board president Don Mackay said he was doing what was necessary to restructure the service. Sturgess said he was listening to advice from the wrong people. Anonymous sources claimed he was choosing only those officers who were favoured by Nixon and Jarratt, and getting rid of those who might be competition for their posts.

Yet even when Ryan came to announce his new top team of Lawson, 56, and Jarratt, 48, as deputies; Nixon, 43, as Assistant Commissioner in charge of human resources and development; Clive Small, 50, Assistant Commissioner heading the new Crime Agencies encompassing all the old crime and child protection units; Assistant Commissioner Mal Brammer, 49, in Internal Affairs; and Paul McKinnon, 54, for Olympics, it was all a bit of an anticlimax. Even the news that the former assistant commissioners Schuberg, Alf Peate, Bill Galvin and Dennis Gilligan were either leaving or retiring was no surprise. It had all been leaked beforehand.

The new team, together with the new set of district commanders, settled quickly into their jobs. Ryan hoped for a period of relative calm to help them bed in, and for him to continue rebuilding and restructuring the service, and winning over the hearts and minds of both officers and the public. It wasn't to be.

On 4 February 1997, Ryan launched a new Code of Conduct for officers, including the banning of free gifts, drinking on duty, and the threat of dismissal for any criminal offence, including drink-driving.

The very next day, he was accused in the press of breaching his own code by accepting tickets to football games and stage plays. The headline dubbed it 'Peter's Gravy Train'.

Ryan was livid. He'd accepted a ticket to the 1996 AFL Grand Final in Melbourne during his first few weeks alone in Australia, after Police Minister Paul Whelan handed him a ticket saying, 'This is a treat on me.' He'd paid for his own flight, and flown back that same night. The next month, he was invited to the opening night of the musical *Crazy For You*. He'd thought nothing of it.

> It was months later that we launched our Code of Conduct. It wasn't like the Ten Commandments – Thou shalt not do – it was: if someone gives you something in return for a favour or it might compromise your position as a police officer, you should think very carefully before accepting it or words to that effect. So, how could I possibly breach a Code of Conduct that hadn't even been thought about, let alone enforced at the time? I thought it was absolutely disgraceful and disgusting, and it was pretty obvious that they were doing their damnedest, in my view, to undermine or target me or show me up in some way or another. It just never let up.

The brewing hositility between Ryan and the press, compounded by their attacks during the purge and then their insinuations about the state of his marriage, hardened into outright mistrust and bitterness after that. A few days later, his cleaning lady phoned Adrienne in Britain. She wanted to quit as a car kept following her home from the Ryans' house, and she was terrified it might be criminals or disgruntled ex-police officers. It turned out to be the media.

But it wasn't only the press Ryan was having difficulties with; it was also the Government. When it was revealed that an investigation into a serial rapist who had attacked twenty-nine women in Sydney's west had been bungled, Whelan immediately called a crisis meeting. New figures showed that crime had risen, so again Whelan issued a public 'Please Explain'. And when Ryan decided to abolish the Special Branch and replace it with a new unit, Whelan's fury took him by complete surprise. Suddenly, he began to feel very, very alone.

CHAPTER 15

'Just get on with the job!'

New South Wales Police Commissioner Peter Ryan and New South Wales Police Minister Paul Whelan seemed, on the surface, a perfect fit. Whelan was one of the most senior, established and experienced politicians in the State, having been elected into Parliament in 1976, and having held four ministry positions before being given police in 1995. He was eager to make his mark and had happily backed the appointment of Ryan the next year. It was in both men's interests to present a solid front in order to reform the police service, stamp out corruption and win the fight against crime.

Yet their relationship was inevitably going to be strained by the tension of its inherent power struggle. Whelan, as the political master, felt that his role was to oversee his public servants. Ryan, as the professional police officer, was always aware of the need to keep Whelan's backing but, in truth, felt that he'd been appointed to the position, he'd have to carry the can if anything went wrong, and so he should at least be given the freedom to get on with the job, away from political interference. They were two proud, determined, ambitious men, both keen to make the tough decisions, but each hoping also to win popular support for their actions.

Historically, it had frequently proved a dangerous liaison. In October 1992, for example, Police Minister Ted Pickering resigned after a spectacular falling out with Police Commissioner Tony Lauer who refuted Pickering's claim that he'd never been warned by police about a TV report on 17-year-old runaway Angus Rigg, who had suffered brain damage after trying to hang himself in police cells. A year later, Pickering moved a no-confidence motion against Lauer in Parliament, claiming he'd been unwilling and incapable of pursuing corruption.

By contrast, Ryan and Whelan managed to present a united front on most issues, although Ryan was disappointed Whelan hadn't put up more of a fight for strong 'Commissioner's Confidence' legislation. But as Ryan's popularity began to slip and his daily battering in the press began to have an impact, Whelan seemed to become increasingly keen to maintain a safe distance. When things were going well, he was happy to share the credit. When things were more problematic, he seemed sometimes a little too eager to shift the blame. And when there was an outcry in the press on an issue, or when he felt his own authority was being usurped, he was quick to go on the offensive.

This was never clearer than in the sorry debacle over Ryan's axing of the notorious New South Wales Police Special Branch. In March 1997 during the last days of the Royal Commission's three years of public hearings, Justice James Wood took evidence from the commander of the Special Branch, Chief Superintendent Neville Ireland, that the exceedingly secretive anti-terrorist unit had kept confidential dossiers on some people, despite the fact that they were never suspected of any criminal or terrorist activity. Indeed, Ireland admitted that among the files on civil libertarians and political activists, there were dossiers on a number of barristers, simply for having undertaken criminal trial work. The admission followed revelations that the Branch had burned hundreds of files at the Waverley incinerator in late 1994, soon after the start of the Royal Commission.

This was the last straw for Ryan, who had ordered an audit of the squad late the previous year after hearing it had protected the late judge David Yeldham, who killed himself in November 1996 after being named in connection with pedophilia. Late in the evening of Tuesday, 12 March 1997, he sent a special squad over to seal their rooms, seize the keys to all the filing cabinets, and cancel the magnetic entry cards of all twenty Branch members. At 6 o'clock the following morning, when they turned up for work, they were denied entry to the premises. The unit had effectively been disbanded. Premier Bob Carr applauded Ryan's decisive move, saying Special Branch officers had imagined they were 'a poor person's ASIO'.

Yet when Ryan, a month later, announced in the *New South Wales Police Gazette* via a recruitment ad that he was planning a new elite anti-terrorism squad to replace them, called the 'Protective Security Response Group', Whelan stepped in. He saw the move as an attempt to revive the unit under a different name; Ryan, on the other hand, had felt it was vital that some of their functions were still maintained, like providing protection for visiting dignitaries and fulfilling the statutory requirements of the national security plan on terrorism. He had given the group a new leader, a clear charter and strict reporting requirements, but Whelan reacted immediately. In what was widely perceived as the abrupt end of Ryan's political honeymoon, Whelan told Ryan such policy matters were the Government's concern, and that he should limit himself to 'operational' issues. 'Let me state clearly,' said Whelan, delivering the final, stinging rebuke via the press, 'the Government wants Commissioner Ryan to get on with the job of reforming the police service.'

Suddenly, the essential dichotomy in relations between the Government and its police chief was thrown into sharp relief. With a State election looming in March 1999, Carr and Whelan desperately wanted Ryan to succeed in cleaning up the force and introducing the changes recommended by the three-year $70-million Royal Commission whose cause they'd championed. It was crucial that their daring gamble of bringing in a total cleanskin outsider for the top job be seen as an astute and judicious move, and they were only too aware how important the issue of law and order would be to the rank-and-file voters of New South Wales. At the same time, however, they simply could not afford to be tied too closely to Ryan, just in case crime figures went too high, or great swathes of corruption were discovered to be flourishing unchecked. Neither could they allow Ryan to become so popular that he could be seen as beyond their control, and operating independently of them. Ryan, meanwhile, was learning to play the media game and was fast developing a freewheeling style that kept him one step ahead of his critics. He stunned supporters and enemies alike when in a February 1997 ABC-TV documentary he said that he'd support a trial legalisation of heroin – not a popular view for a police chief to hold, even if a lot of his colleagues privately agreed. And he triggered a storm among the judiciary by supporting majority verdicts in criminal trials and the removal of the right to silence for the accused. But this could not be allowed to develop unchecked. More and more, Whelan began to call Ryan to heel. With a healthy sense of his own self-worth, Ryan resented it hugely.

> The calibre of politicians in New South Wales wasn't very good. They were well-meaning people, but they were still politicians. It was almost as if they believed that upon election they were anointed with all the knowledge and information and professional analytical ability to question people like me, who spent a lifetime doing nothing else but studying and working in these professional environments. They all have an opinion but, as someone once said, the problem with opinion is, everybody's got one. None of it was particularly helpful. It was all, really, media reaction to something that's got to be done. Something goes wrong and it's 'Somebody's head must roll,' 'I'll get someone as a result of this,' 'Let's knock someone else over,' which became almost an excuse for not doing something. It was very unnecessary. That's not the way to run anything, and certainly not a police force.
>
> There was an obvious lack of strategic thinking because there were no policies on anything. It isn't a policy to say, 'We are going to bring down crime.' Policies are things with procedures actually set out, whereby we *can* bring down crime: things that are going to happen, a train of events that actually translates into some kind of operational activity that brings down crime. And having brought down crime and having arrested people, we then have to think about how we're going to process them through the courts, and think whether legislation in terms of punishment is effective enough. Finally, do we have the prisons to house them? So it's a whole train of events, involving not just one agency. It was this obvious lack of foresight in policing policy that wasn't clearly articulated.

Whelan and Carr thought they'd bought a policeman to police New South Wales. What they'd ended up with was a man who'd sliced a fast track up through the echelons of the British police service with a mixture of determination, ambition, education and the kind of peculiarly English arrogance that was a requisite for good leaders of quasi-military organisations in the UK. Ryan, much to their dismay, wasn't interested in limiting his attention merely to police operations. He felt he had experience and wisdom to bring to all areas of Australian life – and he was determined to make everyone listen.

After his first few months settling into the job, Ryan started broadening his field of interest. He saw the Australian criminal justice system, for example, as a set of British Acts of Parliament amended slightly to fit their new environment.

> But what was apparent to me, and it stuck out like a sore thumb to someone who has been in this game so long, was that legislation in some areas was beautifully crafted to make it almost unworkable. It was heavily biased towards civil liberties of the individuals, as opposed to the practical operational requirement of law enforcement. Take the illegal shooting galleries in Kings Cross. I couldn't understand why on earth we didn't go and shut them all down – until I read the legislation. Police had to know there was someone inside shooting up, and exactly what drug they were using, before they could get a warrant. It made it impossible.

That triggered an interest in looking at the whole range of legislation the police used every day. Drunkenness in a public place, for instance, wasn't an offence unless it was accompanied by violence. Street prostitution was extremely hard to prosecute because of legal brothels operating nearby. There was the presumption of bail for every single offence, other than murder, and even then bail was still being given if the accused had a recognised address. 'This meant that a lot of criminals just carried on being criminals,' says Ryan. 'We could see them coming out on bail and continuing to rob, steal, break into houses and assault people.' What perplexed him even more were the cases where jurors were vulnerable to being swayed by one individual in a case to insist on a 'Not Guilty' verdict, even where the rest of the jury were convinced of a person's guilt. In those cases, there could never be a unanimous verdict, so people were walking out of court free. Then there was the vexed question of jurors being 'nobbled', that is threatened, blackmailed or bribed to find an accused not guilty.

> You would have to be mad to believe that the same couldn't happen, or wasn't happening, here in Australia, particularly given our cultural mix and the fact that people from all sorts of backgrounds, who you've got no chance of examining beforehand, sit on juries. So one of the things to improve jury trial would be to have a majority verdict. So I said we should have that. I also believed that the right to silence along a British model again should be removed, and advance disclosure of the defence case, pre-trial. In too many cases here, you hear the accused saying, 'It wasn't me – I was on holiday in Queensland.' But if you don't say anything till you get to trial, the prosecution can't bring back witnesses to refute the claims, so the story can't be checked.

Naturally, Ryan's stand, outlined originally at a Parliamentary seminar for leading New South Wales legal figures, unleashed an absolute outcry. New South Wales Law Society president Patrick Fair said he wanted to see a better police force rather than a 'softer' legal system. The president of the Bar Association David Bennett QC similarly criticised Ryan's prescriptions for more efficient courts. Carr also joined in the fray, saying he would not support any changes that made it possible for innocent people to go to jail. It's worth noting that three years later, when the tide had turned well and truly against Ryan, new Police Minister Michael Costa managed to secure laws denying bail to repeat offenders after less than a month in office. Where there's political will, it seems, there's a way.

Back in 1997, however, Ryan was unmoved by the outcry.

> People said, 'Who am I to dare say this?' But, remember, I was the person who edited the British police service response to the Royal Commission Inquiry into the Criminal Justice System for the whole of the UK. That's who I am. The attacks weren't on what I said, they were on my right to say such things. They were

saying, 'Keep your nose out of our legal business' as if I wasn't entitled to have an opinion!

Mostly, I got verbal support from the Government, but of course there was a great deal of uncertainty there generally. You can understand it: I was a foreigner, I was brought in, some people might have said I was a rash experiment, a gamble. The minister was supportive as best he could be, and when I laid out my plans for the future, I got verbal support. It all sounded good because it had all the right things in there: more police on the streets; better crime detection; investigation; better management systems; and more efficient processes. All those things, but of course I wasn't given an extra penny in the budget to deliver the changes; there was nothing. Almost every organisation which is going through a massive restructuring would have set aside an amount of money to do it, because you have to hire people to help, you have to get consultants in, and there are generally costs involved when you change a process or alter a system to do something else. The idea being, further down the track, a year later or less, that the initial investment would be repaid in greater efficiencies and effective savings. Not with the police. I had just to manage with the budget I had, to do all the things I was expected to do. There was no additional money at all other than for salaries for officers when they were given a pay rise. But of course the politicians were still hedging their bets each way, giving me support, but at the same time, positioning themselves and wording that support in a way that gave them a back door should things go wrong.

If keeping on the right side of the Labor Government was hard enough, that was still nothing compared to Ryan's problematic relationship with the Liberal Opposition. For someone touted at the beginning as such a Labor prize, it was ironic that, in truth, his personal political beliefs were generally much closer to Liberal philosophies. Indeed, even as he was being constantly attacked by the New South Wales Opposition, and critics like Gary Sturgess, the one-time advisor to former Liberal Premier Nick Greiner who employed him for ten years, he was being approached by the Federal

Liberal Party to mull over an offer to serve as one of their candidates after he'd left the police.

Yet in the meantime, the State Party seemed as anxious as possible to undermine him at every turn. After all, if Labor proved successful in restoring the public faith in law and order, a central plank, and perceived strength, of their own election platform would be gone forever.

The Opposition were never on my side from the word Go. They regarded me as a Labor appointee, rather than someone who could try and steer a middle ground in politics and deliver the goods. So I really didn't have too much faith in them giving me support. In fact, I'm hard-pressed to think of any statements made at any time by them that were supportive. They were constantly critical, which is the way of politics, and when you would meet them, people like [Opposition police spokesman] Andrew Tink and [Opposition Leader] Peter Collins, they would always say, 'It's not personal you know, Peter, it's not you we're attacking, it's the Government.' And I used to say, 'Well, why use me? Why not make generic statements about the police service, rather than about Commissioner Ryan?' But it didn't make any difference.

Meanwhile, the Special Branch files scandal had developed into a full-blown farce. Hundreds of people were suddenly clamouring for the chance to look at the dossiers amidst claims that they contained information far too sensitive for Ryan to be the lone gatekeeper. Ryan was bemused. The files were, in fact, a complete joke, he says, with many comprising little more than scraps of paper with five names jotted down. There had obviously never been any rigorous attempt to keep them up to date or put them into any order. 'We were inundated with requests from people, some famous and some infamous, to demand they have a look at their file,' says Ryan. 'It was almost a badge of honour to be able to say that Special Branch had a file on me. Of course, 99.9 per cent of them had never rated a mention; they were so insignificant, despite thinking themselves so important. Those that were mentioned, the information on them was stupid and pathetic.'

Inside the rest of the service, police officers, angry that so many had failed assessment tests to select eighty new patrol commanders, were considering industrial action. They were furious that the tests didn't take into account local knowledge and experience, and further enraged that Ryan had advertised in the UK for more officers to fill New South Wales jobs. He said he was looking overseas for the kind of expertise that wasn't available at home; they said not enough was being done to give them that expertise.

Ryan's personal style was, to be fair, making him something of a sitting duck too. Just as he'd done in Britain, he liked to court the top end of town, and have regular information-sharing meetings with the State's leading businesspeople. As the head of a huge organisation, he felt it was important to be in touch with other industry leaders. But New South Wales had become used to having its police service run by humble beat cops who'd risen up through the ranks, had little interest beyond their own organisation and knew (and accepted without question) their blue-collar place in the scheme of things. So Ryan became an object of much bemused curiosity. Some regarded him, as he saw himself, as a thrusting corporate professional, eager to learn from the experience of chief executives of similarly large organisations. Others saw it as pure pretension, an assessment exacerbated, at times, by their own prejudices about the arrogant English, his occasionally offhand manner, and his inclination towards self-importance. Frequently, Ryan was characterised as a snobby Englishman, totally enamoured with an elevated notion of his own worth, who became a whingeing Pom when things got tough. He saw that as unbridled prejudice. That was certainly an element, but one of his closest friends, businessman Colin Henson, says, 'I think it was less about being anti-Pom than about parochialism at the end of the day. It was about people wanting someone home-grown from New South Wales for that top job, rather than importing someone from elsewhere.'

Yet Ryan did little to enhance any notion that he was a humble copper at heart. Still passionate about clothes and the importance of always being well turned out, he was amused at having made it on to *Mode* magazine's annual best-dressed list. Jo Hampson saw the danger. 'I tried to explain to him he didn't *need* to be the best-dressed man in Australia,' she says, 'things like that didn't do his professional standing much good at all.' In his time off, he liked to socialise with the celebrity set, and enjoyed – although these days he paid for his own tickets – first nights and openings to such an extent that one columnist even dubbed him the 'Kate Fischer' of the New South Wales police service. Ryan's attitude to that kind of criticism was simple: he worked extremely hard in his job and what business was it of anyone's what he did in his spare time? He saw himself on a certain rung in society – had he stayed in Britain he'd have been looking at a knighthood – with enormous responsibilities and a handsome salary, and was entertaining himself in the same way anyone in a similar position might do. But that wasn't the way public servants in the past had behaved, and he eventually paid dearly for it.

He didn't necessarily want to be out so much in the evenings, but it was often his strong sense of duty that drove him on, says Loretta Henson, wife of his best friend Colin. 'At first, Peter went to a function every night,' she says. 'He did everything he was asked to do, always supporting causes or speaking at functions. He felt under an obligation to do these things, to fulfil people's expectations. It was almost an overdeveloped sense of duty.' But at this stage, the people of New South Wales loved their dashing, debonair police chief. Women, too, would frequently throw themselves at him. Colin Henson once had to rescue him from one trying to follow him into a toilet.

Hampson watched from the sidelines and saw how popular he was becoming, amazed to see a side of him she'd never imagined existed. Back in England, she'd been nervous about accepting the job, thinking of him as distant and remote, someone she found difficult to warm to – particularly as, easily bored and often unaware he was showing it, he spent the whole time during her interview gazing out of the window. In Sydney, however, he seemed to become a different person.

He told me he felt the need to be different there, to be open and flamboyant, and charismatic. I remember being absolutely astounded at the change in him. He was charming and humorous. You could have a good laugh with him. He loves the fame, though, they both do, but there's nothing wrong with that. I remember one day, later on, Adrienne said to me that she really liked being the Commissioner's wife. I told her not to feel guilty about that, she should just accept it.

In any case, if Ryan hadn't had an ego, he would never have got as far as he had. Ryan's high profile was compounded by the way he invariably cut a dashing figure. Next to the portly Whelan (nick-named 'Benny' for his startling resemblance to the late British comedian Benny Hill) Ryan in his uniform, with his buttons gleam-ing, a brilliant white shirt and his trousers always pressed to a knife-edge, was naturally the one who was going to attract the most attention. Besides, he was articulate in a way no Commissioner had been before him, he was witty, he could explain complex ideas in an easily digestible form, and he had a marvellously colourful turn of phrase. Few journalists could resist the kind of copy he made, with his metaphors about being a lone cowboy trying to steer a runaway stagecoach, the single pilot of a huge plane in danger of lumbering out of control or comparing his task with that of Hollywood screen idol Gregory Peck in the classic World War II movie *Twelve O'Clock High* about a US Air Force Marshal trying to boost the morale of a bomber squadron that's suffered huge losses.

There was always one major flaw in such parallels, however. The cowboy, the pilot and the Air Force Marshal never had to seek per-mission for their major decisions before they took them. And they didn't afterwards have to justify them to quite so many masters. For Ryan not only had Whelan, Carr, the assorted media, the public, and his own officers watching him closely, he also had the Royal Com-mission and then, once the old Police Board had vanished, the Police Integrity Commission (PIC) that took its place.

The Royal Commission, to that point, had been a major support. Justice Wood was a strong and influential ally, and Ryan visited the Commission regularly for information, advice and guidance. As the Commission wound down, handing over its final 900-page report to Carr on 15 May 1997 after 453 days of hearings, 640 witnesses and 37 000 pages of evidence, Justice Wood indeed warned of the dangers of the level of political control being exerted over Ryan. Right at the top of his list of recommendations was a concern that the Police Commissioner's responsibility for the management and control of the service was always subject to the direction of the Minister. There was always the risk, said the report, that decisions might then be made for political or electoral gain, or spontaneously in situations where the Minister or his staff did not have access to all the relevant information. Instead, the Police Commissioner's operational functions and the Minister's policy responsibilities should be clearly laid out. This issue would later take centre stage in the debate over policing in general and Peter Ryan in particular.

In addition, said Justice Wood, political parties should stop promising the public extra police to cut crime. The numbers and deployment of police should be the domain of the police alone, with a recognition that increases in crime usually have far more to do with economic and social conditions than the pure size of the police service. Other recommendations contained in the report included lifting the minimum age of recruits from 18 to 21, recruiting better-educated officers, improving the training offered by the Goulburn Police Academy and, in a clause bringing a smile to Ryan's face, establishing a replacement for the disbanded Special Branch.

In handing over the final report, Justice Wood delivered a stern warning that times ahead would be even tougher for any corrupt police remaining, and Carr praised him for making sure 'the people of New South Wales are getting the clean Police Service they've always wanted'. While Ryan joined in the tide of self-congratulation, pledging to work to implement the Commission's recommendations, and ensuring that corruption did not creep back into the service, he did not feel the confidence he displayed. For despite all the good intentions of the Royal Commission, its weaknesses all too quickly became apparent.

There was this huge sense of anticipation about the final report, but also a feeling of disappointment that the Royal Commission had been diverted from its principal purpose of seeking out police corruption into investigating pedophilia. That meant it completely took its eye off the ball for police reform, and some of the good things they could have done to help me chase down bad or corrupt persons or systems, just didn't happen. Their decision to look into the case of Justice Yeldham effectively stopped any further investigations. There should have been a separate investigation under another form of commission, to look into pedophilia.

But I'd arrived in the middle of the Royal Commission, and watched it unfold. They'd had a big revelation, but I'm waiting for names of people whom I can then arrest. Remember, I'm on my own, and I'm in this nest of what felt like vipers, almost, in the police service. I didn't know who was corrupt and who wasn't. Anyway, at the end of the Royal Commission, when it all wound up, there were about 250 people who had been named by the Royal Commission, which meant there was a huge stain on their careers, but often being named meant, 'Did you two people work in the squad together?' 'Yes, we did.' 'Well, who else was in there?' 'Ah, well, there was Jimmy Bloggs, Fred Smith . . .' and you were named. By implication, therefore, you were corrupt.

I then had the Ombudsman and others saying to me, 'Why haven't you locked these people up?' And I'd have to say, 'What for?' Because they usually weren't revealing corruption that happened yesterday or last week; most of it was ten years old, and it was simply illustrating that there was endemic corruption in the organisation. But each case had to be researched and investigated, and who was going to do that, and where was I going to find the people with the skills to do so, people I could have confidence in? I couldn't do it. I was dealing with the here and now, not something ten years ago. These Commissions are very expensive multimillion-dollar organisations; they have police officers attached to them from interstate so they are not New South Wales people, they're stuffed wall-to-wall with lawyers and clerks, and they should be running these sorts of inquiries. But if they've come up with nothing, how am I supposed to?

And did that Commission really stamp out the corruption it had set out to? Ryan soon discovered the shocking answer.

CHAPTER 16

What good was the Royal Commission?

Over the next few weeks, Peter Ryan pored over the 174 recommendations of the Royal Commission, trying to work out how they could be implemented. There was little doubt they were drawn up for all the right reasons, but the more he examined them, the more they appeared to be too vague to offer firm direction, often were completely at odds with the current legislative and union framework and, sometimes, were simply unworkable.

One of the biggest stumbling blocks was known as 'Appendix 31'. This was the set of recommendations prescribing the future management of the police service and the way in which cultural change within the organisation would be monitored. For a start, Ryan wasn't even comfortable with the way the proposal was couched.

The recommendations in relations to management culture, transformational change, and so on, were liberally sprinkled with management jargon and they reflected thinking in the late 1980s and early 1990s. Terms like 'transformational leadership', 'organisational change', and 're-engineering' were thrown about with gay abandon as if everyone would understand, by osmosis, exactly what was meant. In addition, it presupposed that things would remain static from the date the Royal Commission started, and failed to take into account, in my view, how organisations actually work in real life. You can't just change, amend or adapt one part of an organisation without it having a domino effect on other parts of the organisation, rather like when you hit one ball in a snooker game, and everything changes.

That wasn't the intention but that happens, and even skilled professionals make that mistake. It seemed to me there was no allowance built into the recommendation for the consequences of taking a particular course of action. It was generally too vague.

In stating the need for an independent audit, it didn't even give any clues as to who should undertake this, how, where and when it should start. Besides, Ryan had already embarked on his own path of reform.

I couldn't hang around and wait – people were already demanding significant changes. They thought I'd already got rid of the corrupt police, that I was arresting and charging those mentioned in the Royal Commission, that the organisation and structure would be different, and that suddenly the culture would miraculously change overnight. All of that was sheer bloody nonsense.

To confound the whole thing, I was under pressure from the Ombudsman writing me letters saying, 'What are you doing about these 200 people who have been named in the Royal Commission?' But the evidence there wasn't strong enough to support disciplinary charges against some of them. It meant I would have had to investigate all those 200 people all over again. Many of those named were either in the police station on the day something occurred or happened to be a friend of someone who had been otherwise adversely mentioned. I couldn't possibly spare the resources to go back, sometimes fifteen years, into history to reinvestigate these complaints. That I was expected to do something about this showed enormous naivety amongst the staff of the Ombudsman's office.

Even trying to get rid of the people who weren't capable of taking the police service forward was proving problematic, due to both legal hurdles and union agreements that were also obstructing new recruitment. One of the main concerns of the Royal Commission had been that corruption occurred where there was too little supervision, since that's when things tended to go wrong. Ryan's plan for his new, streamlined service involved having inspectors on duty twenty-four hours a day, to make sure there was constant supervision of teams of constables and sergeants, all day, every day of the week. He soon discovered, however, that it wasn't possible to have a selection process for inspectors only. And there was an extraordinarily complex industrial procedure that enabled failed applicants to appeal, which then took forever. More than four years after Ryan launched his project of twenty-four-hour supervision, some of his chosen people were still not in position.

After close study of the 174 Royal Commission recommendations, Ryan came to the conclusion that he could work on 160, but the remainder required legislative change to allow them to be put into practice. 'Making some things happen meant taking on the unions head-on and, for a Labor Government which has historically (as have Liberal governments) been stood over by the police unions in a few marginal seats, saying, "You do this or else [These were the sort of people I had inherited!] we will make sure you are not elected!" was a great concern to the Government and to me. However, I set out to put a group together to address these recommendations and to break them down into manageable chunks.'

The Reform Coordination Unit, made up of Ryan, Jarratt, Lawson and Nixon, with a staff of ten to twelve officers under Nixon's Human Resources division, divided the recommendations into areas of operational reform, cultural reform, Human Resources work, administration and so on. Working with them as an advisor was Dr Peter Crawford, head of the New South Wales Healthy Rivers Commission and a Professional Fellow at the Macquarie Graduate School of Management, who was already deeply involved in the police service in the Executive Development Program, and had advised the Royal Commission on management structures. Ryan gave him a clear brief to run the Unit, tell everyone what to do and how to do it, promising he'd make sure everyone cooperated. In the end, the results just didn't fit with Ryan's vision.

Peter Crawford was a nice enough bloke, but his advice really wasn't useful to me. He told us what we already knew, but was unable to tell us how we should go about implementing reform, and he complained to me after every meeting, saying it was all very difficult and we were not doing it properly. I kept saying, 'What I need from you, you are the expert, you wrote this thing, give us the blueprint that we can follow and I will ensure that we follow it.' But, quite frankly, some of his ideas were straight out of a textbook; they had no real basis in practical application for an organisation the size and complexity of the police. In truth, there is no such a thing as a blueprint that you can slavishly follow to deliver reform of the magnitude we were attempting. You had to think about an action very carefully first, then do it, see if it worked, then implement it elsewhere to see what impact it would have on all the other things that surrounded it. An organisation like the police service had to be progressively reformed in this way.

But Peter [Crawford] kept saying that no one was listening to him, there was too much opposition, and no one would do as he said. I got tired of this. I had enormous pressures on me. I was trying to put together Crime Agencies, rebuild the service into the new command areas and get those bedded in. In addition to that, I was dealing with all the other areas of the Royal Commission recommendations and trying to follow my original blueprint for reform. I wanted him to get on with it. But weeks went by and he eventually came to me and told me, 'I'm sorry, I can't do this. It is all too hard.' I said, 'I know it's hard, but I thought you would be able to help.' He said, 'No, there is too much opposition.' So I eventually said, 'Thank you and goodbye.' And he left.

Ryan then took over the reform agenda himself, but quickly realised it was a full-time job; it would be impossible for him to add to his existing workload. Happily, Nixon and her Human Resources team offered instead to shoulder the burden, arguing that since change always had implications for the work force, they were the right department to take it on. It wasn't long before Ryan started having doubts, however, that they were operating as effectively as they claimed. He'd been receiving a number of complaints for months about the department. Slowly, Ryan began to grow suspicious. Every time he asked for something to be done, it either never happened, or it occurred so slowly it was almost imperceptible. One of the major hurdles seemed to be the disjointed approach of the various units, but there also seemed to be enormous opposition from people fairly junior in the organisation who would be given instructions about performing a task, but would choose not to do so, because they didn't see it as important in their scheme of things.

> So I lost something like nine months of positive change oppor-
> tunity, because of these people deliberately obstructing what I
> was trying to do, and through the inability of Human Resources
> to get their act together and make things work. There was a lot
> of discussion, and a number of well-written papers, but no
> action at the end of it all. One day, Christine Nixon gave me a
> sheet of all the reform projects they were running, and there
> were hundreds – but not many of them had anything to do with
> *my* reform, they all had to do with *their* vision. It was all soft-
> centred stuff, human resource idealism, too futuristic for an
> organisation like the police. It just wasn't practical and certainly
> not for a time when we needed strong, effective leadership.
> More and more too, I felt I was being taken out of the loop.
> I was told Human Resources would sign the certificates of offi-
> cers who were leaving the service after thirty years in the job.
> They would sign the promotion certificates. They would sign
> the new recruits' certificates. So I began to feel, rightly or
> wrongly, that I was being marginalised. They didn't want my
> name on anything. And they also wanted to be totally respon-
> sible for reform.

At the same time, there were a number of leaks to the media of documents that had a very, very limited circulation. Ryan began to suspect they were coming from Human Resources, and were an attempt to slow down, subvert or divert the effort for police reform into an area officers there found more interesting. It was a handful of these people who were later to cause Ryan some of the greatest troubles of his time in office. He, however, made the fatal mistake of leaving them alone to get on with it.

At the time, when it seemed that the police service would benefit hugely from the Commission's inquiry, Ryan was happy to give it as much time as it demanded. But then, following New South Wales Upper House Labor backbencher Franca Arena's questions in State Parliament about Justice Yeldham, it went off at a tangent into pedophilia hearings. Ryan began seriously to doubt whether it hadn't been derailed. He felt it should devote itself to its core business: that of investigating police corruption. In the atmosphere of suspicion and paranoia that reigned after Justice Yeldham's suicide, however – when it was revealed that the judge had been shielded by the disgraced Special Branch – it was understandable that allegations of pedophile networks extending to the very top of the State's power structure began to capture the public imagination. Ryan was soon drawn into the melee when Arena sent statutory declarations to the police to support her claims and the Commission moved to begin investigating her allegations.

It was, says Ryan, a major mistake. It effectively cut off the Commission's inquiries into the police too early. While it was an important issue, pedophilia should have been dealt with by a separate inquiry. The result, Ryan believes, was months of wasted time.

Franca Arena claimed, as she still does, that pedophilia was flourishing in high places, protected by political and legal cover-ups. When Ryan was handed the evidence, at the Premier's personal instruction, in October 1997, he was stunned, but not for the obvious reasons.

A lot of what she said was based on fact, but the frightening thing was some of her informants, it seemed, had read a Dennis Wheatley novel or watched a Hamer horror film, and then regurgitated it in their statements and drawings. There were sketches of famous people dressed in Ku Klux Klan outfits and wizards slashing to pieces a child lying on a table. There were Satanic torture and ritual murders and people bathing in blood with severed limbs floating around. It was just all too bizarre to be true. If those dozens and dozens of people from the statements had honestly been killed, we'd have had a bloody massacre on our hands.

Some of the documents Arena had presented needed further examination, he concluded, but would need a great deal of work to find corroborative evidence. One of the major difficulties was tracing her sources of information. Even where police did manage to find the informants, many led such disrupted lifestyles, as heavy drug-users or rent boys (under-age male prostitutes), it was impossible to tell whether they might be telling the truth. Inquiries were made even harder by the intense level of media interest. Occasionally, officers would turn up to question a suspect only to have a posse of cameras waiting as they'd been tipped off. Then, police were accused of parading that person before the media – and prejudicing the case. In Ryan's subsequent report, he upheld the findings of retired judge John Nader's commission of inquiry, who'd found Arena had no evidence when she accused the Premier Bob Carr and other senior figures of conspiring to protect child abusers.

'I think Arena was a genuinely concerned person, but she found herself being used by those feeding her the information,' says Ryan. 'It was unfortunate she went to the lengths she did with the information. It would have been better if she'd come straight to the police, rather than grandstanding in Parliament. But these cases had to be investigated and laid to rest. It would otherwise just keep coming back to haunt those accused, and the police. Unfortunately, even in the stronger cases, there simply wasn't the information available to pursue prosecutions.' Privately, he felt that the Arena affair had taken up a great deal of his own limited time that could have been much better spent elsewhere, and, moreover, had totally derailed the Royal Commission.

'The Royal Commission ran for years, cost tens of millions and, in the end, sent only a handful of people to jail,' he says. 'Apart from Chook Fowler, the highest-profile person to be sent down was a crook who eventually we sent to jail for contempt, for swearing at a judge. It was a great pity the Royal Commission was so sidetracked in its last few months.'

And, of course, the demands of the Commission meant he took his eye off some of the basics, like fighting crime. For that, he would pay dearly.

CHAPTER 17

Fighting crime

All colour drained from Peter Ryan's face. His heart seemed to miss a beat. It was a question that had come completely from left field. The serial rapist marauding through the western suburbs: did he have any comment to make to the press?

Ryan had been presiding over the ceremonial opening of a police station in Marrickville. He'd tried to decline the invitation, but was curtly told it was an absolute necessity to support new stations in the community. It was invariably a task he loathed, however, primarily due to the bizarre degree of pomp and circumstance that accompanied such occasions, and what he felt was the terrible waste of resources they involved. Marrickville was no exception. When he arrived, he rubbed his eyes in horror. Lined up in front of the station were twelve highway patrol cars and normal-response cars, with two mounted police officers, an awning with chairs inside and a dais cluttered with microphones. As he stepped out of his car, the police band struck up a tune, officers scurried to line up as a guard of honour, and Paul Whelan, the local mayor and various assorted community leaders walked up.

All through the speeches, the singing and the Thai dancing, Ryan could barely contain his impatience, sickened by the use of so many police officers who could, to his mind, be so much better employed elsewhere. When they finally began their tour of the new station, his temper didn't improve on seeing the walls plastered with photos of wanted suspects, perfectly placed for the newspaper photographers. Immediately he barked out an order to take them down before the media saw them, and continued, smiling through gritted teeth, on his way. Halfway through, however, his press officer had approached him with the bewildering request for a comment on the serial rapist. He knew nothing, absolutely nothing, about it.

Every day he received half-hour briefings about serious incidents across the State, but there had never been any mention of a serial rapist anywhere. 'Surely, if we've got a serial rapist out there, I should know about this?' he snapped back to his press officer. Then Whelan's press secretary raced up to Ryan to ask for a comment on the same man. 'I don't know anything about it,' he replied, 'but I'm going to bloody well find out.'

He was infuriated. 'Here I was, with a serial rapist running around who we've obviously done nothing about, and I'm at a carnival with dozens of police, opening a bloody police station instead of policing the community. Their priorities were all wrong. They loved that sort of thing, all this pageantry and fuss, loved it with a passion, with everyone getting very upset if I said I didn't want to make a speech. But I never wanted to do that stuff. I wanted to police. That's what I was there for. Not that kind of nonsense.'

Ryan raced back to his office and started piecing together the evidence. What he discovered horrified him. As the rapes had been spread geographically among various different patrols, no one had thought to put all the reports together and take an overview. Each patrol had instead kept strictly to their own small patch, never apparently considering widening their individual investigations. As soon as he realised this, he called for all the information, and ordered a special task force into the rapes be set up that very afternoon.

That naturally didn't satisfy Whelan. His response, says Ryan, was to declare: 'Heads will roll!' It left Ryan seething as he struggled to find out where things had gone so wrong. It also meant his officers all ducked for cover to save their own heads, rather than willingly cooperating and coming forward with information. And it didn't help that the press had figured out there was a serial rapist at work before even his own officers. Ryan had no choice but to drop his own inquiries and concentrate instead on his new task force, instructing them to profile the offender, work out how he behaved and thought, and where he might have come from.

With a map of Sydney stuck to a wall, Ryan placed a coloured pin at the site of every rape or sexual assault. And even though there were only two or three in each police station's immediate area, as a couple of dozen pins went into the map, a clear pattern emerged. 'There,' Ryan said as he jabbed his finger into the centre of the circle of pins. 'The rapist lives or works within 500 metres of that point there.'

Eventually, a 29-year-old man was charged in March 1997, and finally pleaded guilty in court in February 1999 to raping women who lived alone after he had followed them home. Ryan's task force had profiled the rapist, identified a suspect and arrested him as he trailed a woman from the railway station near where he worked – just a couple of streets from where Ryan had pointed on the map weeks before. Verbal and forensic evidence from the victims proved they'd got the right man.

The whole fiasco did, however, serve to focus Ryan's attention back on the basics of crime detection and on realising just how poor, generally, were his detectives' basic investigative and analytical skills, and how mediocre was the collection of data and intelligence in New South Wales. It proved yet another watershed in the way he ran the service. 'It was a real wake-up call,' he says. 'It was then that I determined to completely restructure all crime investigation, in a manner that was in keeping with my professional standards, no matter how much opposition I was going to get,' he says. 'Besides, I was already getting it anyway, with people going on about "Who is this Pommie to tell us how to investigate crime, when we've already caught lots of bad people?" And they did catch some. But, of course, they didn't do it as professionally as I was used to.'

Ryan ordered that a new head of Crime Intelligence be appointed and set out new procedures to be followed. The emphasis fell on collecting intelligence to solve and anticipate crime rather than merely reacting to it. In the UK, he'd started a crime faculty that was proving extremely effective in identifying and linking series of offences, in training detectives how to follow through such investigations, and in compiling databases for use in the future. Ryan resolved to introduce a similar program in New South Wales, and realised he'd need some experienced detectives from Britain to come over to help him.

With the recognition that the standard of detective work was often so inadequate, he then ordered a complete review of all outstanding murder cases from the previous twenty years, and put a team of people together to start that work. It was a smart move. Over the next year, that team managed to solve eight of those cases, merely by revisiting the evidence, analysing the data and following up lines of inquiry. Even today, however, Ryan worries that there may be cases slipping through the net because they may not be being investigated properly, and alarm bells sound for him every time anyone claims evidence to support charges has been lost. The fear is not only of basic professional incompetence, but that some officers may be deliberately suppressing information to protect themselves or friends who've long since left the service.

After all the attention on police corruption and the Royal Commission, crime-fighting had come thudding back onto the agenda. In May 1997, the reverberations began to be felt everywhere. The New South Wales Bureau of Crime Statistics and Research released new data showing sharp increases in rape, assault, robbery and fraud figures during 1996, after five years of relative stability. Each category had risen by between 21 per cent and 28 per cent. Ryan was shocked, but stayed calm. He felt sure the statistics were up partly because people had been heartened by the purge on corrupt cops and were more willing to report crime. But he also suspected that police had been so distracted by the Royal Commission, often being taken off shift to answer questions, file extra paperwork and have their jobs changed, that they'd actually, as he admitted publicly, 'taken their eye off the ball a little bit'. Carr, determined to yield nothing on his electoral platform of law and order, publicly disagreed. He said the high levels of crime were a result of 'self-indulgent junkies' and high unemployment.

Ryan, however, sensing that many of his officers were becoming jaded with the emphasis on reform, and tired by the massive structural changes he was imposing on the organisation, decided the time was right to refocus the service back onto crime. Resistance to reform was beginning to grow, so he resolved to put the emphasis once again on basic policing. He believed passionately that people needed targets to aim at, clear and unambiguous statements of intent to follow, and solid, basic values with which to identify. The core business of police, after all, was always to combat crime. Now if that could be coupled tightly to the concept of reform, that might provide the momentum for change itself. 'So I gave them the target of crime reduction, crime-fighting and public safety, something that police officers understood, and often the reason why they joined the service in the first place,' he says. The reasons for the rise in crime they would be tackling were clear in his mind.

First, there was probably an under-reporting of crime during the Royal Commission period, because people had little, or no, faith in the police. They thought if they did report crime, the police wouldn't do anything about it, so why bother? Secondly, in the days prior to the Royal Commission, the police probably didn't report crime that was reported to them, just to keep the crime figures down. Then, during the Royal Commission, they were so intent on dealing with its revelations and personal survival, they literally took their eye off the ball and coasted along.

But from 1 July 1997 with the introduction of the new local area commands and the emphasis on ethical cost-effective crime reduction as the watchword of the process, crime was properly recorded for the first time in a number of years. That's because people were fearful of *not* recording it and they had no benchmarks because their areas were different in shape and size to the previous patrols, so people actually began recording crime honestly and properly. As a result, reported crime began to rise very rapidly indeed.

Knowing that the rise in crime figures would trigger outrage in the media and Opposition politicians, Ryan gave his troops a simple target of a reduction in crime below 1996 figures, principally in five categories: assault, housebreaking, car theft, robbery and theft. These were the crimes that affected the vast majority of people in New South Wales, and which inspired the most fear in the community. At the same time, he fought back vigorously against those, behind the scenes, who started suggesting he embrace New York's zero-tolerance policies.

I did not support zero tolerance, as it meant police had to suddenly tackle even minor things like jay-walking, spitting in the street, swearing, and noisy behaviour, the kind of behaviour that police generally would either turn a blind eye to, or just have a quiet word with someone about. In the New York model, the police took action, gave tickets, arrested, charged, and removed nuisance off the streets.

But my belief was that there was a backlash already setting in in New York. The community were frightened of the police, who became the occupying army. It meant that everything that everyone did could be subject to police intervention or sanction, so whilst everyone was happy that the streets were relatively free of drug-pushers or robbers, they found themselves suddenly subject to police control, intervention, rudeness and arrogance. There was also a general intolerance by the police themselves towards anyone who broke the law, and this created even greater criticism that the police service was out of control.

Instead, to try and lift the visibility of police on the streets, more than 110 plain-clothes officers were ordered back into uniform. UK-style community-based safety councils, in place of the old Neighbourhood Watch programs, were announced to help police combat crime, in line with Ryan's conviction that the community also has a role to play in helping get rid of some of the root causes of crime, as well as the opportunities for crime. Limited drug and alcohol testing was introduced for officers. The original regional crime squads that had been found to be the nest of so much corruption were disbanded, and the new Crime Agencies centralised structure was put in place, with Assistant Commissioner Clive Small at the helm. Staffed by a central pool of 600 detectives to investigate major crime throughout the State, they were divided into four specialist units: for licensing, commercial crime, homicide and serial violent crime, and child protection. Another squad, the Drugs and Organised Crime Strike Force, would be assigned to specific tasks in that area. As these units started to hire staff they had many applications from members of the old crime squads. Ironically, a lot of them were found not to have the skills required.

Meanwhile, in the operational area, things were being gradually sorted out, with the new structure of local area commands and patrols, although there were difficulties finding enough good sergeants and inspectors to take the positions.

Even so, when Ryan went back to the UK on holiday in June 1997, he felt relaxed and confident that everything was going well. While away, he was going to attend Adrienne's graduation – she'd just received an honours degree in her course – and start interviewing candidates to fill in some gaps in the new police structure. A few days after he'd left, however, two young constables shot dead a man armed with a knife on Bondi Beach.

The killing of French photographer Roni Levi, and the months of investigations that followed, divided both the police service and the public. Ryan was called at 3 a.m. London time, and he asked immediately for a full briefing. He declined to comment on the case publicly, however, despite pressure from colleagues to immediately leap to the defence of his officers. He'd learnt that lesson from commenting on the case of murdered Lithgow teenager Alison Lewis in March that year. Then, he'd said he was 'convinced' police had done everything possible to respond to reports from a taxi driver that her two friends were being attacked. A report by the New South Wales Ombudsman found, however, that police took more than seventy minutes to respond, and Alison's body was found in a sandpit close to the scene. Ryan later publicly apologised to her family. This time, he was determined to wait until the outcome of a full investigation. 'The initial information provided from the scene is not always accurate or correct,' he says. 'People can slip into a cover-up either intentionally or in a state of denial and it's disastrous for the Commissioner of Police to make a statement, which he believes in good faith to be a true explanation of the circumstances, for it later to be found to be incorrect. It looks then like that person is complicit in the circumstances.' It was a good call. In late 1999, one of the officers involved in the Levi shooting, Senior Constable Anthony Dilorenzo was sacked from the force for failing to adequately explain why he kept company with drug dealers. His colleague, Constable Rodney Podesta, served four months of periodic detention on a cocaine charge.

Ryan was shocked, however, by his first experience of a police shooting, and couldn't help recalling his own experiences as a police officer, being attacked by people with a knife, a sharpened screwdriver, an axe, a bottle and a shotgun when he, as a British officer, was unarmed.

> I'd had to rely on unarmed combat skills to defend myself rather than go for a pistol. So this was something of a culture shock. Obviously, I wasn't too happy about the circumstances, and unconvinced that they'd shot as a last resort, either. I became concerned that perhaps there really should have been better means of dealing with this situation, rather than shooting someone, and then claiming that the officers were fearful for their own lives on account of a knife. But you have to wait for all the circumstances to be revealed before you can make any comment.

Finally, four years later, in the face of powerful opposition from the Police Association, he managed to introduce random drug testing in the service. The issues came back into stark relief in September, however, when another knife-wielding man – this time a 50-year-old from Kingswood – was shot in the stomach by an officer after refusing to put down his weapon. Ryan spoke out in favour of arming officers with capsicum sprays and, this time, to his satisfaction, it was quickly rushed in. Much more complex was the case of police officer Said Morgan, who had used the computer at work to track down a man who'd been charged with sexually assaulting two young relatives of Morgan's, aged 6 and 11 – and then driven to his house and shot him six times with his service revolver. In August 1997, a jury acquitted Morgan of murder, and he immediately declared he wanted to rejoin the police service. Ryan was appalled. 'I was determined that under no circumstances would he be able to come back in,' he says. 'Despite him trying for probably the next nine months or so, I refused to accept him back into the service. The community debate was so intense, I was determined to preserve the integrity of the police service by denying him entry.'

Another lengthy battle was fought over the attempts of another would-be police officer to rejoin the service. Ex-stripper and self-confessed former prostitute Kim Hollingsworth was dismissed from the Police Academy, eight weeks into her training, after blowing the whistle on corrupt officers involved in the sex industry. The police service said she was sacked because she had not revealed her past on her application form, a past that included performing at police functions, but the Industrial Relations Commission ruled that she was dismissed unfairly. Commissioner Peter Connor said it showed a case of double standards in that other officers with dubious records had been allowed to stay. And, after all, neither prostitution nor exotic dancing was illegal in New South Wales.

For Ryan, a man with an extremely strong, old-fashioned and, at times, quite inflexible, sense of morality, it was a terrible dilemma. Hollingsworth's supporters pointed out how she'd obviously helped the Royal Commission ferret out corrupt officers, and that the emphasis should be on male officers serving with her to behave properly rather than saying they'd find it too tough.

Ryan, on the other hand, was outraged by the very suggestion she be allowed back, and immediately appealed. 'How could I, as a reforming Police Commissioner trying to build a corruption-resistant and ethical police service, welcome into its ranks a self-confessed prostitute and stripper?' he says. 'I wasn't prepared to do so.'

Naturally, the media loved the stoush. With her lurid past and her pet rat perched on her shoulder, Hollingsworth always made good copy. She refused to wear a regulation-issue leather police jacket because of her concern for animal rights, and demanded vegan meals in the police canteen, so the contrast between her and the upright Ryan was too delightful to resist. In one interview, Hollingsworth gleefully outlined her ambition to serve under Ryan. A British newspaper even ran photos of the two side by side on its front page, with the headline: 'The Commissioner and the Call Girl.' 'I thought this was absolutely disgraceful,' says an affronted Ryan who, to this day, has never met her. 'I had to tell people to read the article properly to understand the story.' Eventually, Ryan claimed a victory, of sorts. Hollingsworth won the right finally to stay at the Academy, but dropped out of the course.

It was about the same time, however, that Ryan started to make far more influential foes. He was made aware of a little-known authority given to a New South Wales Commissioner of Police under Section 81 of the *Casino Control Act* to ban 'undesirable' people – anyone suspected of obtaining money through criminal activities – from entering and gambling at Sydney's Star City Casino. New South Wales was the only State to have this provision, and it had never been exercised before. But with allegations of loan-sharking, money-laundering and other criminal activities associated with the casino, Ryan started coming under increasing pressure to exercise this authority. Eventually, he signed orders banning forty so-called 'high rollers' from the multimillion-dollar Las Vegas-style gambling palace.

But he was uneasy about using this draconian power. For a start, those people could simply go off to play at another State's casino, which meant they still might be engaging in underhand activities, but that their cash was being lost from a New South Wales enterprise. The State itself therefore, as a result of doing the right thing, ends up suffering lost tax revenues. Convicted heroin-dealer Duong Van la, for instance, gambled $94 million in six months before he was banned. The fear was also that the casino might try to save money by cutting back on security – which, in turn, encourages crime. Indeed, figures released in 2000 revealed that the Casino Surveillance Division cut its staff from sixty-seven to twenty-nine over 1998 and 1999.

> Unless *all* casinos in every State ban people, it seems to me to be a frivolous exercise. They could still be committing crimes here, but simply spending their money elsewhere. So while it might feel good that we're banning them, while everyone else welcomes them and indeed sends them private jets to ferry them to alternatives, it's a strange way of feeling self-righteous. And the biggest problem for me is that if we have suspicions about them obtaining their money from criminal activities, principally drug dealing, why aren't we arresting them? If the power I exercise is challengeable in court, then don't I need proof? Furthermore, having banned them under those provisions, were we not giving them a clear indication that we were on to their activities – and might, or might not, eventually arrest them for it?

Even more worryingly, Ryan knew that, by taking up that veto, he'd made some extremely powerful enemies. He already knew he had many within the police force, within politics, within the media, and within Sydney's dark criminal underbelly. A few more could tip the balance. And those ranged against him were, for the first time, beginning to make significant headway.

CHAPTER 18

A clear target

In the dead of the night, Peter Ryan raced to a clandestine rendezvous with his Internal Affairs Assistant Commissioner, Mal Brammer, and twenty officers sworn to absolute secrecy about their work. The mood in the room was tense as he delivered his briefing to his troops, each the leader of an elite team of corruption 'hunters', about their morning's work.

Whispers had been circulating for months around the New South Wales underworld about Ryan's formation of a posse of untouchables, officers who could be trusted implicitly, who were completely free of the stain of corruption and whom it would be impossible, hopefully, to turn. And here they were, all assembled in one room at 3.30 a.m. on Tuesday, 9 December 1997, shuffling nervously in the thought of what they were about to do.

It was set to be one of the most daring operations ever undertaken by a Commissioner of Police in Australia, and the stakes were high. For the last eleven months, Ryan had led a massive covert surveillance investigation into corruption at all levels of the police service allowing drug suppliers to prosper, including within one of its most prized squads, Task Force Bax, which was probing organised crime networks at Kings Cross.

What he'd found horrified him. 'People seemed to have learned nothing from the Royal Commission,' he says. 'There were still reports of corruption taking place, always broadly along the lines of the Commission revelations of cops giving information away for money, police telling criminals that a drug bust was going down or selling information off the police computer. Criminals were generally being kept informed of things going on, and much of that was coming from the police.' This operation, code-named 'Gymea', was set to blow away a great swathe of that, not only in terms of the men and women it would net, but also as a dramatic show of strength that would deliver the message to everyone else that Ryan had the means, and the determination, to get them.

It felt like one of the longest nights of Ryan's life. But by midday, he knew the operation had been a triumph. Twenty people had been arrested in dawn raids across Sydney and the Central Coast, two amphetamine factories had been closed down and charges laid relating to drugs worth $10.2 million. A few minutes later, another detective was arrested as he stepped out of the witness box at the Police Integrity Commission, and charged with conspiring to pervert the course of justice. Ryan met with the New South Wales Premier, the Police Minister and Justice Wood to brief them fully. Then he held a press conference, reiterating his determination to seek out organised crime and the police who helped it to flourish. It was among the happier moments in his job.

This group of young and untainted officers worked extremely hard on corrupt police and corrupt criminal associates from a secret location. No one knew them or what they were doing; they had to operate in an area where they couldn't even tell their families and friends. The aim was always to maintain the integrity of the investigation because, in the past, there had always been leaks.

I was so pleased how we managed to surprise everyone by being able to operate in such a clandestine and undiscovered way. But to set that up was not easy. We were using an internal police informer as an undercover officer. He'd been approached by some criminal police who were trying to entice him into joining their corrupt activities, but he came to us instead and admitted what the approach had been. I told the Government that there was significant police corruption, and that I needed all the possible help I could get in order to fight it. We couldn't afford to be complacent or think that, because of the Commission, things had been cured.

The difficult operation had been carried out with the help of the Police Integrity Commission (PIC), set up at the end of the Royal Commission to deal with corruption on a full-time basis. Given wide-ranging powers for its task, including the freedom to bug people, tap phones, install secret cameras or microphones, conduct 'stings' or entrapment circumstances, seize police files, and enter and search wherever there was a suspicion of corrupt activity, it proved a formidable ally. Ryan had no formal control over the PIC's activities, but, when they were able to agree on joint operations, they could work very effectively together. The problems came later, when the PIC frequently tried to rein in Ryan – and he saw them as hampering rather than helping the work he was trying so hard to do.

The PIC, headed by Judge Paul Urquhart with fifty-five staff below him, and audited by the Royal Commission's Justice Wood, now working as Inspector-General, also had the power to run continual integrity checks on police. In these, they worked hand in glove with Ryan. Frequently, the results startled outsiders. In one of the first sets of thirty-six tests, for instance, more than half the officers failed – which was instantly taken as an indication that the service was still riddled with corruption. In one case, a constable was targeted and sent to a pub in Taree to deal with a concocted incident. There, he was approached by two female detectives posing as customers who reported their car had been stolen, with a handbag lying inside containing a considerable amount of money. Unbeknownst to the officer, a security camera had been fitted inside the car and, when he found the car, it filmed him stealing cash from the bag. Ryan was at pains, however, to stress that since the tests were aimed at officers suspected of dishonesty, a high failure rate was to be expected.

The news travels fast when someone fails, and officers find themselves wondering whether an incident they're dealing with is real or a test. Officers can then feel that management doesn't trust them, which is one of the downsides of such testing. On the one hand, the service is being told to be more caring and accountable and, on the other, we're clamping down on them with tests for drugs and integrity and so on. I've got to somehow manage those tensions and it doesn't always work. It can create an atmosphere of fear because that's not properly understood. Outside agencies, like the PIC, can require us to do things that place a fairly tight noose around officers' necks at times.

The success or otherwise of such strategies was often dependent upon Ryan's restructuring of the service to try to make it far more trustworthy than it had been in the past, with a series of checks and safeguards. Early in 1997, he'd axed the old Professional Responsibility department and internal investigations, renamed the whole branch of the service 'Internal Affairs', and put it under the command of Brammer. The idea was that it would look into police corruption and serious complaints against the police as they were reported, and it would adopt the new approach of proactive investigations. It would target major criminals and work backwards to find out who their police contacts were, rather than waiting for an incident to occur and merely respond to that. In the case of Gymea, it was an approach that yielded huge dividends.

Yet every time Ryan increased his activities and became more visible, so he seemed to attract more and more criticism. Some saw his activities as pure grandstanding, since no Commissioner before him had ever stepped quite so regularly into the limelight – or appeared to relish it so much. Some couldn't seem to forgive him for being an outsider, referring to him continually by his country of origin and insisting that he couldn't possibly solve the kind of problems that had developed over decades in New South Wales, which needed someone born there to understand them fully.

Certainly, in the way he continually put his head above the parapet, Ryan was a clear target, and a softer one still in his chosen tactic of ignoring his enemies, and freezing them out, instead of either answering them back, or inviting them to engage in personal debate. To some extent, that was understandable. He'd come from a country where police didn't take part in lively discussion about their modus operandi and, indeed, where it was only occasionally, if ever, subject to close scrutiny. In New South Wales, however, everything Ryan did was seized upon, dissected and publicly discussed. Ryan reacted by retreating more and more into the job.

Jo Hampson, Ryan's English chief of staff, said it was a shock when his honeymoon with the press ended. Everyone had been totally unprepared for the turn. The problem then with the media strategy was that . . . there wasn't one. 'In England, we just didn't speak to journalists,' she says. 'Probably few people in London would recognise the Metropolitan Police Commissioner if they saw him in the street, not even his officers. But in Australia, it's quite different, and we didn't realise that at first.'

During a dinner with 2UE talkback radio host Alan Jones, she was shocked at his attitude.

> He told me that I was being ridiculous and naive to imagine Peter didn't have to speak to the press. He said the bottom line is that he'll say what he feels like on the radio, whether it's right or not, and he expected people like Carr, Howard and Ryan to pick up the phone and put him right. That was totally alien to us, and I think that's why we never ended up managing the press. I told Peter not to say anything but, in hindsight that was wrong. When you don't say anything, journalists print crap. You had to be proactive, but it wasn't until later that we realised we needed a strategy. Peter is a sensitive soul. He took it all personally, and he hasn't ever learnt to cope with that, or get to the stage where it stops mattering to him. The press was foul, and in the middle of it, it really felt like a campaign to get him.

His friend, Colin Henson, said that, in any case, he was often hamstrung by circumstances in his dealings with the media. 'A lot of the stuff he was dealing with was secret, so he couldn't tell them about it even if he'd wanted to,' he says. 'But then they construe that as him sitting back and not doing anything. It was absolute rubbish.' Occasionally, Ryan did bite back, but seldom continued beyond one response and, indeed, seemed, somewhat naively to believe that once he'd pointed out how he saw the situation, others would take that on trust. He was totally unprepared for the level of hostility he encountered, and often, at first, bewildered by the aggression.

When, for example, the results of an IBM Culture Survey Ryan had commissioned revealed that most rank-and-file officers were too nervous to discuss problems with their superiors because they feared reprisals, Gary Sturgess was among the first to pounce. He wrote an article for the *Daily Telegraph* the very day the report was released, describing the document as a 'damning indictment of police management'. While the survey found that most officers supported the broad thrust of the reforms, and contained comments from many endorsing Ryan's leadership, Sturgess pulled together nearly every area of criticism that had ever been made about Ryan to launch a vigorous personal attack on the man. Ryan spoke publicly about it only once. A couple of days later, he referred to the onslaught and said, 'Mr Sturgess was a member of the Police Board which had management oversight of the police service for a number of years. I am now fixing the mess that the police service is in.'

It seemed only to whet Sturgess's appetite for a fight and, when Ryan refused to rise to the bait again, it appeared to stir his ire even further. A few months later, it was reported he was in discussions with the New South Wales Liberal Party about coming on board to help leader Peter Collins in the run-up to the 1999 election. Sturgess, however, says he most definitely wasn't working with the Liberals on Ryan. 'Bullshit,' he says. 'I've established a reputation for being, if anything, too independent to belong to the Liberal Party.' He wasn't alone, either, in his criticism of Ryan. At this time another of Ryan's most trenchant critics began to emerge, University of Sydney anthropologist Dr Richard Basham.

Ryan has never had any time for Basham. He has always referred to himself as having been one of Ryan's top advisors, sitting on the Police Community Advisory Group, yet Ryan is aware of having met him only once or twice. He has certainly always been scornful of Basham's attempts to present himself as a trusted aide who once had the ear of the Commissioner. Ryan also points out that while Basham seems happy to be referred to as a criminologist, he is actually an anthropologist, and is not a member of University of Sydney's highly prestigious Department of Criminology. But Ryan was made to pay for his obvious disregard for the academic in February 1998 when Basham's attack on him on ABC-TV's 'Stateline' made colourful copy. He cast Ryan as a tragic Shakespearean King Lear, demanding 'hollow' statements of loyalty from his senior officers. He said he was far too distant from his staff and had cocooned himself in his 18th-floor office at Police HQ, becoming detached from the real operation of the service.

It was an easy enough observation to make. Ryan had made a conscious choice when he came to take up his new job not to trust anyone until they earned that trust. Of course, he was in the unenviable position at first of not knowing who was on his side and who was not. That determination to put himself beyond the usual police mateship networks, however, made him appear all the more isolated and remote at the head of the service. Those below him began to resent what they saw as his self-imposed detachment, and often felt hurt, then irked, that he didn't trust any of them enough to take them into his confidence. The fact that he was English only exacerbated their suspicions. Maybe he felt himself to be too good to mix with the locals in the lower ranks? That healthy Australian disregard for status and authority suddenly started working against someone they construed to be overly conscious of class and position.

This was another area in which Ryan didn't exactly help himself. 'In England, he'd been a very highly ranked and highly thought of person, who went through the ranks very quickly,' says close friend and human resources professional Geoff Officer. 'While he's a very intelligent guy, and he wanted to do a good job, I think there was a little bit of that English attitude tucked in of coming out here to reform the colonies. He's never been backward in terms of talking of his own competence, and he did have a lot to offer.' He was also still seen regularly out on the social circuit. In truth, he didn't much care with whom he socialised – as long as they weren't police officers. But, increasingly it looked as though others were being actively courted at his colleagues' expense. It was the TV-show hosts, radio personalities, businesspeople and high-profile authors Adrienne favoured, the kind of company which kept them in the social pages – a first again for a Police Commissioner. Many saw that as completely inappropriate for a man in such a serious position in society.

And notably, while the Ryans wined and dined with the glitterati, his closest associates, Bev Lawson, Jeff Jarratt, Mal Brammer and Clive Small, were rarely invited over to his house. Adrienne, however, saw it differently. 'In truth, we only went occasionally to social functions, but the newspapers used the same photos of us, over and over. We'd wake up on New Year's Day to find out how much we'd enjoyed Frank Sartor's Masked Ball – when, whilst invited, we'd never gone once! It created completely the wrong impression of us.'

'But he never really learnt that Australian concept of mateship,' says Officer, himself New Zealand-born. 'He always felt, and looked, very isolated. He never took the time to really understand the Australian way. Mateship is something that's held very dear here.' Perhaps suddenly aware that it was time he stepped out of the ivory tower and trusted some of his top people, Ryan had made tentative advances of friendship to Bev Lawson who was fast becoming a trusted professional confidante. Then, on 22 January 1998, tragedy struck. Lawson died suddenly after suffering a massive stroke the day before. No one could ever know for sure what brought it on, but many people suspected it might be the strain of a top job in a profession undergoing unprecedented change. It was quite possible. While Ryan had been on leave the month before, 57-year-old Lawson had served as Acting Commissioner and, since she was absolutely wedded to the service, she tended to take on far too much work, and far too much stress.

Ryan was personally devastated. His one certain ally was suddenly gone, and he was filled with despair for what might have been. 'I really regret – looking back now – that I never made more of a friend of her,' says Ryan. 'I was a boss, a colleague and a supporter and a work-friend but I would have liked to have been a *good* friend of hers. She was really very, very good and I valued what she did. She played an enormous part in the restructuring of the force.' Jo Hampson felt similarly. 'She was the only person Peter had who started doing things differently,' she says. 'I could see everyone else just carried on the same, while saying, "Yes, Commissioner." But she was loyal, and really tried to drive change forward. A lot of the others just went into his office and tried to get him to agree to what *they* wanted, without warning him of the implications. People were always trying to control him, but I wouldn't let them. I think most of them hated me.' Ryan was left with Jarratt as his lone deputy and might, in other circumstances, have taken him into his confidence. But already he had doubts about both Jarratt's capabilities and, more importantly, his support.

In early 1998, Jarratt had led a committee, which included both region and local commanders, and the Police Association, to examine how the local area commands had settled in. All stations at that time were graded at a level between one and three which indicated the difficulty – or otherwise – of the Commander's job which, in turn, dictated his salary. It had nothing to do with the volume of, or the seriousness of, crime activity in each area, says Ryan. The committee recommended that a number of the stations be downgraded. One was Cabramatta.

Ryan felt unable to refuse. The committee had been working long and hard on the project and, while he had his doubts, he didn't feel in a position to argue. 'But I thought it was totally unnecessary and we should leave things alone,' he says. 'It would upset people who might see themselves being punished for doing well. But I agreed verbally, providing Jeff could persuade the local area commanders. Some of them found out beforehand and became concerned. Some asked to see me.'

The storm that followed the revelation that Cabramatta, one of the drug centres of Australia was to be 'downgraded' was eminently predictable, and incredibly damaging.

In hindsight, it was an absolute disaster. Then Jeff didn't help by sending out a memo apologising that people must be hurt and bruised. He should have just said: This is the situation. The way he did it gave the impression that it wasn't his decision – which left only me looking as if I'd done it.

It was a classic example of a service trying to introduce accountability falling foul of others who didn't understand what we were trying to do. They accused us of ignoring crime, of being dismissive of resources. It was a gift to the Opposition and they played it for all it was worth. But it was never intended to be anything else but an instrument for setting salary levels. It was an example of bad ideas letting us down badly. They hadn't thought things through.

When, in February 1998, Ryan left Australia to inspect the security arrangements for the Winter Olympics in Nagano – the last Games before Sydney's 2000 event – relations with Jarratt hit an all-time low. Upper House Parliamentarian Rev. Fred Nile had learnt that police were set to march in the Mardi Gras parade, in uniform and on full pay. His comments set off a storm of criticism of Ryan for allowing such a thing, and particularly at a time of such swingeing budget cut-backs elsewhere in the service. Immediately following the Nagano Opening Ceremony, Ryan received a call from Adrienne, telling him about the controversy in the newspapers and on talkback radio, and saying that Jarratt did not appear to be fighting his corner at all.

Ryan was alarmed. Police had participated in uniform and on full pay at two previous Mardi Gras; the only difference this year was that they'd be marching rather than riding in a bus. He was particularly incensed at the suggestion that Jarratt didn't appear to be defending him. Adrienne called a newspaper to claim that her husband was being deliberately undermined and, in a furious interview with a newspaper, Ryan accused those closest to him of 'white-anting' him, and his media unit of failure to act in his best interests. 'I could have been completely wrong, but it seemed that Jeff just never seemed to share the vision, and I started seriously doubting that he was supporting me,' says Ryan. 'I began to question my trust in him. After all, he had applied for my job, yet he was my deputy and we had to work together.'

He wasn't so sure of another of his top officer's support either, that of Assistant Commissioner Christine Nixon. Indeed, by May 1998, he was convinced that if Nixon wasn't actively working against him, she certainly wasn't actively working for him. Reform seemed to be happening excruciatingly slowly and, despite what he saw as his clear instructions about the kind of changes he wanted to see put in place, he increasingly felt that her Human Resources department wanted to run its own agenda.

One group in particular, Restorative Justice and Behavioural Change, soon to become the notorious Crime Management Support Unit (CMSU), seemed to be running completely its own race, unfettered by any sign of control by Nixon. He believed they were chasing some soft, fuzzy, idealistic notions of change, rather than the hard-edged goals he wanted. 'Let's get the patient breathing and cure the most serious ill-nesses,' he told them. 'Then we can get on and do the other things to make the body healthy.' But still, he felt they weren't coming to the party. What made it worse were the number of leaks to the press that seemed to be coming from the department. One afternoon, at a meeting with the HR managers, he told them the leaks would have to stop because they were derailing the reform process and, if he found anybody talking to the press, he would 'nail them to a tree in Hyde Park'. It wasn't a casual throwaway remark; it was a deliberately strong statement calculated to provoke a reaction. And it worked. Before he'd even reached his waiting car, his mobile was ringing with press inquiries about police officers being nailed to trees.

The speed of that information reaching journalists was phenom-enal. It made it quite clear where the leaks were coming from. That was the last straw. For a long time, they'd chosen to ignore my instructions, they'd offered me no advice at all, and now I knew they were leaking information outside. We were twelve months behind where I'd hoped we'd be in the reform process and we were already suffering the consequences of that. Human Resources really needed a thorough sort-out. It simply was not performing. The Human Resources Command was the source of many complaints from the field as being out of touch with real policing, and it seemed they were trying to be a power unto themselves, empire-building and running their own race. Despite agreements I'd reached with Christine, she still seemed to go off and do her own thing.

He took swift action, and moved Nixon out to a regional position in Greater Hume, under the guise of giving her more operational experience. Ironically, when Nixon later applied for the post of Vic-torian Police Commissioner, Ryan supported her application. And one of the principal reasons she finally won that job, he says, was precisely because he'd given her that edge in operational experience. Nixon declined to comment for the book, beyond drawing attention to her statement released to the press on Ryan's departure, thanking him for giving her valuable experience while in New South Wales, and praising his contribution to the service. Ryan was still having problems with Human Resources to the day he left.

So eager to make changes, Ryan started believing that he just wasn't receiving the support he should from other institutions, too. He rode a storm of internal police protest about his proposal to bring over more British detectives to help shore up the service. He was privately furious that the New South Wales Government hadn't stood by the powers they'd originally given him under the Commissioner's Confidence legislation, and had ended up weakening it to the point where 'it was easier for them to appeal, so it ended up almost like a criminal case where it had to be proven beyond reasonable doubt,' he says. 'So we had some people reinstated who'd committed quite serious offences, and officers were still allowed to resign when I wanted them not to be able to, and face the music. Instead, by resigning, they effectively got away with what they'd done. It was an absolute disaster.'

In addition, the police union was proving a formidable foe in Ryan's quest to put his new structure in place. Because the union wouldn't budge on its industrial agreements, he found the promotion system was taking far too long. If someone was appointed, for example, they still had to wait for verification from both the PIC and Internal Affairs. Even then, the appointment could be appealed by anyone who reckoned they had more right to the job. Every single appointment at one stage was appealed, leaving 680 appeals outstanding at once. Ryan had his own theory as to why the union made it so difficult for officers.

'When the work force is disaffected and disgruntled they turn to the union who can always play the card: "We're doing this for you, but management won't budge." It's a good ploy to have the work force think it is management's fault. And then because it's an industrial agreement and law I can't change it without the Government coming to the party.' The Commissioned Police Officers Association (CPOA) was hardly an ally, either. They were threatening industrial action unless they were offered a pay rise of more than 20 per cent. Everyone had simply assumed they'd received that rise the previous year, along with Police Association members, but no one had realised the two groups were quite distinct. Ryan didn't really believe

they deserved it – they weren't working hard enough – but he battled in Treasury nonetheless. At a very tense and heated Cabinet
meeting, Ryan and Whelan were subject to abuse by the other ministers who expressed their opposition to paying them any more on
the grounds of performance. Ryan tended to agree, but fought on
nevertheless. Eventually, the Government agreed to give them 16 per
cent on condition he found the other 4 per cent. When he told the
CPOA of the result, he was sadly disappointed that they seemed so
ungrateful.

Yet still Ryan didn't baulk at criticising any sector of society he
didn't feel was pulling its weight in the fight against crime, however
hallowed. Even the judiciary came in for criticism. After off-duty
officer Constable Peter Forsyth was stabbed to death in March 1998,
he said people were sick of judges awarding light sentences for violent offenders. Penalties for violent crimes should be much higher, he
declared, with judges applying maximum sentences.

But in April that year Ryan made his most important and influential enemy, a man who was later to drive him to the very edge of
despair. The waterfront dispute that began in Melbourne quickly
spread to Sydney, and caught everyone off guard. Too few police
were allocated to the docks, and a stand-off emerged. Ryan paraded
his commanders in front of him, and tore strips off them for not
being ready. But that day, the port operators Patrick obtained an
injunction to prevent the Maritime Union of Australia from stopping
traffic entering and leaving the port. Ryan read the injunction closely –
and recoiled. 'My previous experience was that in common law
police had the right to enforce an injunction if a breach of it creates
a breach of the peace,' he says. 'Striking generally does. But the
strange wording of this one meant that while the MUA could not
boycott the port, others could. It also didn't extend to the police
forcing the dock to be open. It created some real legal problems for
us, with the mix of public and private land, so I was advised by my
lawyers that we couldn't enforce the injunction as it didn't relate to
the police.'

The next day, the police tried to keep the docks open, but the TV
cameras caught graphic images of officers trying to drag women,
children and elderly men out of the way. Ryan, appalled, ordered his

troops to stay back, but to still maintain the peace. Alan Jones, broadcasting on Radio 2UE the next morning, didn't approve at all.

Alan Jones starts raving at me for being useless, and not taking any action, even though we were trying to sort out the legality of the injunction. But Jones's attack on me continued on and on. He was constantly pushing Patrick's point. It was always Patrick's that were mentioned. I thought this was going well beyond reasonable interest and comment on the matter. He was saying, 'For God's sake, Commissioner, get down there and get blood on your hands.' I rang him and, on air, asked him, 'Whose blood, Alan, women's and children's?'

From that point on, Ryan couldn't do anything right in Jones's eyes. It seemed every day Jones attacked him and Ryan was convinced his condemnations were politically motivated, but bristled, silently, under the onslaught.

Jones was branding me a lackey of the Labor Government, even though I was trying to be non-partisan. It's difficult when the Government makes a point and the Commissioner speaks out. But to be honest, in reality, I'm a Liberal voter. But I could never say what I really felt about those political issues. I was stuck between a rock and a hard place, and he took advantage of that shamelessly.

Ryan had declined to get the blood of women and children on his hands but Jones, the media giant, could smell the blood of an Englishman . . . and it had the whiff of ratings victory.

CHAPTER 19

'Tonight we're going to kill you all . . .'

Nine-year-old Georgina Ryan had been playing by the swimming pool when she heard the phone ringing in the house. She raced indoors but the answering machine in the study had already clicked on. She pressed the button to hear the message. It was a voice she didn't recognise, deep and rasping. 'Hello, Mr Ryan,' it said. 'Tonight we're going to plant a bomb and kill you all . . .'

Georgina felt a cold chill pass through her body. She yelled for her sister and Elizabeth came running in, alarmed by the note of fear in her voice. The two stood there and listened together. 'We both got scared,' says Georgina. 'It was horrible.'

That night, Ryan moved Elizabeth from her bedroom on the other side of the house to the spare room between her parents and Georgina. Normally, she might have made a fuss. But that night she was relieved. 'I slept there for a couple of weeks,' she says. 'Since then, we've had hundreds of threats.'

Often the family would shrug off the threats – phoned, written or cut out from magazine letters – to shoot them, kill them or maim them, but sometimes they would take them a great deal more seriously. One midnight the phone rang and, as soon as Ryan heard the nature of the death threat being played, he called the Protective Security Group. They advised him to get out of his house as quickly as he could.

Adrienne woke the children and told them that, as a surprise, they were all going to stay in a hotel that night. They gathered up a few things, jumped into the car and drove, at top speed, into the city, where they checked into the Hyde Park Plaza, next door to police HQ. 'It was pretty exciting at the time,' says Georgina. 'But I was upset because they wouldn't let me bring the dog.' Adds Elizabeth, 'They told us at the time that they were bored with the house and wanted to stay somewhere else. Later, they told us what it was really about. I was worried. I thought I was going to die.'

At one point, Georgina was bundled off to stay at a friend's house. At another, Elizabeth had to be accompanied at all times by a police-woman. 'It was always such a strain,' says Adrienne. 'The anxiety you feel, especially when the threats are directed against your children, is terrible.' Her closest friend Loretta Henson, the wife of Ryan's best friend Colin – the couples had first met on a holiday at Club Med on Lindeman Island in January 1997 – was often surprised by the elabo-rate precautions they had to take. A particularly handsome birdhouse she admired in the garden turned out to be a closed-circuit camera. When, in December 1998, the Ryans bought a new four-bedroom, $1.35-million home closer to town, but still on Sydney's upper North Shore and next door to the Hensons', they were horrified to see a photograph of the house printed in a newspaper the next day.

Although terribly homesick for her family and friends back in England, and frequently questioning the wisdom of having left the security and comfort of a good job and a beautiful home in Bramshill, Adrienne had taken a full-time job with Westpac as a senior manager, examining recruitment and selection strategies, had enrolled the children in the private North Shore girls' school Abbot-sleigh, and was trying hard to make a go of their new life. She struggled, however, with all the hostility her husband was facing, and what she saw as the constant media intrusion into their family life. While Ryan was away at Nagano in May 1998, the 37-year-old became irretrievably entwined in her husband's public life, by call-ing the media to get involved in the Mardi Gras row. Shortly afterwards, she delivered a speech to a meeting of Sydney business-women that included comments about the difficulties faced in migrating to another country, which had come at 'an enormous cost to us, as a family, not only financially, but what is more important, personally, emotionally and physically.'

She hadn't realised a reporter was in the room and, the next day, the story about her speech was headlined, 'Life Is Hell'. The backlash was immediate. The talkback radio airwaves buzzed with callers complaining about 'whingeing Poms' and the newspapers were full of indignation that she should complain after her husband was paid so much to do a job, and they had such a luxurious lifestyle. Adrienne, hurt and angry, cancelled all her speaking engagements and went to ground. Later that year, she quit her job at Westpac, with onlookers linking that decision to a speech she'd made a few weeks earlier in which she'd mentioned the 'glass ceiling'.

> The extent of the hostility is far greater than I ever thought it would be. The difficulties that Peter faces are greater than anyone could ever have imagined. But this kind of job really hasn't been done before. It's also so lonely here. We do get lots of lovely invitations, but we can't take them up in case people think Peter's on the gravy train. And he has to be so careful whom he socialises with so he'll never be compromised. It can be very difficult to make friends.

At times, it's been difficult for Ryan when his wife speaks out, but he is adamant that it's not his role to gag her. In some ways, he likes it, feeling that no one else understands the difficulties of the job, or has been so prepared to come out and defend him publicly. In other ways, it can complicate life in that she's seen to be entering the political fray. 'But she has her own life and is her own person,' he says. 'And she gets angry at what she sees as untruths and injustice.' In the long run, it probably didn't help at all. While naturally feisty and outspoken, the fact that she obviously felt entitled to play a larger role sat uncomfortably with those used to Commissioners' wives who had been older, more retiring, and knew their place back in the shadows. It also had the effect of making Ryan look weak and drew attention to the fact that Adrienne was there in the background, often influencing his decisions. Now she too had put herself forward to become a target.

Ryan, by now assigned a bodyguard to shadow every move, was also beginning to have serious doubts about the move to Sydney. While his rise to the top in the UK had often been a struggle, nothing

had prepared him for the sheer relentless battles each day as head of
the New South Wales police force.

> I've never been a quitter, and I didn't want to think that I'd made
> such a big sacrifice with my career that I was going to fail. But
> it was very hard. What really used to stick in my throat was
> people saying, 'Oh well, you must have realised how difficult
> this job was going to be.' No one could have realised how diffi-
> cult this job was because, if they had, they would have put some
> fixes in earlier on to make it right. And if anyone did know as
> much as they reckoned they knew, well, they were culpable for
> not doing something about it, either as a politician or a senior
> police officer or a public servant. Nobody knew the problems,
> and daily more and more were revealed. I'd ask a question and
> people would say, 'Oh, I never thought of that!' or 'We never
> thought of it that way' or 'We never thought of tying in this
> activity with that.' They wrote brilliant and beautifully crafted
> reports on what we ought to do, but they left out the 10 per cent
> about *how* we were going to do it, and how we knew when we'd
> *done* it. It was very hard, extraordinarily hard, and no one could
> have known that.

It was lonely there at the top, too. For a naturally sociable man
who enjoys having a beer with mates, he felt himself becoming more
suspicious of everyone and everything. Increasingly, he relied on the
company of Colin Henson, usually just meeting in one of their
homes for a drink. With Adrienne and Loretta, they'd often make up
a foursome for dinner. He drew comfort from the loyalty and support
of his chief of staff Andrew Scipione – later to become a deputy – his
successor Bernard Aust, his secretaries Sina Castiglione, Lynette
Howle and Carrie Di Certo, his policy advisors Helen Ainsworth,
Edwina Cowdery, Gillian O'Malley and Cathi Margherita, and his
bodyguard Danny Hill. Every day he was grateful for their encouragement and determination to stay cheerful against all the odds.
With Alan Hall, his driver from his very first day on the job to his
very last, he forged a strong bond over all the hours they shared on
the road. Hall was more than just the driver, quickly becoming a

friend whose own life was disrupted by the long days and tours of duty. Hall sat by watching Ryan go through hell and always gave as much support as he could. Hall would talk all the time to cops on the street and report back on their feelings to 'The Boss', and officers would often use him as their informal channel to Ryan. 'I always found him very approachable,' says Hall. 'He coped pretty well with all that pressure. In his position, I would have blown my cool and taken someone's head off their shoulders.'

Elsewhere, Ryan was hesitant to make new friends, and didn't feel he could afford to trust anyone. He'd always been someone who kept his own counsel, but still some were surprised at the way he seemed to be able to close down his sensitivities completely. When Hampson told him she was leaving to go back to the UK, for example, because her sister was sick with cancer, she was devastated that, after their sixteen months working side by side through some of the toughest times she could ever have imagined, he seemed totally unmoved by her news. 'I loved him, and respected him, and would have died for him,' she says. 'But he doesn't tend to recognise that, or appreciate that.' Of course, someone who's reached that kind of position, particularly in an organisation as imbued with machismo as the police service, has to be hard to survive. It was only when Hampson went to say her final goodbye that she was gratified to see a glint of a tear in his eye as he stared out his office window towards the harbour. 'He is a very loyal man, and very genuine, with a profound morality and integrity, who can be clever and nice. He does care,' she says, 'but he doesn't often show it.'

To be fair, to do so could have run the risk of being construed as weak, particularly when he was under such sustained attack, and everything he did attracted criticism. When the spotlight fell on the issue of Aboriginal reconciliation and the police service came under pressure to issue a public apology, he resisted being the one to make it. As an Englishman who'd been in the country for only a short time, he felt he really wasn't the appropriate spokesperson, even though he believed to apologise was the right and proper thing to do, particularly in view of the number of deaths in custody and Aboriginal people's grievances about their treatment by police. In the end, he gave in, and read a statement at Parliament House, surrounded by the CEOs of other criminal justice agencies. It set the scene nicely, in any case, for his push to recruit Aboriginal officers a few weeks later. After his speech, other police forces asked for copies so they could use it in their own ceremonies, and he received a flood of letters, many from Aboriginal people saying thanks, and many more from critics questioning his right to make any apology at all.

Chief among those, predictably enough, was Gary Sturgess, who branded him as 'dumb' for having done so. 'What's a Brit doing purporting to tell us how to feel, especially on a complex matter like this?' he said. But Ryan barely gives him the time of day, saying his enmity dates back to his getting the Commissioner job ahead of the Australians Sturgess had favoured, and the dissolution of the old Police Board. Sturgess rarely let up in his attacks, however, and was soon joined by another old enemy, Richard Basham. A constant theme was that Ryan was isolated from the rest of the service below him, was far too formal and aloof, and personally disliked Basham because the academic had once had the temerity to address him as 'Peter', instead of using a more formal title.

'It's absolute bloody nonsense,' says Ryan. 'These things about being isolated and lost, this just becomes a myth. I don't know what they expect. I don't go round to people's houses for barbecues or go to the pub drinking with them. My job is to reform the service, not become best mates with everybody.'

Basham was starting to become a particular irritant. Whenever Ryan defended himself against his critics, or even tried to plug leaks to the media, Basham waded in with ever-more savage attacks. By May 1998, he was accusing him of Richard Nixon-style paranoia, with resources squandered in attempts to ferret out enemies and stop leaks. One of the few conversations Ryan ever had with Basham disintegrated into a heated argument at a Police Association dinner a few days later, with Ryan telling him to stop both his ill-informed criticism and his claims to have been a personal advisor. Ryan assumes Basham went straight to a phone because, even though it was 8.30 or 9 at night, a blow-by-blow account of their conversation appeared the next morning in a newspaper. The row then escalated further when Basham accused him, through the newspapers, of giving Adrienne a confidential police document to read – something the Ryans deny, vehemently. He then suggested New South Wales would be better off with a new Police Commissioner. When approached, Basham at first says he'd prefer not to comment for this book. Then he concedes that while he was in favour of Ryan's appointment at first, he turned after his criticism was taken personally. He felt Ryan was going wrong at a number of points, but the Commissioner refused to take his points seriously. 'My initial critique of Peter about him being a Lear-like figure was meant to be helpful for him,' says Basham, blithely. 'I wanted him to understand that wouldn't do him much good, but he personalises everything. He was surrounding himself with the wrong people, and getting rid of Geoff Schuberg was a real worry. Then he became too concerned about his public image. He was spending too much time with the big end of town and the media.'

Ryan sees Basham as not being qualified to judge his record. 'He's made a career out of claiming he's a personal friend. Then he keeps going on that I don't know about Australian culture. I'm working in the dark heart of Australian culture day in, day out. He's an American, what does he know about it?'

By the time the Ryans went back to the UK for a holiday that June, speculation that he might resign was intensifying. Journalists, perhaps a little out of frustration that he refused to speak to so many of them, seemed eager to whip up the debate about whether he should stay or go. Many were receiving leaks and others were, according to Ryan, being purposely fed wrong information designed to show him in a bad light. Certainly, some long-serving police journalists' main sources were thought of as the 'old' team, with not much of a future under Ryan, and were resentful of having a foreigner foisted on them. Another journalist wrote that he'd been told his phone had been tapped in order to discover the source of the leaks he was receiving. Ryan counters that he'd never have the power to do such a thing, even if he wanted to. His only course was to examine the police phone records to see who was calling news organisations. Yet everyone, it seemed, had something to say on the issue of Ryan's tenure. There were some who said agents of change within large institutions, particularly in one as innately conservative as the police force, were always going to be resented. There were others who said that foreigners were generally welcomed in Australia – but that friendliness could quickly turn to hostility when reform was on the agenda, and that mateship could be used as a weapon against outsiders. Even the notion of bringing a dapper Englishman into the blokey Aussie culture of the police, it was pointed out, could be seen as a touchpaper.

Just as many felt, however, that Ryan was far too sensitive to media criticism, taking much of it personally. He took negative stories as evidence that certain journalists were against him, instead of the more logical possibility that they were merely looking for a fresh angle on a running story. Coming from a culture where authority tends, generally, to be respected, he wasn't prepared for being challenged on every point, which is par for the course for many public figures in Australia. 'He found that very hard, and increasingly believed the world was against him,' says Hampson. He could be paranoid about the media, agrees his management consultant friend, Barry Newton, but that doesn't surprise him. 'All police chiefs are,' says Newton.

> For the media, the police make sexy, interesting stories. But the problem is, at the end of the day, policing only happens by consensus. Police can only police because people *allow* them to. If the media gets so bad that people start to feel alienated from the police, and resent their authority, then policing goes out the window. They can't do their jobs any more. So it's not about Peter flattering Peter; it's about Peter building and sustaining the confidence of the community and worrying that the media will be preventing that from happening.

Shortly after Ryan's trip to the UK, however, he suddenly received an important credibility boost. At about the same time as he had a meeting with the British Home Secretary Jack Straw to discuss security arrangements for the 2000 Olympics and the general issue of police corruption, the head of Scotland Yard, Sir Paul Condon, came under pressure to retire. The British newspapers were filled with stories about likely successors – and his name was prominent. It took him completely by surprise. 'I hadn't been approached at all about it, but I thought it was interesting,' says Ryan. 'I had only been out of the country for two years, so I was still fairly well known. My experience in Australia was thought to have added to my expertise in Britain. But it was all just speculation anyway.' While it was mere speculation, its effect in Australia was spectacular. Suddenly, Ryan looked once more like a feted man with many options, and someone to be prized. The challenges he'd had to face in New South Wales served only to increase his stature.

Meanwhile, the problem of youth gangs roaming Sydney streets was beginning to attract attention, and Ryan welcomed new powers to enable police to frisk anyone suspected of carrying a knife, and spoke out in favour of being allowed to close video arcades that had become magnets for crime. Worried that many of the arcades along George Street in the city centre were becoming de facto headquarters for predominantly Asian gangs, he established a more obvious police presence in and around the games parlours.

In November, after increasing tension about gang activities, violence exploded on the streets of suburban Sydney. Lakemba police station – which is in a predominantly Lebanese area – was sprayed with automatic gunfire in a drive-by shooting, which left two officers being treated in hospital for shock, and one for injuries caused by broken glass. Three days later, Bankstown police station was rocked by an explosion after a device was thrown from a car on to the footpath at the front. Ryan was concerned about his officers, and worried that, left undefended, areas could develop into no-go zones. He ordered bulletproof glass be installed in the windows, and issued body armour to anyone who wanted it – although he privately believed it was far too hot and heavy to wear in Australian conditions.

A major emerging problem, he felt, was the ready availability of guns on the streets. The numbers had grown exponentially in the two years since he'd arrived in Sydney, and he was concerned that historically the legislation on gun ownership had always been relatively lax, and gun dealers were notoriously careless with their records. An earlier firearm amnesty and gun buy-back scheme had not been a particular success. Ryan warned about guns and pressed for tighter legislation, only to earn the ire of the gun lobby. After earlier criticism when he dared to talk about ethnic participation in gangs, even that angle was difficult to pursue.

The morning after the Lakemba police station shooting, to try and dampen down local fears, he went along to Lakemba with Elizabeth and Georgina in tow, visiting the police station, walking through the streets and having tea with members of the local mosque. The children were excited about going along; it made a change to meet other people who were also being threatened.

But behind the show of support for the law-abiding members of these troubled communities lay a steely resolve to nip their problems in the bud. 'It became quite apparent that we would have to deal with these emerging gangs in a very, very firm way,' says Ryan. 'Threats were being made to police; notes were put under windscreens. We had a number of high-profile operations to show them we were serious about beating them. I was determined to win.'

CHAPTER 20

Winning votes, losing friends

The New South Wales election was looming, and the issue of law and order was dominating State political life. The Labor Party had come to power in 1995 by the slimmest possible of margins – fifty seats out of a total of ninety-nine – and had worked hard to shore up a platform that had traditionally belonged to the Liberals. The recruitment of Peter Ryan, particularly now that he seemed to be in demand for the top policing job back in Britain, had been the lynchpin of its strategy. And it seemed to be working handsomely. Labor polling found that voters felt more positive about Ryan than any politician, with a staggering 86 per cent approval rate, and a senior Liberal insider referred begrudgingly to him as 'St Peter' and dubbed him the most popular person in public life in Australia. Deputy Commissioner Jeff Jarratt said if Ryan had stood for Parliament, 'I think he would have been elected Premier.'

Ryan knew this, but was approaching the election, to take place on 27 March 1999, with a feeling of real dread. Attacks on him by both Opposition Police Minister Andrew Tink and Opposition leader Peter Collins had intensified, and Collins even hinted that, if the Liberals won power, Ryan might find himself out of a job. When Kerry Chikarovski deposed Collins in December 1998, there was little comfort; she continued to taunt him at every opportunity. One afternoon, at a cricket match, Ryan found himself sitting next to her. Trying to build bridges, he said that if there was anything she wanted, or needed to know about the police, she just had to ask. 'If there's anything I need to know about policing,' Ryan says she snapped back, 'I'll ask Andrew Tink.' Ryan was taken aback at the curtness of her rebuff. 'What Andrew Tink knows about policing I could write on the head of a match,' he replied of the police spokesman who'd been in his position just two and a half years. After that brief exchange, they hardly spoke again.

For the Liberals, it was imperative that they discredit Premier Bob Carr's law-and-order strategies and, by association, Ryan. Only by winning back that high ground could they have any hope of snatching back power in New South Wales. As the election grew nearer, Ryan started studying his contract closely to work out whether, if the Liberals triumphed, he could indeed be dumped on a political whim.

What he found shocked him. The conditions under which he would be employed – or removed from office – appeared to be little more than a gentleman's agreement. After having given up his career, uprooted his family and sold his home in Britain to travel to the other end of the earth for a job, it seemed he could lose everything on a turn of the electorate. His friend Geoff Officer was surprised when he looked at the contract too. 'He never really sought help in terms of his personal situation; he was interviewed for the job, he was given it, and he leapt on a plane to come and do it,' he says. 'He could be very naive.' Hastily, Ryan called for copies of previous Commissioners' contracts. Theirs were the same. The only difference was that, beyond the contract, they'd all had protection enshrined in law that their removal would also have to be agreed by the New South Wales Police Board and ratified by both Houses of Parliament. That piece of legislation had changed on 1 January 1997 and, with the axing of the Police Board, Ryan could be removed merely at the request of a new Police Minister, without a moment's notice.

Ryan consulted with a number of industrial lawyers, and together they drew up a new five-year contract, which, if he were sacked for little reason, at least meant he'd be entitled to two years' salary if he were given less than twelve months' notice. The tricky part was working out exactly what an appropriate salary might be. Ryan talked to Police Minister Paul Whelan, and agreed they would let the Statutory and Other Offices Tribunal (SOORT) decide. Ryan gathered together figures of what a private sector CEO would earn with an equivalent size staff and operation, and passed them, through a negotiator, to the tribunal. They looked at the figures and came back with a recommendation that he be given a pay rise. In retrospect it was a rise for which Ryan would end up paying dearly.

At that point, however, he was adamant their recommendation for an increase on his annual salary – set at $315 000 when he signed up but, with the annual incremental rises paid to all senior public service executives, now standing at $375 000 – was a fair wage.

> I understood it was a high salary by public-sector standards, but it was not the *amount* that was the point of the new contract. The salary and terms of disengagement were intended to prevent a capricious move on a political whim to sack me. There were no bonuses attached to this, and I did have to pay everything out of that flat rate. Other public sector CEOs weren't far behind, I know that, and they often had bonuses on top as well. Besides, I was like those people who were brought in from outside to do a particular job from the private sector, who were expected to do the job for two, three or four years, and then move on again. I was running a big organisation and had a hell of a lot of responsibility, and I should be recompensed for it. If you are going to attract the right calibre of people, and retain them, you need to pay them appropriately. On top of that, my family and I had sold up everything to come to Australia and to be sacked, without recompense, after only two years would have been disastrous.

Even as the new contract was signed in February 1999, however, there were the first inklings of trouble. Ryan was adamant that his new salary be kept secret; the media demanded to be told. It was only two days before the first newspaper reports emerged putting it at more than $350 000. It was quite a bit off the mark even of his current salary, but Ryan still insisted the actual figure be kept quiet.

> I maintain that salary is a personal thing. It's an agreement between the employer and the individual and, public life or not, I still think that no one else is entitled to know. I don't see any

difference between the public or private sector, because all accounts can be audited. So if it's a proper contractual arrangement, why should it be emblazoned across the front pages of the newspapers, and mentioned in every article ever since? I don't think that's right and fair to any person. No one had anything to hide. I just wanted some privacy. I don't ask how much money editors of newspapers are paid or TV executives or anyone else for that matter. I couldn't care less, but I know it's much more than me.

But the newspapers and the public *did* care. Ryan was a public servant, with a salary paid by taxpayers and so, they asked, what right did he have to keep his salary quiet? How could he possibly compare a career in an organisation like the police, which most people join because they want to serve the community, make a difference, and maybe even assume some power and prestige, to the kind of money earned in the private sector with all the attendant risks and rewards determined by free-market forces? Besides, signing a new five-year contract, just six weeks before an election, when you still had two years left to run on the original, seemed a pretty dodgy deal. Then there was the not inconsequential argument that, since police corruption had flourished in the past in an atmosphere of secrecy, the police service should be as open and transparent as possible. The salary-guessing game became a national pastime, and even Ryan's children suffered. 'Other girls were always coming up to us in the playground and asking how much our dad earns,' says Elizabeth. 'I think they were told by their parents to ask us.'

Newspapers applied under freedom of information legislation to find out the real sum, only to be knocked back, and then reapply. Gradually, it emerged there had even been a major slip-up in the signing of the contract. Anxious to close the deal in advance of the final campaign launch of the election, everyone signed the day before SOORT sent its letter recommending the salary. The amount had been confirmed on the phone, but hadn't been sighted in writing. Immediately, the Opposition demanded an inquiry. 'We then had a Parliamentary Inquiry at enormous expense, resulting in a thick report written at even more expense, to question why we signed the contract before we'd received official notification,' says Ryan. 'The answer was simple: we'd had verbal notification. But they were looking for anything and everything just to, in my view, unbalance me.'

To some extent, however, he'd managed that on his own. While he himself never understood the clamour about his salary rise, the affair marked the real turning point in the affections of an adoring public towards Ryan. With his new contract and a salary many already considered excessive, he was suddenly cast, for the first time, as a man who had taken advantage of a Government fighting an election, and a State struggling to purge its police force, to satisfy his own greed. To Australian battlers, young families struggling on limited incomes, and most salaried workers, $315 000 seemed like a princely sum. To ask for an increase just two and a half years on from signing up, appeared quite unwarranted. Some of those police officers who had always stood by him, quietly moved away. Among the ranks of officers that even Ryan admits weren't paid enough, resentment began to grow. 'He was a police officer and there he was earning huge bucks, mixing with celebrities and going off to things like Kerry Packer's son's wedding,' says a former senior officer. 'What were we all to make of that?'

As the election campaign swung into top gear, Ryan, now branded Australia's highest-paid public servant, found himself press-ganged, often quite innocently, into helping the Government's cause. He was pictured shaking hands with Whelan in an ALP newspaper advertisement. He was named by Carr in a TV political commercial as the man Labor appointed to reform the service. When Chikarovski promised 2500 extra police if elected, and Ryan was pressed by journalists to respond to Whelan's claim that the Goulburn police training college couldn't cope with such a huge extra influx, he found himself trapped. Forced to admit that no, it couldn't, he was instantly accused of getting involved in politics, and told sharply to 'butt out'. It was exactly the politicisation of the police service that Justice Wood had warned about in his final Royal Commission report. Three days later, Carr announced plans for an extra 400 police deployed into flying squads to swoop on problems, and said Ryan had helped him draft them.

I didn't realise this was happening at first, until I started seeing pictures of myself alongside politicians used as a way of promoting them. As far as police numbers went, we'd always said we wanted more civilians rather than more police, to release police for general duties. But when pressed, we did an analysis of how many police we could get through the training system without breaking it or expanding it to an unacceptably expensive level, and 1200 was the number we came up with. Immediately, Carr stands up saying this number was what we could recruit. So Kerry stands up and says she'll give us 2500. When I was doorstopped to comment and said the system couldn't cope with that, this was taken as a direct criticism, and therefore political. It was quite unnecessary to drag me into politics the way they did. Our relationship went downhill from there.

The strength of his relationship with Labor was sealed tight, however, by their resounding election win, with a 6 per cent Statewide swing. Onlookers wondered aloud whether such a convincing victory would leave them unbeatable for almost another decade. But there were perils in being so tightly allied with politicians that Ryan would only fully appreciate much later. And, of course, there was danger in feeling infallible, particularly when you were being feted by an adoring public wherever you went.

In the meantime, it wasn't as if Ryan had nothing else but his political masters, and the escalating row over his salary to occupy him. More and more, he was becoming caught up in preparations for the Sydney Olympics, little more than a year away. He visited Washington, making contacts within the FBI, the CIA, the Defence Intelligence Agency and the State Department in Washington, ironing out the two countries' support arrangements and exchanging intelligence on terrorists, as well as attending the multimillion-dollar three-day Westwind disaster simulation at an old military base near Los Angeles in which one of the potential worst-case scenarios of the Games was played out: terrorists releasing deadly gas at an airport.

'It was a valuable lesson in how we should take charge in Sydney,' says Ryan. 'The interesting thing with the Americans was that no one was actually in charge, and everyone claims to be in charge – until something goes wrong and then there's no one in charge at all.' A seemingly spontaneous, totally unanticipated, series of demonstrations around the world by Kurdish groups chilled everyone, realising how quickly, over the Internet, activists could organise events without intelligence agencies even realising. Later, he visited Israel for secret talks on the terrorist threat, and to reassure authorities that their athletes would be adequately protected while in Sydney. He realised just how seriously they took personal security when he and other members of the delegation were offered a tour of Jerusalem city. They all turned up in casual clothes, ready to mix and mingle with the other tourists. But their escorts had other ideas. They turned out to be soldiers with loaded machine guns who surrounded the group completely, insisted they keep moving at all times, and parted the crowds before them.

Yet Ryan could never forget that however many enemies there might be overseas, there were still plenty back home. When a Sydney newspaper printed the story that Ryan was away visiting Israel, the couple's home was attacked, and the garden vandalised. Opposition police spokesman Andrew Tink also took the offensive. After admitting he'd been refused when he'd tried under the freedom of information laws to find out more about Ryan's new contract, he claimed the Commissioner was putting the Olympics above all else, and neglecting his work in New South Wales.

Certainly, there was always plenty happening back home. In April, the historic Drug Summit was held following a fresh controversy over illegal shooting galleries. Ryan made the opening speech and pointed out how existing legislation was impossible to properly enforce. Before an injecting room could be raided, for example, police had to know exactly who was taking drugs and what kind of drugs they were. There was no way to force arrested people into treatment, and there wasn't the leeway to caution people in possession of small quantities of soft drugs; everyone had to be dealt the same black-and-white criminal approach. 'I said we needed the drug laws overhauled to make it clear what police could do and how, work out the end product of enforcement – treatment, sentencing, drug courts. It wasn't particularly popular with some. The debate was very emotive, with people talking from a moral stance rather than a practical one. In the end, we had three days, but nothing really constructive came out.' Ryan's harm-minimisation approach of trying to reduce the demand for drugs, and improve treatment options for drug-users, was often in stark contrast to Carr's tough 'Say No' stance. Ryan's stand did prove to be influential, however, in helping soften the Premier's approach and eventually the legal injecting room experiment was allowed to take place in Kings Cross.

Meanwhile, the pressure on Ryan to reveal details of his new contract and salary continued unabated. Eventually, New South Wales Auditor-General Tony Harris joined the fray, and asked Ryan to waive his confidentiality clause. Ryan finally agreed, and everyone waited, with bated breath, to find out the truth of his new deal. The revelation would harm him perhaps more than any other single issue of his time in the job.

CHAPTER 21

The end of
a dream

Ever since Peter Ryan joined the police force at the age of 16, there'd been one job he'd dreamed of: the Commissioner of London's Metropolitan Police. It was the absolute pinnacle of British policing – the head of one of the largest forces in the world, with 27 000 officers and 12 000 full-time civilians and an annual budget of £1.5 billion ($4 billion at the rate of the time). More than twice the manpower of the New South Wales force, and more than three times its budget, with it came an automatic knighthood, and the prestige of being responsible for protecting the Royal Family and the British Parliament, as well as 8 million Londoners.

To a boy from the north of England, it seemed an ambition well beyond his wildest imaginings. But suddenly, after forty years in the service, he was almost there. The call had come in May 1999. It was the Home Office in Whitehall. He'd been named as one of four possible candidates for the post, would he be interested? It seemed a ridiculous question – like asking a cricketer if he fancied captaining Australia. And the interview was scheduled for June when he'd planned to be in Britain anyway, visiting family and friends, so why not?

Ryan thought he was in with a real chance of winning the job. He had greater and wider experience than at least two of the other contenders, but he and the serving deputy John Stevens would probably be just about neck and neck. Yet by the time of the interview, held on a scorching summer's day in London, he was in a quandary about whether he truly wanted the job. The Met were just discovering more corruption in the ranks, and wanted someone tough, and a cleanskin outsider, to try and stamp it out. From his experience in Australia, he was perfectly cast, and well used to the challenges and strains of working as a foreign outcast. The week before, however, he'd addressed the annual Chief Police Officers' summer conference in Manchester and had grimaced at the Left versus Right politics of the industry, and the endless debates about the nature of policing, with never any concrete conclusions reached.

> I wasn't convinced I wanted it. I was genuinely committed to what I was doing here in Australia, and was getting lots of support. I also found myself operating as an Australian officer rather than a British one. They were full of mealy-mouthed promises of how they would improve community services, instead of real action. The debate was the same one I had left behind three years ago. Also, they had no experience of the type and complexity of ethnic community policing I'd faced in New South Wales. They saw the problems in simple terms of Afro-Caribbean areas of London being more antagonistic and difficult to police. Nevertheless, the opportunity for a British police officer to be head of Scotland Yard was too good to miss. It had been a personal dream all my life.

The interview went extremely well. He could answer every question the panel put to him, while shuddering at the quality of some of the questions asked by the lay members. He got the distinct impression that the panel had found him a harder, tougher person than they'd anticipated, more forthright and pragmatic. They also clearly considered him an Australian, and someone from outside the British system was exactly what they wanted. By the time he left, he knew he must be one of the favourites for the job. But then came the disaster. Breaking from their tradition of keeping the interview process confidential, and only announcing the successful candidate on his appointment as the new Commissioner, the Home Office announced the candidates publicly. This was immediately picked up by the London and Sydney newspapers.

Suddenly, Ryan found himself under siege. Journalists called him every minute of the day. Whelan rang him to ask what the hell was going on. Ryan tried to stall them all. No, he hadn't exactly gone after the job, he told everyone truthfully. Yes, he was very flattered, but he wasn't sure even if he'd want the post. No, the Met hadn't made a decision yet. Then Bob Carr called. He was furious. He'd just given Ryan a new contract, he barked at him. He'd just given him a huge pay rise. If he didn't withdraw his application and get straight back to Sydney, he might find he no longer had a job to come back to.

As an ultimatum, it couldn't have been clearer. Ryan was distraught. He called the Home Office. Could they tell him if he was likely to get the job? He needed to make his decision immediately. The Home Office would not be hurried. They appreciated his position, and were shocked at the way he was being threatened by his paymasters in Sydney, but they couldn't work through the due process any faster. Ryan was in a terrible dilemma. He'd dearly love to see if he could get the Met post, and then make his decision of where to see out the last few years of his police career, but he could well end up not getting the Met and losing his Sydney job at the same time. He could finish up with nothing at all. On the other hand, this would, realistically, be the last chance he'd have at such an influential post. The successful applicant would sign a five-year contract by which time Ryan would be 60, and considered too old to try again. He didn't know which way to turn. This was clear to the friend with whom the Ryans were staying at the time, Barry Newton.

He was a tortured man. He was so torn, he really was. The phones were ringing constantly, and we sat and talked about it all night. He would have loved that job, Peter is all about making a difference, and he could have done that there. That job would have been the ultimate recognition that you've reached the very top of your career.

But the pressure the politicians from Sydney put him under to withdraw was immense and the abuse and four-letter words they were shouting down the phone . . . I would have told them to shove their job. But he stood his ground – to a point. He was very, very brave. There's a point at which most normal people have to say, 'Enough is enough!' I would have cracked, but he

didn't. At the beginning of the Met interview process, I put a bet
on him getting the job. He'd worked as an agent of change in
Bramshill and in Sydney, and had dealt with corruption and ethical questions. He was the ideal candidate. But all that pressure
from Australia wore him down, I think. It took his mind off the
task at hand. By the end, he was going in an even bet.

Finally, after two days of sitting around talking through all his
options, and nights filled with urgent phone calls to and from Sydney, he called the Home Office, with an extremely heavy heart, to
officially withdraw from the race. Whitehall was shocked. Did he
understand what he was doing, when he was so close to the prize?
'Yes,' he replied. 'I do. But I really have no choice.' Even today, Ryan
resents the position he was put in. 'It was hard to walk away from
that,' he says. 'I've still not really got over it, even though I might not
have been offered the job in the end. That was my last chance.
I found it hard to believe I would ever be treated in such a way.' John
Stevens, the deputy, now Sir John Stevens, was eventually given the
job. Carr always denied to the media that he'd put any pressure on
Ryan to return.

The atmosphere was no easier when Ryan returned to Sydney. He
struggled to put a brave face on the situation, proclaiming himself to
be a true 'Aussie' who'd decided to stay after talking it through with
Adrienne but, in reality, he was devastated. Adrienne too was disappointed, having often mused on the possibility of becoming 'Lady
Ryan'. Worse was to come, too. The Carr Government had been
resisting all the applications to the New South Wales *Freedom of
Information Act* to release details of Ryan's new employment package
but, when it looked as though the Administrative Appeals Tribunal
might take a different view, Ryan was finally asked by the Government
to consent to its release. Ryan's new salary, it was at last revealed, was
$425 000 – more than twice the Premier's salary of $188 000, just
under double the Prime Minister's $231 000 and $80 000 more than
the Met Commissioner receives.

It wasn't until October, however, that the rest of the contract was
made public. Ryan would receive a bonus of an additional year's pay
if he completed his contract, and would walk away with nearly two

years' salary if the Government sacked him without giving him a year's notice. In his defence, he insisted that headhunters had priced him at more – although when it later emerged that his professional executive recruitment advisors had said senior executive roles carried salaries of $600 000 to $700 000, including business-class airfares for wives, and second cars – it only served to fan the flames. Adrienne was indignant. 'This was a tool used in the negotiation – not a demand by Peter but, as is the norm, the media are distorting it to make it look as if that's what he was actually demanding. Peter's biggest concern is that the police might see him as a greedy bastard.' Again, Ryan denied the package was anything other than a man holding such a tough position deserved. Again, the public's warmth cooled just a little more towards him.

It was a controversy that he could not seem to shake off. Towards the end of the year it flared again when the Auditor-General Bob Sendt referred the end-of-contract bonus and damages payout to the New South Wales Crown Solicitor for a ruling on its legality. The Opposition then released independent legal advice claiming the contract was not covered by a State Act, and could be void, and the Legislative Council committee decided to hold an inquiry. Eventually, the Crown Solicitor ruled it was, in fact, invalid, but could be fixed simply by drawing up a separate agreement, which was duly done. Yet even in the first half of 2000, he was coming under attack. Liberal frontbencher John Brogden, later to become Leader of the Party, likened Ryan to Alan Bond.

The job seemed to be getting harder every day. Ryan's deputy, Jeff Jarratt, had been criticised at a Police Integrity Commission hearing for shortlisting former inspector Angus Graham, who resigned from the service after three internal misconduct charges, for the job of commander of New South Wales Police State intelligence. Ryan told the inquiry that Jarratt was guilty of 'very poor judgement'. The PIC ordered him to undertake a course on police ethics, and Ryan sent him on an executive development program at the FBI Academy. Previously, Jarratt had been overseeing the operations of the whole service after the death of his fellow deputy Bev Lawson, which Ryan admits was a huge task. Now, Ryan split the job in half and gave Jeff the role of looking after the general duty operations of uniformed officers and detectives only, and advertised his former role of commanding police specialist operations. Ryan says he'd perhaps been expecting too much of Jarratt, doing two people's jobs at once. He hadn't wanted to fill the gap left by Lawson at the time of her death, but now felt that the time was right.

He'd warned Jarratt about shortlisting Graham, and told him he didn't expect Graham to get the job, but believes that, ultimately, there were far more important issues the PIC should have been investigating. 'It just reflected the paranoia about how the police service operated,' says Ryan. 'Graham didn't get the job, so what was the point of dragging it all up again?' A few months later, however, another complaint against Jarratt was referred to the PIC, this time over an allegation that he 'did not show due prudence' in accepting hospitality from the US Motorola corporation which was bidding for a new $28-million police radio network, although there was no suggestion he had been compromised by the act.

There were also problems with other officers. There were a number of complaints filed against a favoured employee of Ryan's, Chief Superintendent Lola Scott, the second-most senior policewoman in New South Wales, who was known to be a strong supporter. Ryan dismissed the complaints by some of her officers about her management style as 'personal politicking' at a time when the deputy position was up for grabs. There were also problems later with hard-core pornography circulating on the Internet, with officers being suspended as a result. It was an issue Ryan felt particularly strongly about. He'd been angered that 10-year-old Georgina had received unsolicited pornographic emails, and warned other parents to check their children's computers.

On the crime front, life was busier still. When Federal Justice Minister Senator Amanda Vanstone accused New South Wales police of having a far lower arrest rate of heroin dealers than Victoria, Ryan was dismissive. It was simply because the Victorian Police recorded crime completely differently, he said, using methods out of step with the rest of Australia. 'She tried to blame us for rising crime, when we should have been praised for better recording!' he says.

Meanwhile fresh New South Wales Bureau of Crime Statistics and Research data showed there'd been no increase in crime for the first time in a decade, vindicating Ryan's belief that the huge jump in the previous figures merely reflected the fact that crime had been going unreported by a disillusioned public and by police officers anxious to look better on paper than they were doing in reality. At last he felt he was getting somewhere. But Ryan was still having problems cutting through all the bureaucratic paperwork that threatened to swamp his push for reform. However, one major victory was the Federal Government's go-ahead for the national database to track criminals through DNA and fingerprint evidence, and the linking of Australian police force databases through a central source – Ryan's personal brainchild. He'd campaigned long and hard for a National Crime Information System (CrimTrac), a national criminal database to include outstanding warrants, previous convictions, sex offenders, even DNA profiles. At a sporting event in Sydney, Ryan found himself sitting opposite Prime Minister John Howard. 'A few minutes of your time please, Prime Minister,' Ryan called over. Howard agreed, and Ryan sold him his idea. Howard was enthusiastic and later pledged the $50 million needed.

In September 1999, Ryan triumphantly announced that a major crime syndicate had been broken after 150 police took part in raids and arrested nine people over a spate of murders, woundings and drive-by shootings. In his continual quest to free more police for beat duties, he also founded a police call centre – the Police Assistance Line, or PAL – for the phone reporting of non-life-or-death incidents (such as car theft). Although the Opposition decried the experiment, Ryan says it has worked well. It now receives around 75 000 calls a month, saving countless hours of officers' time on station front desks. The only problem seems to have been some officers becoming too lazy to take down details of a crime themselves when the public actually rings stations, and referring them to PAL instead.

Yet still Ryan never quailed from stirring controversy. At one point, he started a huge debate when he accused Australians of being rude and selfish. At another, he spoke out in favour of juveniles committing serious crime being 'named and shamed'. 'The purpose was to explode the myth that serious offenders were not innocent little kids in shorts and short socks – quite the opposite,' he says.

Preparations for the Olympics were also still taking up much of

Ryan's time. Speculation that $16 million would be cut from operational spending to fund security arrangements for the Games and pay rises was causing alarm in the suburbs, particularly those with ongoing crime problems. There was outrage over a plan to axe one-man police stations, and to draw an extra 400 police from busy metropolitan stations to help out security at Games venues, bringing the total allocation up to 4900. The year before, Ryan had started a novel program for officers in the city to effectively stalk each suburb's worst repeat offenders in a bid to curb their activities. It was a fairly blunt tactic aimed at letting them know they were being watched, so they would realise that they wouldn't get away with any crimes that they did commit. The intent was to persuade them either to reform or, more realistically, to leave the city. The results were already promising. Only one class of criminals were never likely to reform, says Ryan: pedophiles. During the uproar over the release of John Lewthwaite, who murdered a 5-year-old twenty-five years before, Ryan said little. Lewthwaite had to be rescued from his home after an hysterical mob threatened to drag him out on to the street and lynch him. And while he abhorred mob justice and vigilantism in any form, as a parent himself, Ryan could understand the fears of Lewthwaite's neighbours. 'Pedophiles never reform,' he would say privately. 'They will always re-offend.'

The first indications of trouble from another front, however, passed completely unnoticed. A five-person unit called the 'Behavioural Change Group' was complaining at being gradually phased out, and had contacted some journalists asking them to write stories about their plight. They seemed to be suggesting that Ryan, incredibly, together with other senior officers, was working covertly to undermine their pioneering efforts to ensure that reform was taking place in the New South Wales service. Ryan was *blocking* reform? That was big news and in a few months everyone would know the names of his accusers.

CHAPTER 22

Cabramatta claims another victim

Peter Ryan was growing increasingly depressed about how his new life in Australia was turning out. Every day, he seemed to be angry, hurt and disappointed about some new obstacle to change, the constant close journalistic scrutiny, and the way his critics always appeared to receive far more sympathetic hearings in the press. He and Adrienne began arguing more and more as the strain began to tell on their relationship. Friends told the couple to let the criticism and the attention wash over them. They tried, but they still couldn't help devouring the newspapers every day and taking every disparaging word to heart. They itched to hit back, and put the record straight but, whenever they did talk to the press, it either seemed to prolong the discussion or make the situation worse.

Ryan was also missing his elder daughter, Elizabeth, 12. She'd begged to be allowed to return to England to the private girls' boarding school, St Swithun's in Winchester, to be close to her old friends. She also needed to get away from the pressures at her Sydney school of being the New South Wales Police Commissioner's daughter. It had been a difficult decision but, in the end, they had let her go, even though they dreaded the press finding out and accusing them of being poor parents to boot. Ryan and Elizabeth had always been extremely close. 'Dad had always read me stories about the girls' boarding school, Mallory Towers, and I really wanted to try one out,' says Elizabeth. 'I thought it would be cool; no one would know who Dad was. I didn't want to come home every night any more and hear what they were writing about him in the papers.

Ryan is announced as the new Police Commissioner of New South Wales by Premier Bob Carr at a press conference in June 1996.

Photograph: Rick Stevens, Sydney Morning Herald

The family, with Georgina (left) aged six, and Elizabeth (centre) aged eight, pose for a last photo at Bramshill together, in July 1996, before Ryan left to take up his new post in Sydney.

Ryan is sworn in as a member of the New South Wales Police on 30 August 1996.
Photograph: Andrew Taylor, Sydney Morning Herald

Ryan's bold move in January 1997 to interview all his senior staff and tell them bluntly whether they had a place in his new structure sparked fresh controversy.
Cartoon: Courtesy of Warren Brown and Daily Telegraph

Ryan's appointment caused a sensation in the press, with many seizing on the issue of appointing an Englishman to head the New South Wales police.

Cartoon: Courtesy of Warren Brown and Daily Telegraph

Ryan returned to Britain in June 1997 to proudly watch Adrienne graduate with her BA in Politics and International Relations.

Ryan announces in June 1998 that Ken Moroney will join Jeff Jarratt as a Deputy Commissioner, five months after the death of Bev Lawson. Left to right: Ryan, Moroney, Police Minister Paul Whelan, Jarratt.
Photograph: Rick Stevens, Sydney Morning Herald

Ryan visited his officers at Lakemba police station shortly after the building was sprayed with gunfire in November 1998 in a drive-by shooting after an increase in gang activity in the area.
Photograph: Steven Siewert, Sydney Morning Herald

During Ryan's visit to the 1998 Winter Olympics in Nagano, Japan, a row over whether he was being white-anted at home flared.

Photograph: Jason South, The Age

Ryan visits Israel in February 2000 to consult with the Government and Mossad about the likely terrorist threat during the Sydney 2000 Olympics.

Full of relief after the 'best-ever' Olympics, Ryan fools around at the home of his best friend Colin Henson, with Henson's daughter Fiona looking on.

The Ryans share their Australian Christmas celebrations every year with their close friends, the Hensons. The year 2001 was typical. Left to right: Georgina, Elizabeth, Peter, Adrienne, Alex Henson, Loretta Henson, Fiona Henson, Amanda Henson, Colin Henson.

A rare opportunity to relax with a family holiday at Port Stephens in January 2002. Georgina is sitting; Elizabeth stands.

In this 2002 cartoon, *Sydney Morning Herald* artist Alan Moir nicely captures how the new Police Minister Michael Costa seemed to be constantly sidelining Ryan. Moir often portrayed Costa with a parrot on his shoulder pointing the way, in a blunt reference to radio host Alan Jones's perceived influence on policing policy. Cartoon: Alan Moir, Sydney Morning Herald

The announcement on 10 April 2002 that Ryan's tenure as Commissioner was being terminated two years before the end of his contract came as a complete surprise to many onlookers. Carr speaks at the press conference while Ryan looks on.

Photograph: Andrew Taylor, Sydney Morning Herald

17 April 2002, and Ryan struggled to hold back the tears as he left police HQ for the last time to the stirring strains of a lone piper, the salutes of his officers and an applauding crowd.   Photograph: Andrew Taylor, Sydney Morning Herald

It had really been getting to me. I'd started developing headaches. Whenever dad got upset, I'd get upset too. It was like sympathy pains.' Ryan missed her terribly. Talking weekly on the phone was a very poor substitute. Of course, Georgina was still at home, but she was often quiet and withdrawn.

Her father found it hard to buoy her, or anyone, up. The interminable rows over his salary were fast dragging him down. One newspaper asked readers to write in with their views of Ryan, and he came home that evening in a very black mood. 'We ended up having a fight about nothing in particular,' says Adrienne. 'I blamed it on him brooding about the stories, but he denied it. The following morning, he told me to put the house on the market as, when the time came, he wanted to leave Australia, and didn't want to be tied to a property.'

On the surface, Ryan was trying to put a brave face on life, but every day it was harder. Trouble had been rumbling close to the surface all the way through the run-up to the Olympics, only to erupt with a vengeance after the Games.

In February 2000, the first signs had come with the re-emergence on the political scene of the 1998 downgrading of the notorious Cabramatta police district. New South Wales Opposition police spokesman Andrew Tink claimed he had been told that the lower ranking meant fewer resources were allocated to the station. Ryan continued to insist it was purely an internal measure gauging the effectiveness of a particular local area command. Overseas on business, he phoned his deputy Jeff Jarratt, whom he'd just signed up for a further five-year contract, to ask his advice. 'I had told Jarratt to run the police force while I concentrated on the Olympics,' says Ryan. 'I believed he knew what was going on, and I took his advice on trust.'

Ryan then went straight on the offensive on two Sydney radio stations, saying that crime was down in the area. 'We've reclaimed the streets in Cabramatta to a large extent,' announced Ryan. 'We've had such a success [there], it's no longer regarded as dangerous or as [the] difficult place it used to be.' It was a statement that exposed him to instant ridicule in the press, which pointed out that there had been a number of shootings and two murders in the area in the last four months, and by sections of the local community, angry still about the level of crime. Cabramatta Chamber of Commerce president Ross

Treyvaud accused Ryan of abandoning the area. Ryan, however, insisted on his return to Australia that it still wasn't necessary for him to visit the area. That, of course, wasn't a popular position to take.

That night, he didn't sleep well at all and by 2 a.m. he was lying wide awake. An hour later, he went downstairs and started working through his papers about the behavioural and cultural change of the service, a subject that was being increasingly sandwiched in between Olympics commitments, police changes, and having to respond to media criticism about Cabramatta. Eventually, under increasing pressure, he indicated he'd visit the troubled suburb – the same day the Sydney *Daily Telegraph* discovered he'd agreed to sit as a subject for the art world's prestigious Archibald Prize.

He was furious at the juxtaposition of the two issues. 'The headlines intended to indicate I was sitting in my office for a portrait for ten hours while there were burnings and shootings in Cabramatta,' he says. 'But that had been over five sittings while I'd been doing paperwork, and the artist had been thrown out a couple of times when I was busy.' One area command faxed over their support for Ryan and other regional commanders phoned in to sympathise. But Ryan was devastated. He'd had meetings with a couple of editors, imploring them to lay off the personal attacks and said they'd agreed to stick to comment on operational policing matters. He was hurt; he'd believed them. Then a few more reporters called up asking for interviews, and saying how they'd thought it had been most unfair. He was heartened by their concern. Another journalist, this time from the *Daily Telegraph*, eager for a follow-up audience, rang his press secretary, saying that everyone now regretted it had been put on the front page.

Showing the same extraordinary naivety he'd always had when dealing with the media, Ryan took all their expressions of support in good faith, and used them as evidence of being hard-done-by, apparently not realising that the vast majority of journalists, eager for an interview, will say virtually anything to capture the confidence of their subject. For most of his time in office, this lack of understanding of the media, allied with a lack of professional expert guidance from a person strong-willed enough to make him comply with their advice, compounded his problematical relationship with journalists. Instead, he continued to judge them by his own simplistic rule of thumb: if you weren't for him, you were against him. It didn't take long for any favoured journalist, after writing a positive story, to be cast back into the wilderness as a traitor for any faintly critical report. Was he being paranoid? Well, as the old joke goes, just because you're paranoid doesn't mean they're not out to get you. His public popularity was Ryan's greatest strength at a time of open hostility to the change he'd been brought in to expedite. As that started to slide, his enemies in the police, politics and media were realising that they had found a substantial chink in this white knight's armour.

The irony is that Ryan's Jesuit education had given him a very strong belief in honour and duty. The sense of right and wrong literally beaten into him made it hard for him to understand why anyone would even question his motives. And that steely core that allowed no self-doubt and which had sustained him throughout his meteoric rise through the ranks of the British police would prove an instrument of his undoing. For while the true politicians around him could bend and shift in the wind, Ryan felt no need to be diverted from his goals. And while he felt compelled to be honest, sometimes painfully so, he was bewildered by the way the facts were either ignored or twisted beyond recognition to always present him in an unfavourable light. The very idea that he could have a 'gentleman's agreement' with journalists, however senior, betrayed an almost Pollyanna naivety. Ryan still took it as a bitter personal betrayal if anyone else seemed to be acting what he might see as unprofessionally. 'The Jesuits' training is all about morality and crusading,' says his friend Geoff Officer, who was once a Catholic priest. 'The idea of being some kind of saviour, of the police, of those who wanted to do good, is very attractive to him. He's a very *good* man, with a simple morality, but there is a naivety about him that makes him totally unprepared for those ready to play gutter politics around him.' Friend Colin Henson says, 'He's an extremely honourable man. When he bought his house in Killara [next door to Henson's] at auction he suddenly realised he'd forgotten his chequebook. I said I'd write a cheque for him, but he said that wouldn't be appropriate at all. Instead, our son drove him home to get his own chequebook.'

But often circumstances prevented Ryan from defending his corner. At Cabramatta, for instance, the Local Area Commander Peter Horton was facing a threat of industrial action and a vote of no-confidence from his own officers because of dissatisfaction with his management style. When Ryan was pressed by the media as to whether he still had confidence in Horton, he said he was doing a very fine job. Ryan felt he couldn't say anything else. He understood a complaint had been made to the PIC about the way Horton was running Cabramatta, so felt to cast any doubts on his performance could prejudice any subsequent inquiry. 'I was stuck,' says Ryan. 'He wasn't doing a bloody fine job at all, but I couldn't say so. [Police Minister Paul] Whelan and I looked at each and said, "This is going to come back on us."' Before the no-confidence motion was cast, Horton asked for a transfer out of Cabramatta. He was gone by the end of May.

Meanwhile a new figure had just emerged in the Cabramatta melee. His name was Sergeant Tim Priest, a former drug-squad officer and the son of New South Wales RSL president Rusty Priest. He'd sent a letter to New South Wales Police Association president Mark Burgess, which was passed on to Ryan, claiming senior officers were covering up the true crime rate to win promotion and that: 'They are prepared to destroy any decent police officer willing to fight the odds and continue to make a difference . . . if you speak out or don't agree with the policies, you get cut to pieces.' This presented a whole other nightmare for Ryan. He claims an internal investigation was being conducted into Priest on another matter – something later confirmed by Priest – and that his outburst was directly related to this fact. If Ryan were to reveal this, however, doubtless Priest would complain to the media that the move was exactly the kind of cover-up tactic he was trying to expose. Ryan felt trapped and his inability to deal with Priest or his complaints would give the anti-Ryan forces not just another issue but another, credible, voice of dissent.

Even the appointment of Superintendent John Sweeney to the Cabramatta commander's post failed to calm unrest at the police station. In August, officers started planning another vote of no confidence, this time in Sweeney. Jarratt was called in to thrash out a resolution.

On a completely different front, the gang issue was threatening to explode. Ryan had blamed a spate of gang-related violence on the streets of Sydney's south-west on Lebanese gangs, calling on the community to 'own' their criminals in the same way as they claimed their sporting heroes, a cry that unleashed the ire of many in the Lebanese and Muslim communities, as well as civil libertarians and politicians. Later, the Australian Bureau of Criminal Intelligence started work on a report about gang violence, asking officers specifically to list any ethnic link to gangs and, the following year, Carr – who'd once criticised Ryan for linking crime and ethnicity – actually talked of migrants being responsible for many of the problems. Ryan felt exonerated. 'The problem with ethnicity and crime will always be with all our societies,' he says, naming Triad groups from Southeast Asia, Middle Eastern gangs, 5T Vietnamese gangs and the Russian Mafia which, he says, is quietly and slowly also emerging in Australia. 'Following the arrests of some of the dangerous people, my office received many threats against my family and me.'

His long-term prognosis is, however, pessimistic. 'I don't think we can beat gangs,' he says. 'We can make some important inroads. People make a lot of fuss about areas being made dangerous by gangs, but the truth is that most people are safe, as it's usually gangs fighting each other.'

But the problems continued to come hard and fast. During the Queen's visit in March 2000, he was accused of behaving like her 'lap-dog'. A quarter of his police patrols were still without leaders. He was feeling enormously frustrated by a chronically slow and outdated promotions process. His thoughts on providing an early retirement plan for those over 45 were greeted with howls of derision by those who said experience should be just as important as youthful energy. A police officer, Constable Matthew Potter, was accidentally shot dead by a colleague while working in the station. In its first review of the reform process, the PIC said more than a quarter of internal inquiries into complaints against police were 'unsatisfactory'. And a new report found that there'd been a twenty-fold increase in the number of officers on stress leave in the past five years. Ryan, who remembers clearly the days from his own early career of picking up body parts from railway lines after a suicide and being threatened, as a young unarmed rookie, by men with bottles and knives, has little sympathy. 'The job is obviously stressful, but often these people don't work hard at all,' he says. 'If you profile those on leave, it's most often those who joined before 1988, and therefore they have enormously generous pensions. If they don't get promotion, for example, they choose to go off on stress leave. Some of them are just wimpish people.'

The bright spots, since they seemed increasingly few and far between, were to be cherished: the planned establishment of an Institute of Forensic Science; New South Wales joining the national CrimTrac program; Adrienne launching *A Silent Love*, her book on miscarriage; Ryan being presented with an honorary doctorate of law by Macquarie University; an extra $189 million from the State Government, earmarked mostly for new technology; the installation of mobile computer systems in 750 police cars; new laws to allow wider DNA testing of criminals; and the charging of a man for the bashing and rape of a 93-year-old woman in Wee Waa as a result of the historic mass DNA screening of the town's 600 men. 'I thought it was a good idea, and worth testing to see how far people were prepared to go to support the police,' says Ryan.

In August, on the eve of the Games, the news leaked out that, despite Bob Carr telling Parliament less than a fortnight before that police stations would not be closed, Ryan had refined his plans to do so. In mid October, the announcement came: seven suburban stations – Woolloomooloo, Pyrmont, Broadway, Paddington, Randwick, Mascot and Malabar – would close and be formed into three 'super-commands', operating out of Waterloo, Kings Cross and Surry Hills. 'Some of the stations were in a terrible condition,' says Ryan. 'This would give us better service and provide more officers for beat duty. But I didn't have much time to argue the case.' The community revolt was immediate. Local residents, big business and even police held public meetings to discuss the proposed changes. The battlelines were being drawn.

Trouble seemed to be coming from all directions. New claims emerged of misconduct at the Goulburn Police Academy, and the Australian Institute of Police Management at Manly was revealed to be under investigation. Then, after the Olympics, in October 2000, the small Behavioural Change Group that had been complaining the year before about being gradually phased out, went public, and all hell erupted. They claimed the reform process was being deliberately stifled, an allegation that, within the atmosphere of paranoia and distrust that reigned in the police service, was sure to grab headlines. And it did.

CHAPTER 23

The Sydney Olympics

When Peter Ryan first arrived in Sydney, he'd been thrilled at the prospect of organising security for the 2000 Olympics. It had been one of the main reasons he had taken the job – a massive challenge that could very well end up crowning a glittering police career. The Games were at a critical point in their history. If there was any repeat of the kind of tragedies that marred Atlanta in 1996 or the Munich Games in 1972 the chances were that it could finish the Olympics forever. No one would believe a trouble-free event on such a massive scale could ever again be staged.

Yet when Ryan started in New South Wales, he felt full of confidence. While he had never been to a Summer Olympics before, a contingent of 100 Australian officers had worked at the Games in Atlanta, some in quite senior positions, so he knew they would have valuable experience on which he could draw. A command structure, with Assistant Commissioner Dennis Gilligan at its head, was already in place. The New South Wales Government reassured him that everything was in an advanced state of preparation.

It wasn't long before he started feeling uneasy. Every time he asked direct questions about the security arrangements for the Games, he was assured, 'It'll be right, mate. Don't worry.' There were rarely any concrete answers. Whenever he managed to get Gilligan, who always seemed to have a million and one things to do, in his office, the response was the same: 'She'll be right.' Early in the process, Ryan consoled himself with the thought, however, that the man below Gilligan, Superintendent John Garvey, seemed bright, intelligent and a really good operator. If anyone could sort things out, it was him. But in 1996 Garvey was sacked, after being criticised by the Wood Royal Commission over an incident in 1985. Charges were dismissed in 2001, after a magistrate found the witnesses to be unreliable and the alleged victim a 'despicable person'.

'I never got a decent story out of Gilligan,' says Ryan. 'With Garvey gone and Gilligan still in charge, I was beginning to lose confidence. I wasn't getting any answers. Everyone was telling me things were going all right, but no one could show me how. I thought I needed someone in there I could trust and have confidence in that they could do the job.' So his first task was to clear what he saw as an obstruction and Gilligan left the service in the January 1997 restructure of the senior command.

But now Ryan started growing even more nervous. The two main men for the Sydney 2000 Olympics were gone, and he had little idea of what they'd put in place. Everyone around him was nonplussed. 'Oh well, it's still three years away,' they repeated, over and over. 'Don't worry about it. We'll get there in the end.' But for Ryan, the vague hope of perhaps getting lucky by the due date simply wasn't an option. His own time was already being overwhelmed by the demands of restructuring the service, purging it of corruption, organising promotions – and dismissals – and trying to give the Government instant results in the crime figures. He started looking around for someone he could trust to kick the run-up to the Games into gear.

Paul McKinnon's name cropped up time and time again. He wasn't an obvious choice. He had appeared twice on drink-driving charges in the 1980s, and been criticised by ICAC for his 'alarming' attitude to security when confidential police dossiers were leaked to the underworld by the State Intelligence Group he commanded. But there were not many senior officers left who'd be up to the job, and McKinnon struck Ryan as a man of a very high intellect and organisational ability, who had a rare flair for motivating the troops below him. Ryan called him into his office. From the look on McKinnon's face, he was preparing himself to be sacked. Ryan, however, gave it to him straight. McKinnon was equally direct in his response. He'd take on the job,

work on the Games until it was over, and then retire. He'd also have
the choice of officers he wanted to work for him. Ryan agreed, and the
two men solemnly shook hands.

It was a long, hard road. Many officers weren't interested in working in the Olympic Planning Unit (OPU); the massive upheavals in
the service meant there were a lot of fast-track opportunities for
bright, capable candidates, and the OPU was seen as a bit of a back-
water. To lure them over, many were given promotions well above
their ranks, and some couldn't cope with the demands of the work,
or were then poached back into mainstream policing. A number of
American 'experts' claiming to have held key roles in organising the
last Games volunteered their advice, until it was discovered that
many of them had spent the entire duration back in a crisis centre in
Washington. The FBI offered their expertise, and veterans of the
Barcelona and Seoul Games came forward. 'It was simply remarkable,' says Ryan wryly, 'just how many people claimed to have held
critical roles in all of these previous Games. Many of their roles were
completely exaggerated.'

McKinnon, as Commander, Olympic Security – responsible for
the command, control and coordination of security arrangements –
faced up to each fresh setback with cheerful resilience.

He did extraordinarily well. I hold him in great regard. He has a
reputation much bigger than the reality. He has had a chequered
past, he can be abrasive, he doesn't suffer fools gladly – *ever* –
he has his own way of speaking, McKinnon-speak, which you
have to learn to understand. But the bottom line is that he gets
things done, and he inspires enormous enthusiasm and loyalty
in people.

The pair would have weekly meetings sorting out plans, working
through proposals and deciding who to recruit from both inside the
service and beyond. The team grew as the Games approached, with staff
from ASIO, ASIS, the Australian Defence Force, the Australian Protective Service, the Australian Federal Police and the Australian Customs
Service all brought into one big unit, with a clear structure of command
under the single leadership of Ryan – a structure deemed necessary

from observing past Games. Underneath him, 5000 police would have responsibility for core issues such as security at venues and the Olympic Villages, while the non-core security roles, with their 3500 volunteers and 4000 private security guards, including controlling car access, were supervised by the police.

There was, naturally, much jostling for position, posturing, rows over poaching key personnel and personality clashes. Private security companies, realising they'd have a big role to play, started enticing police officers to join them with better salaries. Some sections of the service refused to hand over their best officers, while staff from other agencies had sometimes to be moved on after trying to insist their organisation was the one running the show. One afternoon, Ryan was sitting in on a presentation in Canberra by quite a junior member of the Australian Federal Police, and was shocked to hear, the AFP officer declare himself in charge of security for the Games. By early 1997, Ryan had managed to manoeuvre himself into the position of chair of the Olympic Security Working Committee, and put the focus on collaboration between the various key players: SOCOG, the Olympic Co-ordination Authority (OCA), the Federal Police, the Federal Government, the military, the New South Wales Government and the intelligence agencies.

> The main problem was that people kept trying to take over. But, at the end of the day, I knew if it all went wrong, you wouldn't be able to see them for dust – the blame would stop with me. So I made it clear there was one person in charge. I'd have to carry the can – I couldn't afford to expose myself through anyone's incompetence. A lot of people were still in a state of denial in any case that the Games would actually take place. And there was all the constant distraction of the restructuring, the Royal Commission, police officers shooting people, prisoners escaping, criticism, crime, the media, politics . . . I used to get cross, thinking, 'How much more do you want me to do? I'm reorganising police, and dealing with corruption, daily operational problems, Franca Arena, an election, storm, fire, flood and bloody mayhem, and I've still got to deliver the Games.' No one understood that workload.

Ryan brought back expertise from Israel, the UK and the USA, tested the planning and methodology against the Australian–New Zealand Risk Assessment Process, finetuned strategies and ensured everyone was working in the same direction. He launched major anti-terrorist exercises to rehearse a dozen possible scenarios, including a boat hijacking and a Games venue being captured by terrorists who threatened to release toxic gas. The problem seemed to be that many of the police involved didn't react appropriately since, unlike in Britain and the USA, they'd had so little real-life experience of terrorism in Australia. He held talks with the Prime Minister and Cabinet and every agency involved. By the time the Games were almost upon him, the Americans declared they were so impressed with the planning, that they were going to use it as a model for their Winter Games in Salt Lake City.

His masterstroke came, however, when he and McKinnon presented the detailed 'concept of operations' game plan to a board meeting of SOCOG late in 1997. 'This is the foundation of our entire operation,' he told the meeting. 'Change one aspect of it and, like dominoes, everything else will begin to fall over. So only in absolutely exceptional circumstances will we move from this position. If you insist later that anything is changed, and I don't agree, then I will transfer the risk of the Games to you in writing, so you assume the risk, and if anything goes wrong, it is your responsibility.' In the following years, various people tried to chip away at the framework, but Ryan always resisted the pressure.

Often unforeseen problems cropped up, and generally they were thrown at Ryan and his officers to solve.

Collaboration with SOCOG was very good, though sometimes tense. We were all planning for something outside of our experience. Whenever they found they couldn't work things out, like how the venues would operate and how they'd be managed, what would be the reporting lines from the main operating centre, the movement of goods and people, they asked us for advice. We gave them a police operational methodology on how we manage incidents, venues and structures, so many of the structures that went towards Olympic operations ended up being based on our original work. Many of their consultants knew about managing a business from an accounting base, or a product base, but they didn't know about managing an operation like delivering the Games. We manage operations all the time, and know about crisis management and we aren't averse to risk. Nevertheless everyone worked together as a team, everyone learned quickly and the results spoke for themselves. There were some extraordinarily good people among the SOCOG team, highly professional and competent operators, like Jim Sloman, Sandy Hollway, John Quayle and Bob Elphinston. But if others tried to interfere, I would go back to that original statement and say I'd transfer the risk to them. If anything went wrong, I was aware that I'd be the person to be pilloried; it wouldn't be any good to say, 'Well, *he* told me to do it.'

Yet by the eve of the Games in September 2000, Ryan still felt nervous. He hadn't slept properly for months. He'd been up by 3 o'clock every morning, nervously pacing the house. He'd tried sleeping tablets, but they rarely worked. Elizabeth, who'd eventually been brought back to Australia in July 2000 to live, was no longer talking to him, saying he never had anything nice to say to her. He was moody and aggressive, and none of his family could remember the last time they'd seen him smile. After one particularly bad argument, Adrienne told him to move out for a while if he would find it less stressful. But Ryan simply felt anxious all of the time, saying he felt as though everyone was drawing their strength from him to the point where he had nothing left. He'd prepared everything and everyone as well as he could, there were good people in charge of intelligence, venues and operations, but there were still so many unknowns he could do absolutely nothing about.

There had been threats of demonstrations by Aboriginal groups – with Charles Perkins talking of the Olympics being 'in jeopardy' from violence and riots on Sydney's streets – by environmentalists, by anti-globalisation groups who were due at the World Economic Forum in Melbourne just days before the Games, and anyone who seemed to have an axe to grind about absolutely anything. More than 300 individuals and groups had been identified as potential security threats, and ASIS and ASIO had been working closely with Interpol, the CIA, MI5 and Israel's Mossad. Locally, the person who'd placed a bomb on a Sydney ferry in 1998 had never been caught, a bomb packed with chlorine and left on a peak-hour Sydney train was discovered and defused just days before the start of the Games, unemployed artist Peter Hore was a long-term serial pest, disrupting numerous sporting fixtures as well as Michael Hutchence's funeral in late 1997, and, despite constant briefings by global intelligence agencies, Ryan knew a suicide bomber could walk into a crowd, pull a cord on his jacket, or open a bottle of fizzy drink that turned out to be a toxic chemical, and suddenly he'd be left dealing with a massacre.

At the turn of the new year 2000, an Algerian had been stopped by customs officials as he tried to cross from Canada to the USA, and his car was found to be packed with explosives. He was traced back to a terrorist cell connected with Osama bin Laden's Al-Qaeda terrorist organisation operating out of Jordan and, among a list of contacts found in his pockets, were two names and addresses in Australia. On investigation back in Sydney, they were discovered to be two overseas students who appeared to have no visible means of support and who, despite their protestations that they would be arrested as political prisoners if they dared to return home, had been back to Algeria and over to the Middle East six times in the past year. The Federal Government withdrew their student visas, and they both left the country. A few days before, on New Year's Eve, another man was arrested in the heart of Sydney in possession of a home-made grenade. It may not have killed anyone, but it would have caused a number of injuries.

In the strategic Olympic Security Command Centre, three monitors were constantly playing BBC World, CNN and Sky News, so police were aware of every change on the international political scene all hours of the day, and feeding it to their huge intelligence cell, coordinated by the Olympic Intelligence Centre, to analyse whether it would have an effect on Australia, and work out likely scenarios. Tensions in the former Yugoslavia were being carefully monitored in case a member of the community decided to use the Olympics as a publicity opportunity. Reports were being made daily on the conflict on the West Bank. Security plans for Israeli officials and athletes were being stepped up daily, while at the same time they were being told they could not bring their own guns and bulletproof armour into the country. Everyone was being prepared for every possible eventuality: biological, chemical, radiological warfare, even attacks by planes from the air, with some of the world's most sophisticated anti-terrorism equipment hidden away in Sydney – just in case.

The ringleaders of S11, the international group of anti-globalisation activists, were also being tracked through the FBI in the USA, and MI5 and MI6 in Britain. There'd been huge demonstrations around the world, often with associated violence and damage to property, and everyone feared the Olympics could be targeted, with indications there were plans to block entry to the Olympic Stadium and disrupt competition with sit-ins. Two known activists from Seattle were stopped from entering Australia, but others still managed to slip through the net and set up cells in Melbourne. Various intelligence sources reported they were training people how to instigate large-scale civil disobedience operations, how to disrupt police communications, and how to chain themselves together with large locks around their necks so they couldn't be moved. Most experts believed that, after the Melbourne meeting, most would move on to the World Summit G7 meeting in Prague rather than up to Sydney for the Games, but no one knew for sure.

The IOC visited regularly to examine progress on the Games. One of their two security advisors would visit every three months and make occasionally outlandish suggestions, for example, that mini-submarines be placed in the Harbour. Ryan would gently advise him every time that he would have Navy underwater search teams, there would be high security around the super-yachts and cruise liners due to visit from all corners of the globe, there would be dozens of people in the water during the Triathlon and sailing events, 200 extra water police were being selected to help and a whole new fleet of boats and jet-skis were being purchased to help. 'I think eventually he got the message that we weren't too interested in mini-submarines,' says Ryan. 'The last enemy submarines we had in the Harbour were the Japanese in World War II – and they didn't fare too well.'

Ryan was especially concerned about security at Sydney Airport.

He'd been trying, ever since his arrival, to take over security there, particularly during the Games when 300 000 international visitors were due to arrive, but the Government resisted, awarding the tender to the Australian Protective Service (APS). Ryan was not impressed that a couple of APS members had recently been found asleep on the job at Kirribilli House, the Prime Minister's Sydney residence, downloading pornography while guarding Defence offices in Canberra, and failing to prevent a man throwing a Molotov cocktail at Parliament House. 'All the airlines have their own security, and then the airport is guarded by a bunch of men in Ninja suits with little training in terrorist response,' says Ryan, tightly. Then there were fears about masses of spectators being disgorged from venues at the same times, with all the dangers of people falling and being trampled, stampedes and children being crushed, not to mention the presence of large overexcited, often inebriated, crowds all around Sydney every evening. The VIPs attending the event would also expect tight protection, while the 10 000 athletes, particularly the Americans and the Israelis, would be obvious targets – especially if they wanted to go out and party when their events were over. 'Eye in the sky' helicopters would be constantly buzzing overhead. 'As we've got closer, all the worries, all the fears are now coming home as people are at last realising how huge it all is,' said Ryan, two days before the Games' Opening Ceremony.

I'm very concerned about what could happen. I've considered bringing in more police from interstate, but those forces were going to charge us, and there are problems with accommodation and feeding the extra numbers. We've put our people in boarding schools, university dorms, and training facilities, but we've now run out of space, and I can't put constables in the Ritz Carlton. We've had to send some country officers back as, if they don't have digs or family in the city, I can't use them. As for the criticism from politicians, I can understand the concerns of those in rural areas worried about police leaving the bush, but I have no time for the politicians in metropolitan areas who are saying their police stations are going to be short-staffed. That's cheap, nasty politics. I didn't ask for the Olympics to be

here. They're going ahead, and I have to use the number of
police I think we're going to need. I don't need some newly
elected MP with no experience of running even a bloody raffle
to tell me how to police the Olympic Games.

The day of the Games' Opening Ceremony on 15 September, Ryan
visited the Aboriginal Australians living at the Tent Embassy set up in
Victoria Park. They were surprised by his visit, but pleased that a
Commissioner of Police had taken the trouble to call on their elders
personally, and held a ceremony burning gum leaves as a gesture of
friendship in his honour. If they were intending to hold any protest
marches, Ryan offered to remove any obstacles for them, to ensure
they would be peaceful and non-disruptive. Indeed, a couple of days
later, some of the S11 crowd arrived in Sydney and tried to join the
Tent Embassy. They failed completely. The Embassy dwellers made it
quite clear they didn't want them. Another demonstration in the city
by people protesting against Israeli policies in the West Bank was
watched carefully to see if it might trigger sympathy actions. For
months before the Games, Lola Scott had been liaising with those
groups most likely to protest during the Games. 'She wasn't too thank-
ful for the job initially,' says Ryan. 'But she is intensely loyal, so she
went off and did an outstanding job. She got to know all the different
people and we allowed small protests to take place and the boat with
the Aboriginal flag to sail up and down the Harbour but, in the end,
there was no trouble, and they attracted very little media attention.'

The evening of the Opening was clear and bright, and after the
spectacular display seen on television in hundreds of millions of
homes around the world, Ryan, Bob Carr, Sydney Lord Mayor Frank
Sartor, SOCOG chief executive Sandy Hollway and his deputy Jim
Sloman stood in the foyer of the Regent Hotel where they were all
staying, and had a drink together. 'I felt this massive euphoria,' says
Ryan. 'It wasn't just that we'd just witnessed something spectacular,
it was also that the Games had started without a hitch. Thousands of
people were thronging the streets, incredibly happy. After all those
years of planning, and the feeling, "The Olympics are coming, the
Olympics are coming," all of a sudden we'd arrived. There was no
turning back now.'

That night came the first trouble, at the live site in Martin Place. Mindful of the bombing which killed one and injured 110 people at the live site in Atlanta, Ryan had always been against the six live sites as they hadn't been catered for in the original security plan – the idea of putting up giant screens to show the Olympic events and adding bands and entertainment for afterwards had come late in the preparations. His main worry centred on the combination of the availabilty of copious amounts of alcohol through the relaxed licensing laws, excitable young people and, particularly, heavy-metal music. That first night after the Opening Ceremony fulfilled all of his expectations. Flower beds were trashed, all the bins were pulled up, the bunting was torn down and the place ended up littered ankle-deep in broken bottles. At times during the night, the police came close to losing control completely.

The following morning, at the daily GCOG meeting, Ryan insisted heavy-metal music no longer be played, and the site close down at midnight, with no more alcohol for sale afterwards. Public safety should be the first priority, he asserted, whereas the organisers had obviously put it last on their list. The other members protested, but he stood his ground, saying his officers would not police the area if this wasn't agreed to. The row rumbled on for a few days. Eventually, they reached a compromise and more family entertainment was provided at the sites instead, and a couple of bomb-search exercises were run through Martin Place in the early evenings.

From that moment on, there was hardly time to breathe. A group of Korean team officials was hijacked by two prison escapees from Silverwater Gaol. An average of fifteen threats started coming in each day, people saying they'd planted bombs on a train, on a bus, on an athletes' coach, in the Village, at the Opera House, on the Bridge . . . Each one had to be taken seriously and checked out thoroughly. Police worked around the clock to trace the threats arriving daily for Olympic President Juan Antonio Samaranch and Olympics Minister Michael Knight. Many came on email via elaborate routes through China, the former Soviet Union, the USA and New Zealand into Australia, in a bid to avoid detection. Two people in Australia and the USA were eventually questioned. Bags, parcels and packages were discovered and had to be carefully examined. Areas due to be visited by high-profile people, such as the American President's daughter Chelsea Clinton, or where there was a sporting clash between two hostile countries, had to be scoured minutely.

Even the Harbour ended up causing a few problems. There was a report one day of divers swimming beneath a catamaran that was used to host functions for the Prime Minister, his ministers and heads of business, half an hour before a high-level lunch meeting. The Government representative on board tried to insist the lunch be allowed to go ahead; Ryan refused point-blank. 'If the threat had been real, we could have ended up with the smoking ruin of a ship,' says Ryan. 'We had to make a decision and we made it. It was hard, but when you're dealing with people's lives, you have to make those tough decisions.'

Ryan was constantly walking around, always in uniform, telling all the officers on duty, the security guards and volunteers to stay alert, and not to let people through without tickets or passes. 'In my mind, I was constantly thinking, "Things must not go wrong." If anything did go wrong, I was intensely aware that could finish the Games forever. The responsibility was huge.'

Inevitably there were tensions between the organisers, now known as 'Sydney 2000'. The group would meet daily at 7 a.m. to discuss issues and problems that had arisen. Michael Knight, well-known for his abrasive style, would often be quite ruthless to those he thought should have solved the problems, says Ryan. He would be backed up by OCA Director-General David Richmond, the man who held the highest public-sector role in the Games, and SOCOG Deputy CEO Michael Eyers, in trying to apportion blame first rather than find solutions. 'I was lucky because I did not work directly for them,' says Ryan. 'In any case, security was going well and we were helping to solve other people's problems. We never came in for criticism.' Only once did Ryan suffer Richmond's ire. At the threat of a boycott on fuel supplies, Richmond barked that the police were slow and ineffectual when this had happened once years before. Ryan barked right back that there was a new regime in these days, under new management. 'Others round the table smirked and winked at me, as if to say, "Good on you!"' he says. Despite the tensions, it was a good and cooperative team effort. 'Michael Knight was a hard taskmaster, but he did have a hard task to do,' says Ryan. 'None of us could fail. The reputation of the country depended on us.'

Because the Games were running so smoothly, the IOC were able to find few problems. Their main obsession seemed to be how the Olympic family were transported and whether it was in a dignified enough fashion, and the pronunciation of French, the first language of the Olympics, at all the Games venues. 'That was a huge bone of contention for the IOC and they mentioned it in every single meeting from the first day to the last,' says Ryan. The next major concern seemed to be whether there were enough seats for IOC members at events, particularly the swimming.

Journalists were a constant headache. They'd try any subterfuge to get into restricted areas and Ryan, on visits to venues, found himself ejecting journalists from places they didn't have accreditation for. Invariably, they'd make a fuss. One American group even smuggled prostitutes into the media centre, and then claimed the sex workers had breached security, even though they'd been brought in as their guests.

The biggest problem loomed early. Ryan, starting work at 5 a.m. each day for the daily series of meetings and briefings, would make sure to spend as much time as he could walking around Olympic Park. By the Tuesday night of the first week, he became worried about two or three spots where the crowds were being crushed as some tried to leave and others arrived. As the evening venues began to open, he could see the problems would grow much worse. When Ryan raised the issue, Eyers responded that he'd just need to put more police officers in.

Ryan argued that wasn't a solution at all; there had to be a drastic revision of crowd-routing plans, particularly for Fridays, Saturdays and Sundays, when the number of visitors would double. He ordered that a senior officer from the Olympic Security Command work with relevant SOCOG staff to draw up a completely new plan and insisted on its implementation. Overnight, flower beds were torn up, new signs erected and barriers placed to completely change the flows of people, so that they could only move one way on any of the major through-routes. It gave them all an extra kilometre to walk to the railway station, but thinned the queues to make sure they could keep moving. It was a triumph.

I don't think GCOG appreciated exactly what happened, because after the Friday night when we had 450 000 people in the park, they all congratulated each other on how well it had gone, and completely ignored the fact that it was the police service working with one individual in the bowels of SOCOG that had actually made it happen. They'd ignored me for months on the issue of crowd movement, and we moved in and fixed it overnight.

Ryan also felt annoyed that SOCOG wasn't thanking the police for virtually running the venues for it, and was claiming all the credit for the smooth progress of the Games. But it was the police, he says, who were marshalling people, moving entertainers, looking after the entry and exit points, and who even ended up guarding the venues when it was all over – when that certainly wasn't part of the deal. 'That was supposed to be the venue managers' job,' says Ryan. 'But they all went off and had a party and then went home, leaving thousands of dollars, sometimes millions, worth of assets sitting there – TVs, computers, cameras, microwave links, everything that ran those venues. Some stuff did go missing but because of our presence, very little.' Eventually, towards the end of the Games, Ryan felt his anxiety lift, and allowed himself to start enjoying the occasion. He couldn't relax completely, however. He'd become so used to the press criticism by now, he didn't feel he could be seen to be having a good time.

'My experience with him was an extremely good one,' says McKinnon. 'There was the presence of trust between us and I knew if I cocked up he would tell me immediately. He listened to what I had to say, and he operated everything like a general and always behaved with impeccable dignity.'

A few days later, on 3 October 2000, Ryan sat down with his top officers at the Olympics breakfast for several hundred Olympic staff and volunteers to pay tribute to the organisers. He felt happy and relaxed that the Games had been such a massive success, and his officers had done a magnificent job to make it so. The organisers of the Athens Games had begged him to help them, Salt Lake City were asking for his contribution, and the IOC were inviting him to consult with them in the future. But, in Sydney, as he listened to the lists of people being awarded honours, he was shocked never to hear security mentioned once. The Games could never have taken place without all those security preparations, and with all his officers working so hard to put the procedures into place. Anything could have happened with 1.5 million excitable people milling around the city – people falling into the water at Darling Harbour, hysterical crowds at Circular Quay, people being trampled on at the railway stations . . . anything.

And although the police came close to losing control on a couple of occasions, in the end only four arrests were made in the biggest police operation Australia had ever seen, the world's biggest peacetime event. Yet Ryan sat at the breakfast with his contribution and those of his officers being totally ignored. The problem was that, since the police had effectively ensured nothing had been allowed to disrupt the Games, the organisers had simply assumed there had been no difficulties. It was the ultimate irony: Ryan would only have become a hero if something had gone dramatically wrong, and he'd solved it. Solving problems before they became difficulties didn't count.

> My staff were absolutely furious. We didn't want to walk away with laurel leaves around our necks, but we wanted to be mentioned for the way we supported, managed, changed, and fixed the Games. Many of my staff wanted to walk out, but I kept them at the table until the end. Then we were the first out of the room.
>
> I'd like to think it was deliberate, but I think it's just typical of the way this society treats the police. They are expected to be there and to do things to make us all safe, but get no thanks for it. They are the police, and they *should* do it. We'd been, as a police service, on our knees, hated, reviled, and blasted as corrupt, ineffectual and useless, yet while we were rebuilding the whole command and structure and fighting a rising crime rate, we'd delivered the Games. Against all the odds, we did it. It gave us a completely new spirit and sense of purpose. I think we performed miracles at those Olympic Games and now we were being completely ignored.

When Ryan arrived home that afternoon, he sat at his kitchen table, put his head in his hands, and wept.

CHAPTER 24

The chooks come home to roost

The relationship between Peter Ryan and the Police Integrity Commission was already a tense one. Despite their apparently complementary roles, with the PIC investigating corruption in the service and providing the checks and balances, and Ryan continuing his reforms, they'd frequently clashed, and Ryan felt they were often straying into his territory and hampering his investigations. A lengthy inquiry he'd been running into a notorious underworld figure, for example, had to be aborted just a few days off its conclusion when a PIC investigation crossed over. Ryan had been unimpressed, and his senior legal officer, Michael Holmes, advised him to lodge an official complaint. 'When the target walked, it made them the laughing stock of the underworld,' says Ryan, absolutely furious at the time.

We had to completely pull back because of them. It's pathetic. They could have been the biggest help to us in saving this police force and putting the criminals away, but they've become the greatest hindrance. When the PIC was first formed I used to have a good working relationship with them. That changed after I complained about them claiming the credit for a police internal affairs inquiry that resulted in officers going to jail. It had been purely a police operation, but their report implied they had been totally responsible for the inquiry and its outcome. Since that point, it seemed that, instead of working with me to solve the problems of the service, they worked alone.

This was very disappointing because I didn't see any of their corruption inquiries delivering tangible results.

Used to running his own race, he found it difficult to have such a huge body looking over his shoulder. The old Police Board had been axed to give him more authority over his officers; now the PIC, with its unprecedented powers to investigate police, seemed to be actively cramping his style. He was meant to be the most powerful New South Wales Police Commissioner in history, but now he railed against having dozens of statutory bodies, including the PIC and Ombudsman, and all the various civil liberties, privacy, ethnic and women's groups, scrutinising the service. And he resented their presence hugely. 'Each of the bodies had their own agenda and the recommendations they made often contradicted each other,' says Ryan. 'And it was a case of "do as I say, or else" – a bad report would be made to Parliament.'

Naturally, top of the list was the most powerful, the PIC, under Judge Paul Urquhart, which had been charged with auditing the progress of reform, as per the Royal Commission's recommendations.

This audit should have started when I commenced as Commissioner so that it could effectively measure the changes in the service from that time. Instead, it began nearly two years later when so many things had already been put in place. The auditors once wrote to me asking how reform was progressing. I wrote back explaining we'd decided to move on – without forcing transformational change upon people – to a period of what can be called in the new management thinking 'dynamic stability'. In other words, you get the organisation feeling relatively stable without massive upheavals; people are feeling comfortable and confident in what they're doing. It still has this dynamic feature of change going on all the time, but at a pace – and in a way – that doesn't disturb and upset everybody with the smash, bang, crash changes. We did all that when we disbanded the crime squads and restructured the commands.

But the PIC is composed principally of lawyers who probably know little about managing large organisations. With the greatest respect to them, it's unlikely there are many management graduates among them. They wrote back and said: 'Could you please inform us of the date on which you made the decision to give up transformational change and embrace dynamic stability? Could you please also say at what meeting this took place, who was present at the meeting, any notes that were taken at this time . . .' I thought, 'God!' Do they think it was a case of: 'Right lads, this morning – make a note of this Smith – we've moving from . . .' It's never as simple as that. You make changes in an organisation to push through progress all over the place; it's like playing chess on a massive scale. To try and look at things in such simplistic terms is absolutely ridiculous.

The real crunch came, however, when a few members of a unit that was set up to promote behavioural change among police officers called a remarkable press conference on 20 October 2000 to claim that a group of senior officers within the service was actively working against them to obstruct reform. They announced that Internal Affairs was involved in a deliberate smear campaign and payback in a 'world of total incompetents; of drunken, threatening, bullying, hand-picked members of the Commissioner's executive "team".' They then approached the PIC with their potentially explosive allegations – and found a willing audience. The PIC took their allegations seriously, and launched a lengthy investigation into the work of the unit, into the attitudes of their superior officers, and into Ryan's part in their downfall.

The Crime Management Support Unit (CMSU) had been brought together by Ryan from a tight-knit group of people who'd been working on a ground-up model of policing called the 'Behavioural Change Program'. They'd begun to feel like the real architects of change within the service, and were angry that their role was being gradually phased out. Terry O'Connell – awarded an Order of Australia Medal for introducing community conferencing to deal with juvenile crime, and championed by the former head of Human Resources, Christine Nixon – quit the New South Wales police service in April 2000. Senior Constable Peta Blood resigned from the service in September 1999.

James Ritchie, an academic and consultant, a former ASIO officer and failed Liberal aspirant, was far more combative. Often branded a maverick, and once described by Liberal federal director Andrew Robb as 'a bitter and failed political groupie', he responded by taking two years' worth of emails and memos and reports to complain to the PIC. Detective Superintendent Ken Seddon, a British police officer seconded from the Greater Manchester Police in 1998 joined him. It was immediately billed a 'civil war' for control of the police. Gary Sturgess, once again, emerged to declare it would be a 'tragedy' if the CMSU was disbanded.

Still glowing with the albeit unrecognised glory of having helped deliver the 'best-ever' Games and believing that the new buzz of pride and team spirit in the service would help it leapfrog forward, Ryan had not known anything about Ritchie's plans to go public with his allegations. Watching his dream of a newly invigorated police service slip through his fingers, Ryan sat back in horror at the press coverage of the unbelievable allegations and the damage it was doing to the service. He didn't imagine anyone would have taken Ritchie seriously, and was stunned by the uproar.

He had known about the group since the beginning of 1997, when he first heard of O'Connell and his restorative justice system, an idea imported from New Zealand, bringing together victims and their assailants to forge a better understanding. The idea was that the victims might achieve some sort of 'closure' while the perpetrators, confronted for the first time by the emotional fallout from their crimes, might be deterred from reoffending.

O'Connell had introduced it in the western New South Wales town of Wagga Wagga but, says Ryan, the State juvenile justice department had also moved forward on a similar idea, and it was their model that was taken up by the New South Wales Government rather than O'Connell's. Ryan claims O'Connell's enmity towards the service's hierarchy started at that point. He went over to Canada and the UK to talk about his model, constantly leaving behind questions about who'd given him permission, as a New South Wales police officer, to go overseas to talk about restorative justice, and who was paying for the travel. 'We've never been able to establish the answers,' says Ryan.

O'Connell and Ritchie had approached Ryan in 1998 to say how well their work was going in the Waratah local area command, near Newcastle. They talked about their methods of bringing managers and staff together in a circle to establish open dialogue with each other. Ryan thought it sounded most laudable, but had his doubts about expanding the program.

It had taken them two years to achieve results in Waratah, so with eighty local area commands, it would take 160 years to do it everywhere. I asked if they'd be able to distil what they'd learned in that two years to train disciples to carry the message elsewhere, but [Ritchie] said they were planning just to go to Shoalhaven. I told them to come up with a proper business plan – how much it would cost, how many people they needed, how long it would take, a broad overview of the project – so I knew exactly what I was letting myself in for. They saw this as resistance. They argued they should just go there, get more people and do it.

Eventually, they came up with a half-page report. That was it. I said, 'No, I need more.' They had to be held accountable just like everyone else. They had to have their travel authorised; they had to have their resources authorised; we needed to know what they were spending, and why. They were unhappy with this. But every time I tried to contact them afterwards, they were never around. They used to travel around in police cars, and no one ever knew where they were. These were the people claiming to be the drivers of change, yet they'd only been in two places, and they'd spent years fiddling about in one of them. We couldn't see any changes of great benefit at all. Nevertheless, the concept might be made to work if properly introduced.

Ryan, having came to the conclusion that the Human Resources Department under whose aegis they operated had been a source of leaks to journalists and having moved Nixon out to operations, also sent in the Audit Group to check out whether their claims of instituting change had much merit. Their report said they'd found minimal change. 'At that,' says Ryan, 'they went berserk, saying a conspiracy was running against them. Without Nixon there, they could see they didn't have as much support, and they started to implode. The trouble was, I still believed in behavioural change as one element of reform, but I didn't believe in the people giving the message.'

In October 1999, Ryan assigned Seddon to the group to give them a little more credibility. The task came with a stern warning: he told Seddon not to end up under their spell. 'But then he did,' says Ryan. 'It was as if he had been converted by a cult. Then they all started claiming to be the gurus of reform, but they weren't.' Ryan then moved them out of Human Resources and into Crime Agencies, so they could come under the tighter control of Assistant Commissioner Clive Small. The questions continued to come, from Ryan and now from Small, too.

> The questions may well have been put in a robust way, but this is the police force after all! I believe they were upset because they were being held accountable. Their unit had a history of just running around the State, like stray cats, doing exactly what they wanted. We just can't have staff behaving like that, no matter how important their alleged role is.

Internal Affairs began investigating alleged travel rorts, tax claims and motor-vehicle expenses. After the October 2000 press conference, Seddon's secondment was terminated, Ritchie was sacked on 22 December, and a Supreme Court injunction was obtained to silence them. It was only partly successful. Seddon's wife Pam, a few days later, spoke freely to a newspaper, saying the opposition to her husband could well have sprung from the fact that some saw him as a future contender for Ryan's job.

Angry that he wasn't being allowed to just get on with his job, furious the PIC had given Ritchie such a public platform, and annoyed that something he felt was a minor managerial shortcoming should have blown up into such a major issue, Ryan lashed out on a November 2000 radio interview on 2UE. 'I get oversighted by people who haven't got a bloody clue,' he said. 'They couldn't run a chook raffle and they are oversighting me, and looking at what I'm doing after thirty-seven years of policing internationally . . . I get more advice

than people playing golf, or learning to drive.' Few newspaper commentators doubted his comments were aimed directly at the PIC.

While Police Minister Paul Whelan later told Parliament that Ryan
had spoken out of frustration, Ryan claims that Urquhart called him
directly. 'I'll never forget how his voice was shaking with rage,' says
Ryan. 'He said, "How dare you say we couldn't organise a chook raffle!" I suggested he get a transcript of the radio interview – I hadn't
mentioned the PIC in that comment. But he just said, "You make a
retraction!" I said, "Is that a threat?" He said, "You just do it, Commissioner, or you will see."' Ryan held a press conference to pledge
support for the PIC and the Ombudsman, but Urquhart a few days
later entered the fray. At a parliamentary committee hearing, he said
he could find no evidence to support Ryan's contention that there
needed to be fewer bodies monitoring police performance. Indeed, he
felt police had neglected proposals aimed at preventing corrupt conduct in favour of giving more attention to the Olympic Games.

Finally, in March 2001, the PIC began its Operation Malta public
hearings into the affair. It was scheduled to last eight days and ended
up lasting a year, generating nearly 5833 pages of transcript, 7000
documents, fifty-one witnesses and costing an estimated $8 million,
with the final report not expected to be presented to Parliament
until, at the earliest, the end of 2002.

At first, the hearing attracted enormous publicity, with the sensational accusations by Ritchie and Seddon – later reported to have
resigned from the British police force amid allegations of fraud. Ryan
could only sit by and watch, in enormous frustration. The PIC had
warned him he could be held in contempt of court if he spoke out. He
longed to be called into the witness box to give his version of events,
but his appearance was delayed and cancelled, then delayed again.
Meanwhile, the press was having a field day, construing his enforced
silence as a sign of either guilt or a complete lack of concern. Ryan was
seething, having been advised that he couldn't even say that he wasn't
allowed to speak. Privately, he was beside himself with the damage the
hearing was causing his reputation. 'The whole thing is based on a
false premise. I'm constantly talking to lawyers which is taking up all
my time, and then I'm criticised for not running the force. It should
be stopped before it's allowed to destroy me and the reform process.'

A failed legal bid to have the hearing cut short fuelled his anger. 'The PIC wants a high-profile scalp,' he says. 'In all this time, they haven't had one and they have to prove they haven't been a waste of time and money. Now they want my scalp. The Ombudsman and the PIC – their oversighting of the police needs a complete review. They haven't come up with any corrupt officer of any significance. The only people going to jail are the ones who my police have arrested, and I've handed them to the PIC.' At the end of June 2001, Urquhart had his term of office extended to finish the Malta inquiry. He declined to comment for this book, saying he was not able to speak about Ryan because the PIC hadn't yet given their Malta report to Parliament.

Ryan was forced to sit and fume for an astonishing sixteen months after the press conference first aired the damning allegations, until he was finally invited to have his say at the PIC on 4 March 2002. Even then, he was alerted by journalists to the date he was to appear; he hadn't even been told. But by the time he finally stepped into the witness box – and raised a laugh among the mass of journalists and lawyers present by responding, when he was ticked off for speaking too quickly, 'I've got so much to tell you, really' – many people had simply lost interest in the saga. Hearing Ryan deny the claims made by Ritchie and Seddon had none of the drama, and commanded none of the headlines, of their original lurid accusations. Much of the intricate discussion was lost on the audience. It was all a sorry anticlimax, and Ryan felt absolutely cheated.

He, and the police service, had been done enormous damage by the group's claims. A difference of opinion on how to deal with the CMSU had caused friction between Ryan and Clive Small. Ryan and Mal Brammer had fallen out over their evidence, with Brammer eventually leaving the service to join the Independent Commission Against Corruption. It had taken up an incredible number of hours of Ryan's time, and cost the police service a small fortune in legal bills. And, considers Ryan, it had trashed a reputation that had taken him years to build. 'At the end of the day, it was a matter that should have been dealt with very quickly,' said one legal onlooker. 'It did Mr Ryan a grave disservice that he had to wait so long to counter the allegations.'

Ryan still can hardly believe it happened. 'This was all because a group of people wanted to rail against the service, and they had a high-profile body there that felt obliged to take them seriously and give them such a public platform,' he says. 'It was stupid that it was allowed to go so far and was made to be so important. This was essentially a management problem that should have been dealt with within the service. How could any company possibly survive if employees who are unhappy with the way the business is being run, can end up almost bringing the company to its knees?'

The damage, Ryan felt, had been done. 'Ever since that chook raffle comment, I think there have been certain elements within the PIC – not Judge Urquhart, I never thought he was involved – but other people there who have been out to get me,' he says. 'This Malta inquiry is payback.' Even if it wasn't revenge, it certainly had that effect.

CHAPTER 25

White knights . . .
dark days

Peter Ryan's dramatic reshuffle of his top cops at the end of the year 2000 took everyone by surprise. With Clive Small moved from his beloved Crime Agencies to the Greater Hume Region (an area that covered the poisoned chalice of Cabramatta), Mal Brammer from Internal Affairs to Macquarie (before he left to join ICAC), Graeme Morgan picking up Small's old job, and Ryan's former chief of staff Andrew Scipione to Brammer's, the press was alive with speculation that Ryan was trying to destabilise his rivals. Ryan announced that the spring-clean was simply to give his Deputy and Assistant Commissioners broader experience, but everyone else discussed conspiracy theories that he'd demoted the pair of 'white knights', or at least sidelined them, to cement his own position, to harm theirs or to ensure they wouldn't obstruct his reform process. Reports of Small being privately irate, and Brammer being devastated after three and a half years in his post, seemed to lend credence to the theories. But Ryan insists the truth is far more prosaic.

The moves were reported as having some kind of disciplinary overtones, but it was just normal management practice. I'd wanted to do it before the Games, but that would have been too disruptive. We'd had problems at Cabramatta and while I found Clive Small a very difficult person to manage – I could never get close to him and never felt he was wholly onside with me – it needed someone with his determination to sort it out. As for

Mal Brammer, he'd begun to see only the dark side of policing because he'd spent so long in Internal Affairs, so I moved him to broaden his experience and to give him a break from the work of IA. Neither was particularly happy. They didn't want to move, but these areas were where they were needed. Brammer saw it as an insult, and that probably coloured his attitude toward me from that moment on, and hence the declaration he wrote. I even sent him to the USA for professional development as a means of showing him my support and that he had a future. But then he started saying things behind my back. He's been frustrated as hell by me because I criticised the quality and speed of IA investigations.

Brammer's declaration – in the form of a chain email sent to officers across the State, saying he held Ryan in deep regard 'as a person and in his role as Commissioner' – was seen by Ryan as damning him with exaggerated praise. A month later, Brammer applied for, and was given, a new job as director of investigations for ICAC, seeking out crooked Government officials. In June 2001, Christine Nixon was appointed Victoria's Police Commissioner.

It was easy to believe there were enemies everywhere. While assembling his blueprint for the future of policing, 'Future Directions', the draft copy was leaked to the newspapers. Ryan was dismayed, feeling he had to defend material critical of other organisations that was never intended to be kept for the final version. When it was eventually released, the five-year plan involved outsourcing some police functions to civilians to free up more beat officers, buying up more technology, closing police stations, major industrial reforms to allow change to sweep more quickly through the service, and rationalising the 120 audit reports compiled to just two for the PIC and Ombudsman.

When a confidential Internal Affairs report into the promotions process appeared in a newspaper, it felt like par for the course. Even though it was about how the promotions process had been corrupted after four executives of the New South Wales Police Association had circulated a list of the interview questions beforehand to canvass for union votes, Ryan, who for years had been trying to overhaul the promotions process against fierce union opposition, felt sure that somehow he would be held to blame. He was.

Christmas 2000 was a miserable one. Ryan had just revealed to the press that he and the family had become Australian citizens in a private ceremony, and said he planned to stay in Australia and retire there, but his heart wasn't really in it. In truth both he and Adrienne felt at rock bottom. One evening, he went to a function for a few drinks, but ended up staying for dinner without letting her know. By the time he eventually arrived home, she was sitting sobbing at the kitchen table. 'Sometimes it gets me down and I can't stop crying,' she said a few days later.

> I want to go home to England. I want to go where I have family and long-time friends because I feel too lonely here. The problem, of course, is that his work is here and any future work is here. But maybe I should insist, for the first time in our marriage, that we should do what *I* want. What I want is some peace and at least some feeling of stability. I wish, with all my heart, we'd never come here.

Adrienne's unhappiness was a huge weight on Ryan's shoulders. She'd never really adjusted to life in Australia and, in her darkest moments, called Australians shallow, with many 'lacking decency'. Ryan loved her desperately and felt terribly guilty for what he'd put both her and their children through. 'It's a whole different story for men who marry younger women,' says his friend Geoff Officer, who himself has a wife thirteen years younger, similar to the Ryans' sixteen-year age difference. 'You may have reached a point of stability in your career, but your wife hasn't. Initially, it's about pleasing her, and there can be guilt too.' Here, the situation seemed intractable. Adrienne wanted to return to England; Ryan, despite the misery of his job, loved the Australian lifestyle, weather, and sense of optimism. 'Even the depressed areas of Sydney, compared to depressed areas in Britain, are paradise, absolute paradise,' he says. 'It's just the job. I'd be happy driving a bus, right now. No job is worth this much misery.'

During the good times, Adrienne parlayed life in Sydney into some great opportunities she may not have had back in Britain, like having her book published, appearing regularly on the panel of TV's 'Beauty & The Beast', heading an osteoporosis charity and having a spot on Mike Carlton's Radio 2GB show, talking about health. She loved their home and hosting dinners for crowds of people, even though Ryan would sometimes have been happier eating a curry and curling up with his daughters in front of the TV. But the bad times were bad. 'Maybe I was just looking all the time for friends,' says Adrienne.

> I was so lonely most of the time. It's hard for the whole family. At the moment, I can't even decide what to do about the girls' schooling. Should I send Izzy back to England, or should I let her stay here with us? Do I send Georgina over to join her? It would work out so incredibly expensive. There are so many decisions to be made but the future looks so uncertain, I can't work out what to do. I feel like I'm trapped, and I'm going mad.

There was also the fear that everyone would find out about Elizabeth having been away at school in the UK, and somehow use it against them. The Opposition apparently knew, and a reporter had phoned asking leading questions. The Ryans watched the newspapers each day with dread. Finally, when they had decided to bring Elizabeth back, Georgina had said it was only fair that she be allowed to go too. A compromise was brokered: Elizabeth would return to board at her old school of Abbotsleigh, and Georgina would board too. It seemed an odd solution – after all, their home was only fifteen minutes away – but the girls both really wanted to escape the stress at home.

Ryan had gone to see his doctor over a persistent ear infection that wouldn't clear up and the doctor had insisted on giving him a complete check-up. The news wasn't good. He told Ryan bluntly that the job was killing him. He could risk only another year in it, at most. The stress was exerting a terrible toll on his health. He had to get out soon. His deputy, Ken Moroney, who'd served as chief of staff to both John Avery and Tony Lauer, had warned him right at the beginning about the toll the job would take. His words had an eerie ring about them. 'I told him the pressures of the job had destroyed

John and destroyed Tony,' Moroney recalls. 'And now, I said they'd come after him too – and his successor.' Still Ryan had not been prepared for the stress to be affecting him physically quite so badly.

Shocked, he and Adrienne talked the situation over long into that night. Although he loved his work, he'd already seen several of his senior officers falling by the wayside with stress and heart attacks. 'I finally got him to agree he should leave soon,' says Adrienne.

His biggest concern is about letting down the public. They still come up to him – after all these years – and shake his hand and tell him not to let the bastards get him down. The trouble is, he's very aware that there really isn't anyone to take over. He believes that this will still be the case even if he lasts till 2004 because the succession planning has been so bad in the service. He believes the ideal would be to recruit another outsider, and then the next time have a local ready. He has only managed to get a leadership plan in place in the last twelve months or so.

I'm very, very worried about him. He's so withdrawn and moody. He says he's severely depressed and suicidal. I think he feels really fed up and says he's trying to run the service on his own, with no support. I ended up telling him to take some time off, sick, unpaid, anything, but he says it'll just look like he's running away. Truth is, he thinks things will go even more wrong if he's away from the helm for too long, like they did with Cabramatta. Now he's saying we could always just pack up and go. We'd leave the house, and just go to England and start again. Anything would be better than living like this.

Their friend Loretta Henson agreed. 'You could see the strain in his face,' she says. 'It's aged him, and they're both so tense now.' Another friend of theirs, radio host Stan Zemanek, also worried. 'Peter's always been a really good fellow, a terrific host and a man who loves a good laugh. But you could see both their personalities changing over the past couple of years. It was the strain of what was going on behind the scenes.'

There were the same old personal irritations too. After eight and a half months, one newspaper finally won the right to see Ryan's personal diary, but glumly reported how dull it turned out to be. Ryan was angry, but philosophical. 'I'd said they shouldn't see my diary because there are people's names and details of sensitive operational issues there that people shouldn't see,' he says. 'It was merely an attempt to embarrass me. I was constantly harassed for details on everything: how much money I spent on the corporate credit card – Answer: almost nothing. Who I might be going out with – Answer: no one. It was a stupid waste of my time.' He was outraged too that he was questioned by Opposition politicians about how many holidays he had taken.

Both Ryan and Adrienne started doubting themselves – and each other. For the first time, Adrienne started asking herself whether her husband really had made the right decisions. Was he honestly justified, for instance, in sacking the three men from the CMSU? He began asking himself the same questions. The whole affair was costing him so dearly, wouldn't it have been better to have lived with the consequences of their continued involvement in the police service, instead of sticking his head out from the parapet to make the tough decisions? But quite apart from the CMSU saga, the troubles at Cabramatta and the rows over closing police stations, the biggest immediate cloud on the horizon was the upcoming QSARP (the Qualitative and Strategic Audit of the Reform Process), an historic independent audit of Ryan's first four years set up by the Royal Commission and backed by the PIC, which he knew, from seeing a pre-release copy, was critical of his progress in instituting reform. 'But the report would be more than twelve months old,' he says. 'We have actually come a long way since then.' With a sick feeling in his stomach, he waited, believing it could well prove his downfall.

In the event, it came and went with little fanfare. It was critical that the progress of reform had been fragmented and limited, but said it had given way to Ryan's determination to bring down crime. Police Minister Paul Whelan and Premier Bob Carr both defended Ryan's corner vigorously and, coupled with the declaration that crime figures had stabilised or fallen in a number of categories for the first time in a decade, Opposition police spokesman Andrew Tink's call that Ryan's employment contract be renegotiated went almost unheard.

Far more damaging was proving to be the Upper House Standing Committee Inquiry called into the situation in Cabramatta. In February 2001, Detective Sergeant Tim Priest gave evidence, claiming that warnings the suburb was about to explode into bloody gang-warfare were ignored by Small, and that people were being murdered, shot, kidnapped and injured because of police inaction. He said Ryan had been misled about the situation and was not to blame, while Small vehemently denied the accusations. Priest had the valuable backing not only of other officers at the Cabramatta station, he also had the support of outspoken local publican and Chamber of Commerce chairman Ross Treyvaud, who freely admits passing information about the police in the area to Opposition politicians. Both were fans of the New York zero-tolerance model. Towards the end of March, the establishment of a ninety-strong super-squad of police was announced, with police given extra stop-and-search powers to try and foil drug dealers. Treyvaud was still critical, however, saying he'd received threats from police. Ryan is dismissive. 'He'd had a meeting with a police officer who'd said, "You're making a lot of noise, and you have to be careful about making yourself a target." It was innocent, but it was taken the wrong way. This was all about an internal squabble about who was to blame. It got blown up out of all proportion.' Treyvaud continued to be active, a few months later leading a movement for Cabramatta shopkeepers to turn vigilantes to arrest heroin users and dealers themselves.

Then came the biggest debacle of the whole affair. Deputy Commissioner Jeff Jarratt claimed that crime had dropped, contradicting the findings of the head of the Bureau of Crime Statistics and Research, Dr Don Weatherburn. Weatherburn hit back that very same day, saying that crime had gone up in all categories except murder, armed robbery and store theft. Jarratt then claimed he'd been using different police data. Ryan felt compelled to intervene, declaring Weatherburn to be the expert and rebuking Jarratt for using internal statistics that shouldn't be quoted publicly. 'Some of Jeff's decisions worried me and I felt he wasn't always ready to take responsibility for them,' says Ryan. At around the same time, the police were forced, because of public outcry, to abandon plans to close six stations.

Two weeks before the release of the parliamentary committee's report, in what was widely seen as a pre-emptive strike to defuse the anticipated criticisms, Carr lashed the police for 'taking their eye off the ball' over the drugs problem at Cabramatta. This, says Ryan, felt like a turning point in their relationship. On 26 July 2001, the parliamentary committee released its final report into the mess. It was damning. It said police senior management had failed the people of Cabramatta and their frontline officers, and criticised Ryan for his comments that police policies had been successful in the suburb. The inquiry chairwoman, Ms Helen Sham-Ho cast doubt on the efficacy of reform, saying there was a clear lack of openness and communication in the service. Ryan conceded the buck stopped with him, but urged everyone to look to the future instead.

But the affair just wouldn't go away. Ryan was attacked for not attending the inquiry and, after astonishing scenes where Whelan tried to stop him explaining why to journalists, eventually insisted the invitations were never passed on. In a radio interview he quoted an 80 per cent clear-up rate for serious crime, another figure immediately contradicted by Weatherburn. An unidentified young man, code-named 'James', who claimed that he'd been recruited as a boy into the Cabramatta-based gang 5T to sell heroin, that he rarely went out on the streets in the suburb without a knife or machete, and that hand guns were freely for sale around schools in western Sydney, was championed by Richard Basham as further proof that Cabramatta was sinking into a desperate state of lawlessness. He was touted around the media, appearing on current affairs shows, including one sensational appearance in July 2001 with Ray Martin on '60 Minutes', on radio and in the *Daily Telegraph*. It wasn't until much later, after the announcement of Ryan's departure from the service, that a new report into 'James' drafted by Small, was finally revealed to have cast doubt on some twenty-seven or twenty-eight of 'James' thirty lurid allegations. He was described as 'highly unreliable', a finding that attracted barely a murmur in the previously outraged press.

But, at the time, the damage being done was phenomenal. At an angry public meeting hosted by TV's '60 Minutes' in August, also heavily featuring 'James', Ryan looked tired and uncomfortable. One newspaper ran a series of letters from police on the beat, highlighting all the problems of crime in the city. In his first private meeting with Priest, Ryan urged him to stay on, but was himself coming under louder and louder calls to resign.

It was perhaps the watershed of his term as New South Wales Commissioner of Police. He was starting to look embattled, defensive and alone at the head of a service completely beyond his control. Even more importantly, his critics were starting to band together. Radio 2UE's Alan Jones, who seemed to have turned against Ryan in the middle of 2001, just after John Marsden condemned the police service for the investigation into his life, was savaging him with an incredible degree of venom every morning. In a broadcast on 20 July, he said, 'This business has to stop.' He had Richard Basham on his show that day, who made an extraordinary call for the police service 'to be put into receivership in order to protect the community and all of the thousands of officers who still have some confidence'. He branded Ryan as 'a hollow man' preferring to surround himself with 'people who will crawl' every morning. A few days later, Jones made his first call for Ryan to go. 'The time has come to bring down the curtain on the five-year reign of Peter Ryan.'

Jones was by now having meetings with disaffected police, including Tim Priest, and Basham and Treyvaud. James Ritchie, yet another failed Liberal would-be, was providing a second convenient rallying point with the ongoing PIC inquiry into the CMSU. Things were starting to slip away. Ryan felt it keenly too.

They can sense I'm a wounded animal and they're coming in for the kill. I think Alan Jones is disgracefully biased. People should care that they have a decent, honest police service meeting their needs. They're not buying me, or voting for me. I don't want to get down into the filth and dirt and name-calling that some people in this country thrive on. Jones would take calls from disaffected police, and swallow what they said wholesale. Then when officers with contrary points of view phoned, he wouldn't take their calls, and, once the campaign against me started, would never give me the right of reply. He wouldn't let us past his switchboard, no matter how hard we tried. One of my advisory staff went to see Jones to ask if we could talk privately, but he said no. What do I do? The other day, a bloke came up and said he'd been complaining about a drug house. So I got together a group to raid the house that afternoon: the first time the new drug house legislation was used. Drugs were seized and people arrested. And then it was reported that the place was raided before I arrived! Whelan doesn't say a bloody thing to back me up. Why is everyone turning against me? I'm at my wit's end.

Was it a conspiracy, or simply a group of people thrown together by circumstance? Ryan had no way of knowing. Certainly, Treyvaud had been feeding Opposition politicians with information about Cabramatta, while Jones was a failed one-time Liberal candidate. It did not help that Ryan could scarcely hide his contempt for a man whose own integrity had been seriously questioned in the 'cash for comment' scandal, revelations that very likely would have seen him off the air back in the UK. Jones declined the invitation to comment for this book, saying, 'With respect, I would rather not be involved.'

But he *was* involved. Jones was an old friend of Tim's father Rusty Priest, the New South Wales RSL president. Priest junior had always been doggedly apolitical – even expecting a fine for forgetting to vote in the last election – but he was certainly angry with the Labor Party since being dismissed by Cabramatta Labor MP Reba Meagher as 'a disgruntled officer' with an axe to grind. Priest insists, however, that he had never been personally critical of Ryan, feeling he was simply, as he'd said, poorly advised, and maybe should have gone to the source earlier to check that advice.

'But I'm not part of a cabal against him,' says Priest. 'I've never gained anything personally from this whole thing. Probably, though, I was gathered up in the hysteria and my name was used by others. That's hard to say. I suppose, in a way, the police forced me into the arms of the Liberals because they were the only ones willing to listen to what I had to say. They radicalised me in that way.' As for the Internal Affairs investigations into him, Priest says that's true, but all detectives end up having complaints against them. Meanwhile, at the time of going to press, he and Basham are reputed to be writing a book, which, according to Basham, at least, will be highly critical of Ryan.

Nonetheless Ryan couldn't be sure who was working with whom. While he was mulling it over, he was completely taken aback to be blasted by another one-time Liberal candidate, solicitor John Marsden, after he emerged victorious from his long-running defamation case against the Seven Network which falsely alleged he'd had sex with boys. 'Go back to England, you're a disgrace to humanity,' he growled one time to Ryan via the press. He then deluged him with long letters accusing him of leaking information to the Seven Network, each missive dripping with vitriol, saying that police officers despised him, politicians hoped he would disappear, the public dismissed him as a 'show pony', and he should be ashamed of himself for ruining the service. He claimed Ryan had 'ruined' his life, and hoped he could sleep peacefully at night. Ryan was mystified. 'I was stunned when he came out of court and blamed me,' says Ryan. 'I only got involved when directed to investigate the Franca Arena case and was forced to release documents. The whole of the Marsden affair happened long before I came to Australia.' When this is put to Marsden, however, he is unflinching. 'I blame Peter Ryan totally for what happened to me,' he says. 'I'm very aggro about him.'

Ryan felt bewildered, angry and frustrated that he was coming under such ferocious attack, but he didn't know what to do. He called Carr and Whelan. 'If you're looking for a scapegoat, I'll go,' he told them. 'But you'll have to pay me out of my contract.' They wouldn't hear of it. It did, after all, oblige them to pay him two years' salary. Ryan was bitterly disappointed. 'I'd had enough of the evilness, the vileness and the obscenity of what had been done to both me and the service due to, in my view, political people led by Jones, Schuberg, Priest, Treyvaud and Basham.' Ryan knew now he'd have to continue, and thought long and hard about how he could move forward. He tried his best to swallow the bitterness of the Cabramatta disaster, feeling, like so many of his colleagues, terribly let down by the way his subordinates had handled the affair, quickly standing back out of the way when the criticism fell on his shoulders. He considered moving some senior people, but was worried that it would be seen in the press as the actions of a dying man. Reluctantly, he granted a stay of execution. 'But my confidence in those people responsible has decreased significantly,' he says.

Today, Schuberg says he's never had anything personal against
Ryan and, indeed, felt they often had similar views about policing.
'I never criticised him personally, I just said how policing should be
done,' he says. 'I think initially he took some bad advice. It's unfortunate that in the early days, Peter Ryan didn't give himself more
time to listen to more people rather than make hasty decisions in the
first few months of his arrival.'

With the critics' onslaught, there seemed little cause for cheer, however, even when he received support from some unexpected places –
being called, one day, by former Prime Minister Paul Keating, and the
next day by the Federal Liberal Party asking if he might be interested
in standing for them at some point in the future. The problems were
mounting. Ryan talked about how the war against drugs was being lost.
There were new fears of Sydney becoming an international money-
laundering hub led by Russian crime mafioso, of a rise in the number
of gangs fighting for control of the city's heroin, sex and extortion
markets, and of Sydney becoming the drug capital of Australia.

Everyone was worried about the consequences of a sharp increase
in the number of hand guns on the streets and, as if to illustrate rising crime figures, just over the road from the Ryans' home, a
neighbour's house was attacked by a home-invasion gang. There
were more threats from a former police officer that the service considered dangerous, and the children stayed at friends' houses, while
Ryan started wearing a gun again. Then, like a ghost, the figure of
Seddon rose once more. From England, where he was apparently
living in a tent with his wife and five children, he wrote an open letter
to Ryan via the newspaper, accusing him of having an 'overdeveloped and overinflated ego'. Ryan received the letter two days later,
mysteriously with a Sydney postmark. Adrienne was beside herself
about the lurid damning headlines every day. 'Sometimes I find
myself daydreaming about Peter getting shot,' she says. 'I wonder if
then they'll be sorry for treating him like this.'

Ryan was still thinking about how he could move forward. He
decided to set up a unit to double-check information given to him by
his officers and, ten days later, he held a meeting with Whelan and
Carr who wanted to discuss the Cabramatta issue. The outcome was
that Jarratt had to go. Jarratt was terminated, leaving Ken Moroney as

his lone deputy. Jarratt – an officer for thirty-six years, one of the few survivors of all the changes, and widely seen as Ryan's most likely successor – didn't seem surprised and told Ryan that, in a way, he was relieved. Although sad in many ways, Ryan too was relieved finally to have removed someone he'd had doubts about since first taking up the job. These doubts had grown with the way Jarratt first pushed the controversial Cabramatta change in the crime index, was responsible for the two key appointments (of Peter Horton and regional commander Chris Evans), which came under so much criticism at the parliamentary inquiry, and then the confusion over the crime figures. It was the kind of decisive action he hoped might repair the damage done by the disastrous Cabramatta episode. But it was too little, too late.

Three days later on 8 September 2001, at a by-election in Labor's western Sydney heartland of Auburn fought on a bitter law-and-order platform, there was a 13 per cent swing to the Liberals and independents. In another blow to Ryan, Carr attributed the swing to community concern over crime rather than any other issue, including Labor's much-disparaged stand on refugees. Then Jarratt, who said he was left to endure the brunt of criticism for decisions signed off on by his boss, launched legal action against the police service for unfair dismissal, claiming unspecified damages. Ironically, a month later at a PIC hearing, Jarratt had nothing but praise for his old boss, describing him as 'keen and astute' with a 'keen insight into the police service'.

Yet Ryan was convinced he had an ace up his sleeve. For the past three years, he'd been steering a major undercover operation to expose a group of corrupt police officers on Sydney's northern beaches. Operation Florida had proved a spectacular success, with twenty-five arrests and hundreds of thousands of dollars of cash and drugs seized across the State, and he was itching to unveil it. He hoped it would show that the service under his stewardship had the means, the determination, the knowledge and all the safeguards in place to ferret out corruption, wherever it might occur. 'But with the luck I've had lately, I bet the press will find some way to turn it back on me,' he said grimly, one evening, a few days before he was due to reveal the operation. 'I can't see how, but I bet they will.' His prediction was correct. Some sections of the media ignored his involvement in the operation completely, while others pointed to it as proof the service was as corrupt as ever, rather than effectively dealing with a culture even the Royal Commission had said would take a generation to change.

That evening, Ryan sat in his kitchen, his head in his hands. 'What can I do?' he asked. 'They twist everything and there's no way I can win.' In that, if nothing else, he was right.

CHAPTER 26

Handing over the keys to the asylum

If Peter Ryan thought he was having it tough, there was worse to come. Much worse. At 10 a.m. on Monday, 19 November 2001, his phone rang. It was Police Minister Paul Whelan asking him to come up to his office. As he approached the door, and saw the Minister's staff in tears, his heart sank. The rumours were right: Whelan was about to leave him.

While their relationship had, at times, been tense, Ryan genuinely liked Whelan, and felt they'd worked well together. He became even more nostalgic about their partnership when he heard who was replacing him: Michael Costa. Ryan knew nothing of Costa, but he had a sneaking suspicion that, as New South Wales Labor Council secretary, Costa had been involved in that first 'Send the Pommie home' march. They had met only once, at a formal function three weeks before. Costa, present as Bob Carr's representative, had been sitting beside Adrienne at dinner. When she started making small talk about the number of events they had to attend, and asked him if it was the same for him, she says he snapped back, 'You think this was so bloody popular we had to draw straws for it?' She'd been shocked at his apparent hostility. Later, when they again started up a conversation, she mentioned that she'd always wanted to get into politics. 'Which Party?' he asked. 'I don't know,' she replied. 'I don't understand politics enough in this country; both Parties seem so centrist.' 'Right,' she says he replied, 'that's the most honest thing you've said so far.' Adrienne was furious. 'Are you saying I'm lying now?' she barked back, as she immediately stood up and walked outside to have a cigarette. It wasn't the best start to a new relationship, but later the pair managed to have a much more amicable conversation, and parted on good terms – something she was grateful for when the announcement came that Costa was to be the next Police Minister. Then, she wondered whether Costa had been purposely sent that evening by Carr to check the couple out. 'I wonder if he was nervous about us, and that made him over-react all the time?' she asks.

Later that day of Whelan's resignation, Ryan heard that Costa had been at a meeting, approved by Carr, the Tuesday before at Alan Jones's house with Jones, Tim Priest, Richard Basham, Geoff Schuberg and Ross Treyvaud. He was livid. Carr had never even let him know that Costa had been appointed – he'd found it out, the same as everyone else, from the newspapers. And it now sounded as if Jones was able to dictate, or at least approve, Government policy. What were they up to?

Costa's rapid elevation to Police Minister after only seventeen days in Parliament had left many people asking that exact same question. With a fearsome reputation as an abrasive firebrand who lists 'arguing' among his hobbies, and a chequered past that has included, in his youth, membership of the Trotskyist Socialist Workers Party and, in latter years, of the Right-wing faction of the Labor Party, he was still very much an unknown quantity in Parliament. Many on both sides of the political divide see him as an outspoken stirrer, but Premier Bob Carr is known to view him as a thinker who won his gratitude for heading off big wage demands before the 2000 Olympics. With Jones also agreeing to give him the nod, however, a smoother run for Costa seemed assured. That would mean less of a savaging of Labor in the ears of Jones's faithful battlers in Sydney's west. In three short years Peter Ryan had gone from being a political asset to an electoral liability and there was an election just twelve months away. But no one knew the consequences for Ryan.

Whelan thought he did, however. At his farewell party the following night, he took Ryan aside. 'Whatever you do, Peter,' he whispered to him, 'don't resign! Are you listening to me? Don't resign!' Ryan thought about his words for a long time and came to the conclusion that Whelan was warning him they were trying to pressure him to leave, but that he should resist.

Ryan waited for the Minister-in-waiting to call. It was two days before Costa eventually sent for him. It was a cool meeting. Costa constantly referred to him as an academic – Basham's chosen description of Ryan – and Ryan, irritated at 'all that claptrap that group had obviously been feeding him', countered that the only academic experience he'd ever had was during his last British posting at Bramshill. Gradually, the atmosphere between the two grew frostier. Ryan decided to be straight with his new Minister. 'Look, I believe you've been sent to get rid of me,' said Ryan evenly. 'I've already offered to go quietly, but on my terms. If you're going to chase me out, then it's going to be hand-to-hand combat all the way.' Costa seemed startled at such frankness. 'No,' he replied, 'we want you to stay. You're the most popular Commissioner we've ever had. You're doing a good job. You've just got to deal with the critics.' Ryan bristled. 'That's all very well, but we haven't got off to a good start if you're going to listen to the critics yourself,' snapped Ryan.

Thereafter relations became more cordial. Ryan then went on to brief the new Minister about what the service needed and what regular police officers on the beat wanted – the two not often being the same – and warned him against making promises he'd be unable to keep. One of the greatest problems, Ryan told Costa, was the police union. Indeed, it had taken him nineteen months, a PIC Inquiry and seventy-five subcommittee meetings before he was even able to change the promotions structure late in 2001.

> Their antiquated industrial agreements are inhibiting progress and reform in the service at every turn. They refuse to work single-manning in cars. We're the only police force in the western world like that, even in sleepy hollows. They refuse to work anything but twelve-hour shifts. They prevent me from posting officers from quiet areas to busy areas and pull in the industrial dispute procedure that says it's an enforced transfer. All the things that can fix the problems, certainly for the cops in terms of resources, are industrial agreements.

He ended by telling Costa that, with his union background, he should be able to sort out the mess.

The Minister went off to tour police stations but, instead of returning to Ryan to talk over the problems, he immediately made a public statement about on-the-spot fines. Ryan was taken aback and, when asked about it in a radio interview, had to confess he knew nothing about it. Then he had to backtrack to make sure it didn't look as though the two men were in conflict already. But it was the first of many such changes that Costa decided with absolutely no consultation with Ryan, leaving the Commissioner and his officers scurrying around trying to work out how best to make them happen. Almost as bad, he occasionally seized upon Ryan's recommendations, announcing them to the press as his own initiatives.

The irony is that Ryan is convinced there's actually little philosophical disagreement between the two men. They both want the best for the police service, and want to solve problems that inhibit the way forward.

> In the meetings we've had, it's clear that there's little difference in what we both want to achieve. I try to explain that we do know there are problems. It's not that we're deliberately *not* fixing them, it's due to other hurdles. I've been dealing with similar-sized police authorities for years, and he has no idea of the issues. He just tries to force them too quickly. He announces things every five minutes; then we have to try and facilitate them. It's not that easy. In some cases, the Government just hasn't provided the legislation. Costa has to make a name for himself in politics, I can't hold that against him. All he has to do though, is to try and work in conjunction with us.

More and more, however, Costa appeared determined to go his own way, and take over the New South Wales Police Commissioner's role in making the decisions on operational policy. He announced that Ryan's planned super-commands would not go ahead and that the police stations earlier earmarked for closure – and later reprieved – would stay open. That had already been publicly announced by Ryan, but it still made headlines. The next day, he pledged to reduce paperwork and put police back on the beat, the same promise that Ryan had continually made, and for which he'd drafted plan after plan to bring in more civilians to enable it to happen. Two days later, he said he'd give more officers to troubled Redfern.

In December, however, Costa dealt Ryan a blow that left him reeling. He announced he'd have a seven-person Police Minister's Advisory Council to oversee the police service, which would include Ryan's old foe Geoff Schuberg, the man he moved out as Assistant Commissioner during his first executive purge in the job, and New South Wales Police Association president Ian Ball, representing the union Ryan considered had been obstructing reform so vigorously. Two days later, and another humiliation for Ryan: Tim Priest was given a job as a special advisor within the Minister's office.

Schuberg chose to leave in a fit of pique and now, five years afterwards, after several other jobs, he was back. This committee is amazing. I can understand the rationale of how it's better to have your enemies inside the tent than outside, causing problems, but it's bizarre to have Schuberg there, taken out of total oblivion just because he's joined the fray with Jones, makes me question their motives. Will Basham be next? I've never felt betrayed in my life, ever, but now I know what massive betrayal feels like. I don't know any organisation with so many tiers and advisory groups and overseers. If they all agreed something was wrong, and agreed on the way to fix it, it would be good, but they don't. People within the service keep talking to me about all the positive change they've seen, but now that could all be given away. We've given away the keys to the asylum.

Every day, Ryan saw as delivering another slap in the face. Costa announced new laws denying bail to repeat offenders – exactly as Ryan had urged in 1997, when his proposals had caused such an outcry within the legal profession. He approved a three-month trial allowing police to moonlight as security guards, regardless that the Wood Royal Commission had ruled that secondary employment was dangerous. It wasn't long before he began to be talked about as the knee-jerk police minister, anxious more to appease critics and court the press than to safeguard the long-term interests of a corruption-resistant police service. Yet he had his fans. Remember Gary Sturgess? From London, he says, 'Costa is undoubtedly a true reformer.'

Later that month, Ryan was called into a meeting with Costa, their two chiefs of staff Bernard Aust and John Whelan, Director General of the Police Ministry Les Tree and Deputy Commissioner Ken Moroney. Costa told Ryan he wanted the vacant position of the second Deputy Commissioner – at the time with Peter Walsh acting – filled. Ryan replied that he needed to carefully consider the structure of the service and advertise the position prior to making the recommendation. The service needed stability after years of change. They needed to consolidate what they'd done, fix the promotion system, complete what projects were already under way, concentrate on reducing crime and increase visibility. Costa shook his head. He wanted the post filled immediately. Ryan resisted, arguing that the more appropriate course of action would be to advertise. Finally, forced into a corner, Ryan suggested several good candidates, including Internal Affairs head Chief Superintendent Andrew Scipione and the head of police education Dave Madden. 'Those will do nicely,' said Costa, and told Ryan to summon them to a meeting the following morning so he could promote them. This, he duly did, with Moroney in the new post of *senior* deputy.

But if Costa's modus operandi that day amazed him, what followed at a meeting on Friday, 1 February 2002 absolutely stunned him. At midday, he was summoned to an unscheduled meeting, together with the three deputies, in Costa's office. When he arrived, the subject on the agenda turned out to be the restructuring of the regions. The week before, Ryan, after long discussions with his senior executive, had put a proposal to Costa that there should be a gradual reduction in the number of the regions from eleven to seven, as the regional commanders took retirement. The plan was carefully drawn to minimise any disturbance and upheaval that the restructure might entail – since it would result in the disappearance of a number of very senior and experienced members of the police service. Costa, however, had apparently made up his mind. He said he did not want to wait for the retirements; he wanted all of the regions to be abolished. Ryan was appalled.

The Minister said we should do away with the regions because constables in police stations he had visited had complained that regions were taking up all the resources for what they considered to be little effect in terms of crime-fighting. I said while they could be improved, and we were already working on ways to make that happen, there were a lot of people involved in regions who did provide a good service, like our freelance flying squads who went to trouble spots and dealt with issues as they arose, and who were performing extraordinarily well.

But no, the Minister was adamant that the 900 or so people in the regions should be put in local commands. We all objected strongly that you can't move 900 people who were working in tactical teams or anti-theft groups and so on back into the local commands and then start claiming you had 900 extra officers, it would be a lie. They were doing valuable work where they were. In the previous couple of weeks, the tactical action group had literally swamped Campsie and Burwood, which had an enormous impact on crime.

But Costa and (John) Whelan weren't in the mood to listen. The Minister insisted that, despite what anyone was being paid, they should be out driving squad cars. He then named Edd Chadbourne, the head of Human Resources, and public affairs chief Liz Blieschke. They'd have to go.

Ryan feared that were he to sack Chadbourne just after he'd complained at the PIC's Malta hearing about the police service, it would look dangerously as though it were a payback. He should be counselled about his performance and, if it still hadn't improved, his employment should be re-examined then. 'I'm not going to sack him,' said Ryan bluntly. 'I'm not having anything to do with it. If you want him to go, you get rid of him!' As for Blieschke, Ryan protested that there'd been such a huge turnover of media staff, it was amazing that anyone from that field ever worked for the police service – or ever would again. He wanted her to stay if for no other reason than to try to keep some semblance of stability. Again, he refused to sack her.

The argument raged on all afternoon, until it took a completely unexpected turn. There wasn't one regional commander, said Costa at one point, who had the confidence of the Minister or the Minister's staff. Reluctantly, Ryan finally agreed to reduce the number of regions to five, and then the debate started over who should run them.

'The Minister was quite adamant: he did not want Clive Small as a regional commander. He called him a self-promoter and said he didn't want anything to do with him.' Fortunately, Ryan had heard that the Premier's Department had a job for Small, the Assistant Commissioner who had frequently been criticised by Alan Jones. 'But I didn't want him to be moved from his region command,' says Ryan. 'Clive is clever, bright and sharp and he does get the job done. He was doing a very good job in Cabramatta and I didn't want to lose him. Despite his faults, and I've never liked him talking to the media as much as he does, he was still a good operator.'

Ryan refused to sack him, then left the meeting for another appointment. The meeting continued and eventually Moroney, who had been briefed by Ryan, mentioned the Premier's Department job, and Costa, caught unawares, sat back in his chair. Obviously, he hadn't known a thing about it. Costa has always denied he sought the sacking of Small and the other senior officers, but the allegation was never challenged when it was later repeated in a summons to the New South Wales Industrial Relations Court. But, that day, Costa quickly recovered and continued on with his list. As well as Small, he wanted a number of other senior officers, the Assistant Commissioners Graeme Morgan, Chris Evans, Eric Gollan, Doug Graham, Peter Walsh and John Laycock removed from the service, or notified they were going to be removed by the following Friday. 'We can't lose that much experience!' Ryan exploded, explaining later, 'That's no way to treat people who have done years and years in the service, but who might have upset Alan Jones or the Minister or said something wrong in a press conference. I said they should be spoken to properly and allowed to retire with dignity, knowing their contribution has been valued.' Ryan flatly refused to sack them.

A few days later, Small's move to the Premier's Department to advise the Government on the fight against crime was announced, just as Ryan left the country on leave. In Salt Lake City, where he was

attending the Winter Olympics as the IOC's independent expert on
security, he was besieged by journalists asking whether Small's new
job meant his old rival would now be the de facto Police Commissioner. Ryan bit his lip, and said how they were looking forward to
working together. Privately, he thought the move was ridiculous.

Clive'd been better placed staying where he was, and keeping
on top of the crime problems in one of the most sensitive areas
of this city. He was good at dealing with things on the ground.
He has good ideas. He gets people to follow them through. He
makes them think differently. Now he's being wasted, and I'm
being asked to micro-manage everything. But Jones had been
campaigning for Clive to be sacked, Costa didn't like him much
and Priest was after him. So this lifeline that was thrown to him
was a godsend.

While Ryan was still in the USA, Costa announced the restructuring of the service, with the regions reduced to five, saying that the
plan had Ryan's full input and approval. The humiliation was complete when Costa outlined the new requirement that every police
officer, including the Commissioner, would have to do shifts on the
beat. That merely served to fuel the press speculation over how long
Ryan could now last, given that Costa seemed to be intent on kick-
ing him at every turn. The question that kept being raised was: who
is running the service? Ryan gave a clue when he was asked under
cross-examination at the PIC hearing on 12 March 2002 whether he
was the Commissioner of Police. Without a flicker of emotion, he
replied, 'Probably not, no. I have doubts these days.' The question
continued to be asked publicly, more and more. And the answer was
that no one was quite sure.

CHAPTER 27

Out, but
not down

Peter Ryan, spat Dr Edd Chadbourne, was spineless, cowardly and a poor Police Commissioner. What's more, he said, 'This will send a message to many people in the New South Wales Police Service that, if you tell the truth, you will get sacked. They can put any spin on it they like; this has really marked a turning point.'

Exactly what Ryan feared might happen, just had. Both Chadbourne and Liz Blieschke, despite his pleas to the Minister, had been sacked while Ryan was in Salt Lake City, and now Chadbourne was out for blood – *his* blood. Senior Deputy Commissioner Ken Moroney had declared that the move had been made only after consultation with Ryan, who was still overseas, and the decision was final. Chadbourne had immediately assumed this was payback for his evidence against Ryan at the PIC hearing, and leapt on to the offensive, announcing that he and Blieschke were now taking legal action. The newspapers joined the fray, slamming Ryan for his disastrous timing in choosing to sack the pair just as Costa was struggling to have his restructure accepted. 'I pleaded with the Minister not to do it,' says Ryan, bewildered.

Yet publicly, Ryan would say only that legal restrictions prevented him from commenting, and he stayed silent on who had taken the decisions. It infuriated Adrienne that he seemed to be accepting all the criticisms so stoically. Time and time again, she urged him to speak out, to tell everyone it was Costa who was responsible for making such radical decisions. But still Ryan maintained a dignified silence. As a police officer all his working life, he had a deep,

ingrained sense of propriety, and an unshakeable respect for authority, however abused. The police service, like the army, has always
been a very authoritarian organisation, with its central tenets of obedience, deference and loyalty providing the nerve centre from which
everything else flows. Ryan didn't believe it was his place to criticise
Costa or Carr, certainly not publicly. The more Adrienne begged him
to speak up, the more determined he became not to. Even though
the anger might be eating away at him inside, outwardly he was
impassive and unresponsive. That apparent indifference only
seemed to encourage his critics to become even more aggressive.

> I have a great sense of loyalty. I have never spoken out, for
> instance, against any staff I've got rid of, whether for criminal
> conduct or lack of performance, whatever, even though the first
> thing they have done is to rush to the microphone and the cam-
> eras and castigate me. I've never spoken out against the Govern-
> ment because the Government of the day is what I've sworn to
> support. The easiest thing in the world for me to say would be
> that I don't agree with those changes and that they were forced
> upon me, but that would cause bloody chaos, wouldn't it? It's
> not my way. I've always sat quietly and taken it on the chin and
> held my dignity. It doesn't do the service any good to cause a
> fuss. It distracts people from the main game and merely gives
> the media another week of stories.

Yet with Costa rushing through such major changes, and often
against all advice, the question has to be asked: was this a deliberate
Government manoeuvre to force Ryan to quit, knowing he just
refused to bite back? Ryan doesn't know.

> Part of me thinks, Yes, but another part thinks, No, they are just
> being stupid in rushing forward and trying to look very busy in
> a state of blind panic about the 2003 election. They are deter-
> mined to get elected. When we issue a note of caution or
> concern, they're interpreting that as us saying we don't want to
> do these things. Sometimes, that's true, but sometimes we're
> saying that you can't change things overnight; you have to

consider the consequences of such moves carefully. I don't think
they realise what a huge organisation the police is. Concern out
there is huge. People are wondering what on earth's going on,
and I'm trying to calm their fears, and telling them to get on
with the job of fighting crime.

Other onlookers, particularly those closest to Ryan, have little
doubt what was happening. His closest friend Colin Henson, for
instance, says, 'The Government big-noted him; they were using him
as a drawcard. That has come back to haunt him now.'

Ironically, one of the few politicians at this time to have any sympathy for Ryan was Opposition Leader Kerry Chikarovski. She
approached him on Australia Day for a friendly chat – something the
pair had never had before. She suggested that Costa was a gift to the
Liberal Party. Ryan was noncommittal. She also assured him that, if
the Liberals won the next election, his job as Commissioner was
safe. He tried to look grateful. Sadly, her newfound support turned
out to be of little comfort. Two months later, on 28 March 2002, she
was deposed from the Liberal leadership by 33-year-old John
Brogden, who was soon to start attacking Ryan with exactly the same
ferocity as his predecessor in the early days.

But there was more bad news waiting for Ryan back at the office.
His new media adviser Justin Kelly, who'd begun a proactive campaign with the newspapers and radio to turn public opinion around
since taking the post four months before, had quit. Ryan was just
beginning to feel they might be on the verge of making headway, but
Kelly, originally with Alan Jones at Radio 2UE, was taking a new job –
over at Jones's new station 2GB. Ryan had no idea who he might
recruit to replace him, since the money was not good enough to
attract a top-flight professional, yet the demands of the job were over-
whelming. He was still, however, unable to move beyond his own
preconceptions, despite what he'd learnt over the past six years. One
of his primary conditions for any candidate was that they be well
groomed and smart, which immediately discounted most of the best-
qualified possibilities among those hard-nosed newspaper and radio
police journalists with the media contacts to make a difference, the
knowledge of the service, and the passionate interest.

In public, Costa continued his frenzy of change, including the formation of an armed hold-up squad and flagging plans to lower the entry requirements for recruits – both directly contrary to the recommendations of the Wood Royal Commission. 'In the public service, you have so many bosses, and often they're all saying different things,' says entrepreneur Geoff Morgan, one of the founders of the recruitment company Morgan & Banks, now TMP, and a personal friend of Ryan's. 'Peter came here because he thought the job would be challenging and exciting, but politically it became far more difficult than probably he'd ever estimated. He genuinely tried to do his best but, in that environment, he became something of a pawn.'

That night, Ryan appeared a broken man. He was tired, depressed and, for the first time, just couldn't see any way forward. Alan Jones's attacks on the radio were unstinting. The PIC Malta hearing had dragged on so long that, by the time he took the stand, everyone had seemed to lose interest in what he had to say to set the record straight. Costa, who now hadn't even spoken to Ryan for around six weeks, seemed to be making every operational decision he possibly could, leaving Ryan to pick up the pieces – and cop the flak. When approached to comment for this book, Costa's spokesperson said the Minister had nothing to say on the matter.

Ryan, too, was fast running out of words.

If this doesn't change, I have to look for a way out now. I need to either be left alone to do the job, or to leave long before the election takes place. I don't want to harm the Government, but I just want out of the job. I've had enough. I can't deal with the treachery, the lying, and the publicity. I feel sad because there are a lot of genuine people in this organisation doing their best to make it work. But I just can't go on any more. For all intents and purposes I am no longer the Commissioner of Police. I have lost my authority and my staff are totally confused about who is running the force.

Adrienne was completely behind him. 'This job is killing him. He's a different man now to the one who came out to Australia. He's aged so much. His health can't take much more. We can't take it.'

The girls felt the same. When Elizabeth was asked about her relationship with her dad, she talked about how close they once were. 'Now,' she said, suddenly bursting into tears, 'we don't get on so well. Dad's always tired and miserable and he doesn't laugh any more. All he wants to do is eat or sleep or sit in front of the television. He's so stressed and bad tempered. He doesn't talk to me much any more.'

Ryan took initial legal advice on his contract, and was devastated to discover there was no way out. The Government had made it watertight to make sure they'd be able to keep their most popular Commissioner way past the election, until 16 February 2004. He then approached another solicitor, top employment lawyer Joe Catanzariti of legal firm Clayton Utz to see what his legal rights were in the circumstances. Catanzariti examined the contract closely, and came up with a daring plan. A Bill had been tabled at State Parliament for the next week to amend employment legislation that allowed an employee to challenge the fairness of their employment contract on the grounds that they were being prevented from doing their job. If they prepared a summons to the New South Wales Industrial Relations Commission immediately, before the change could go through, he said, they could legitimately either demand the Government terminate the contract, or demand that he be given the job back he was originally contracted to do – with damages for the hurt and humiliation he'd endured in the meantime. That would mean the Minister would have to agree to consult with Ryan on all matters relating to his duties under his contract, and would agree not to interfere with, or obstruct, Ryan in the performance of those duties.

Suddenly, there was a real urgency to the task of varying the contract. And, in a final irony that, at last, favoured Ryan, Costa's headkicker tactics had played directly into his hands. If anybody doubted that Ryan wasn't being allowed to do his job they only had to read the newspapers. Costa was making operational decisions on an almost daily basis and he had admitted, albeit reluctantly, that he hadn't spoken to Ryan for weeks. Costa could not have been helping Ryan's cause any more if the two had sat down and planned it together.

So Ryan listed all the ways in which he had been prevented from running the operational side of the police service. It grew longer and longer. He had been unable to make his own decision about deputies, the service had been restructured into five regions against his wishes, he had not wanted to remove those Assistant Commissioners, and he had not wanted Chadbourne's employment to be terminated. In addition, the Minister had set up an advisory committee that now seemed to be deciding policy, and he had never consulted Ryan on issues like the secondment of Tim Priest to his office; the appointment of former Police Minister Peter Anderson – one of Ryan's old, axed New South Wales Police Board members – to review police recruitment; the appointment of Clive Small to the Premier's office; the establishment of a school-gang task force; spending $2.4 million on issues related to policing in southern Sydney; changing the costs of policing special events to a user-pays basis; the proposed purchase and trial of a different uniform for officers; the use of drug-detection dogs; initiatives in drug education; against noisy exhausts on cars . . . The examples in the summons ended up filling over seven pages, with the last two showing how far out of the loop Costa had cut Ryan. Point 43 is that Costa makes announcements of changes without even considering whether the police service has the funds to afford them. Point 44 is the claim that Costa fails to communicate with Ryan and summons his deputies to meetings, while cancelling previously arranged meetings with the Commissioner. The final summons for relief under Section 106 of the *Industrial Relations Act 1996* was set to be presented to Carr on 1 April 2002.

As the paperwork was being drawn up, however, a tragedy was being played out on the roads. A young constable, Glenn McEnallay, was shot twice in the chest and once in the head after being ambushed during his pursuit of a stolen car at Hillsdale, in Sydney's south. Ryan, who was always affected emotionally whenever 'his' officers were hurt or killed, was visibly distressed as the news came through. He visited the young man twice as he lay in a coma on life support at the hospital, and talked to the young man's parents and his fiancée at his bedside. The next day, he had to leave the country to attend talks in Athens on the security of the next Olympic Games. He'd taken annual leave for the task, anxious that the experience of Sydney's safe Games be used to help the next. But, as always happened whenever he left the country, politicians on both sides started baying for his head. Last time it had been when he went to Salt Lake City, and Costa's restructure and sackings were announced. The time before, he'd been overseas when the row over Cabramatta exploded. This holiday was no different: why was the Commissioner gallivanting overseas when one of his men lay fighting for his life in hospital? Ryan was inconsolable. Did everyone expect him to sit by the young officer's bedside constantly, despite any wish his parents and fiancée might have to be left alone to deal with their grief privately? McEnallay didn't even know he was there, in any case. Lost in his coma, his doctors had all agreed: it was hopeless. His family was simply hoping for a miracle in the face of the inevitable. Only the machines were keeping McEnallay alive. Indeed, McEnallay's father later called Ryan to thank him for his support in the face of the controversy.

It wasn't as if Ryan wanted to be in Greece, either. It had been a pre-arranged meeting that he didn't feel he could cancel at such late notice. In truth, he wanted to be home with his family, waiting to see what the Government would do in response to the summons. The tension was becoming unbearable. Adrienne cried easily, and often. The children were so unsettled that she let them stay home a few days from school. New crime figures just released showed a marked 34 per cent rise in the number of armed robberies, and politicians renewed their attacks on Ryan for being overseas when Sydney was facing yet another crime crisis. In response, Costa said the police service could function quite effectively without Ryan, thank you. Ryan himself, however, was on the phone constantly from Greece, to check on McEnallay, who died while Ryan was overseas, and find out if there was any more news on his job. The Greek Government was even now putting pressure on him, asking him to stay to help them with the entire lead-up to the Games. Psychologically and emotionally exhausted, he confessed he couldn't even think beyond the end of the week.

The negotiations between his lawyers and the Government seemed to be taking forever. There was delay after delay. When he finally arrived back in Sydney a week later, he went straight to McEnallay's Mascot station to give his support to his colleagues. Then he talked to Catanzariti: it looked like the Government was going to agree to terminate him. The next day, Ryan drove to Taree for Glenn

McEnallay's funeral, on the way up dropping in on another officer, Matthew Nixon, bravely battling cancer in hospital in Foster. The Minister, who flew up, barely looked at him as they sat together in the small church, filled to overflowing with Glenn McEnallay's relatives, friends and colleagues. As he read a eulogy to his fallen officer, Ryan remembered what it felt like to be a policeman rather than a politician. And, as he sat back down beside Costa he realised that the ambitious new Minister still did not know that the end of his long and distinguished career was nigh. He wondered when Carr might tell him.

That night, Ryan, Adrienne, Elizabeth and Georgina sat around their dining table together. The mood was sombre. Gently, Ryan told the girls he was about to leave his job, what did they think? The two girls started to cry. They were scared, they said. What would he do? What would people say? What would happen to them? It was an evening of mixed emotions. On the one hand, Ryan felt like a burden might be about to lift off his shoulders. On the other, he was nervous. He still felt unsure of Carr's reaction, and knew Costa would be furious, particularly since he'd been kept in the dark so long. He also worried about what the press might make of his sudden disappearance. Georgina, her thin face pale, had another worry. That week another girl at her school had told her: 'My mummy says if your daddy hadn't gone to Greece that policeman wouldn't have died.' Ryan and Adrienne hugged their daughters tight. 'It's going to be all right,' Ryan reassured them. He didn't sound too certain himself.

The next morning, Wednesday, 10 April, Ryan left home early for Carr's office at Governor Macquarie Tower. After two hours of talks, and crucially aware of the political damage a fight in the Industrial Relations Court might do, Carr agreed to the termination with a payout of a year's salary, rather than the two the contract specified in the event of an early termination. At 11 a.m., Ryan hurriedly phoned Adrienne. They were calling a press conference in twenty minutes.

Calls went out to the TV and radio stations and newspapers that there was a big announcement about to be made. In the tower's conference room, twenty journalists gathered, all wondering why they had been called in at such short notice. They started taking bets on the subject. The majority verdict: some new statement on stem-cell research.

When Ryan and Carr walked in, a hush settled on the room.

A press statement with sketchy details of the deal that had just been made was circulated. No one could quite believe it. Carr delivered the bombshell news that the Police Commissioner's contract had just been terminated by mutual agreement, and spoke of how Ryan had been the man for the time. He had tried to persuade him to stay, he said, but Ryan had been determined to go. Ryan then spoke, not being able to resist one last barb at his critics in the press. He felt full of emotion in this, the same room in which Carr had triumphantly announced his appointment in 1996. He spoke in a firm controlled voice, but no one doubted tears were not far away. When a journalist asked from the back of the room whether the Premier still stuck by his verdict that Ryan was the best Commissioner New South Wales had ever had, Carr hesitated. Ryan jumped straight in, insisting that yes, absolutely, he was. Behind the jocularity, however, was a clear determination that the Premier should acknowledge his contribution. He was not going to be cheated out of his last hurrah.

Later that day, Ryan and Adrienne agreed to one radio interview, with Adrienne challenging Jones to meet with her and tell her exactly why he had turned so virulently against them. Then the pair went to ground as controversy raged over the size, and legality, of the payout, and Costa tied himself in knots by claiming, at first, Ryan had resigned, but having to concede later that he'd been terminated. Finally, Ryan agreed to speak to '60 Minutes', a tense little interview in which he looked anxious not to give too much away. There was only the tantalising hint that he may well have been able to sue the Government had they not agreed to his termination, and such a blunt refusal to comment on Costa that no one was left in any doubt about the true nature of the relationship between the two men.

On Ryan's last day in the office, on Wednesday, 17 April 2002, he took calls from a number of well-wishers, including the father of slain highway patrolman Glenn McEnallay who thanked him for his support and said that they, at least, knew the truth about Ryan's concern for their son. It was a pity, they said, that no one had asked for their opinion. A Greek police uniform, a souvenir of his last trip to Athens lay over a chair. Ryan joked that maybe he should put it on as he left. Moroney confided that he could feel 'a concrete block' descending on his shoulders, as he saw it lift off Ryan's. As Adrienne and the couple's friends, the Hensons, arrived, Ryan handed back all the property of the newly named New South Wales Police – the word 'Service' was no longer to be used, according to another of Costa's one-man dictates – and said a sad goodbye to his weeping personal staff.

At the front door of Police HQ, his Police Protocol Unit Inspector Maurice Green, tears streaming down his face, leaned over with the few last words of advice he'd ever give him. 'Stiff upper lip, Sir,' he said, his whole mouth quivering. 'Just keep walking.'

Ryan stepped out into the sunshine and walked through a guard of honour made up of his staff and officers, to the lament of a lone piper and the spontaneous applause of everyone present. With his own eyes now full of tears, unable to hide the emotion of the moment, he held up his two hands together in a fist of salute to the crowd, as if to say: I'm out, but I'm not down. You've tried, but I'm not beaten.

Where did it all go wrong?

Three days after Peter Ryan brought down the curtain on his forty-one-year career as a police officer, he was sitting in the garden of his home on Sydney's North Shore, the table in front of him piled high with letters, notes and faxes from well-wishers.

'Much of our achievement to date and what we go on to achieve . . . will be due to your vision,' wrote one police officer. 'You have inspired so many people in this organisation,' wrote another. 'I have great admiration for your tremendous leadership,' said the next. As Ryan sorted through them, he was clearly moved. 'If my critics could see this, they'd realise they were always such a long way off the mark,' he says quietly.

> There are large numbers of officers in the service who've given me their total allegiance and carried the torch forward in terms of resisting corruption and crime-fighting techniques. They always were, and will always be, the silent majority. They don't want to get tangled up in the politics. They just want to do the best job they can. I only hope the foundations I've laid are deep enough and strong enough to carry them, and the service, forward.

It will, in truth, be years before an accurate assessment can be made of what Ryan achieved over his six years in one of the toughest police jobs in the world. And even before then, history will be rewritten by politicians, the media, and police officers both within and outside the force. As for Ryan, however, turning his back on a lifetime's passion – the simple aim to be the best cop he possibly could – remains an intensely painful experience. It's the saddest end to a brilliant career he could ever have imagined, and it's hard not to allow the bitterness to creep in.

So does he have any regrets about taking on the job at the head of the New South Wales police service? He hesitates, then chooses his words carefully. 'I'd have to say, I wish I'd never come here,' he says, sadly. 'I didn't imagine I'd ever think that, but I do. I could have had the job in the [London] Met. I could have gone to the West Midlands. In all probability, I would by now have had a knighthood and I would have retired later, and with far more dignity than I've been allowed to here.'

His supporters certainly believe his tenure here was always doomed. The task was too massive, the odds too heavily weighted against him. 'I'm not sure he ever, really, stood a chance,' says Jo Hampson, the English chief of staff he brought over to Australia with him. Says his Olympic Security Commander Paul McKinnon, 'I've never seen anyone score off a hospital pass. When you're running into three gorillas who you know are going to jump on you and break your bones, how *can* you make it?' It makes recruitment mogul Geoff Morgan fear for the future. 'If we don't allow people from overseas coming here to succeed, then in the end, they won't come, and this country needs, like every country, world expertise.'

There are many, however, who believe Ryan made considerable headway and left the New South Wales force in far better shape than when he arrived, despite the State Government backing down when he really needed their support on two fronts: the strong Commissioner's Confidence legislation that the Wood Royal Commission believed necessary to allow him to purge the service of corruption; and introducing the kind of industrial reforms he needed. 'He did the best he could in extremely difficult circumstances,' says one highly placed insider.

Ryan calls it much the same way. He needed that Commissioner's Confidence power to remove those officers on whose honesty and integrity the Royal Commission cast doubt, or who were blocking progress. He needed to be able to change the police's industrial agreements so they could work much more efficient shift patterns, with proper supervision, accountability and a decent promotions system. 'I should have insisted on that from the word Go,' he says. 'But can you expect a Labor Government to go head-to-head with the trade unions to insist on that change? That's very difficult politically for them.'

Maybe it might have helped if he could have persuaded the police unions to come onside from the beginning. Maybe he could have done more to have wooed his predecessor Tony Lauer, a past Police Association president. Maybe if there'd been a Liberal Government in power, things would have been different. Who knows?

Yet undoubtedly Ryan has pioneered many valuable advances. The deputy who took over from him, Ken Moroney, says Ryan had a futuristic vision and introduced crime-fighting techniques, operational processes, communication systems and forward planning far in advance of what had previously existed. As far as ridding the force of corruption, 'I believe it's a different organisation six years on,' says Moroney. 'The Mascot/Florida exposés demonstrate that today the police are capable, over a long, sustained period of time, of identifying corruption and investigating other police. Pre-Wood, it was something akin to a state of denial.' Moroney also sees the problems with human resources as proving the major obstacle to Ryan's reformist zeal. 'He came here with great expectations and a very reformist view,' he says. 'He thought he'd be able to say things should be done, and they would be done. But they often weren't. He was constantly frustrated.'

Ryan was also done no favours by the unwieldy system set up to safeguard reform, expose current corruption and prevent future corrupt networks from being formed. The paranoia and distrust surrounding the service meant the newly established Police Integrity Commission seemed to feel obliged to investigate every suspicion. When a small knot of officers claimed that senior officers were stifling reform, the PIC launched a major inquiry. It damaged Ryan irreparably as he was forced to sit on the sidelines, enduring the mud-slinging and banned from saying a word in his, and his senior officers', defence. That the resulting inquiry lasted nearly a year and a half was inexcusable, say many onlookers in both political and legal circles. Those claims should have been investigated swiftly as a matter of the most urgent priority, and laid to rest straightaway.

Ryan believes that while it's essential to have a body like the PIC, it should be able to make up its mind quickly, and at least have trust in the one person charged with introducing reform in the service. 'Why the hell would I be interested in working against my own reforms?' he asks, incredulously. 'It was bloody stupid.' It didn't help that neither the public at large, nor the vast mass of police officers beyond the PIC, ever seemed to understand the issues, especially as all the participants were soon bogged down in a morass of detail, claims and counter-claims. Instead, everyone involved ended up tainted by association.

For the future, Ryan would like to see the New South Wales Commissioner being allowed to work much more in tandem with the PIC. They should be able to share the secrets of the service. They should be kept in each other's confidence. They should be working together to achieve the right results, not against each other to weaken them both. When that is allowed to happen, only those intent on exploiting the resulting fragility for their own ends thrive. And Ryan feels strongly that PIC investigations should all come to a definite conclusion.

> I know of inquiries that have begun, officers have been affected and the service has stalled because we can't move on until they come to a decision. But too often inquiries are started, and then just die away. They never bring out a result. I know one officer who wanted a particular job but, when I was told the PIC were investigating him, I had to intervene without giving the game away to anyone else. I had to move the person to another job – but I've never discovered, to this day, the outcome of their investigation. People's lives are ruined like this.

Looking back, however, Ryan sees the point where it all went irre-trievably wrong for him as the Cabramatta furore. He'd been told one thing, and believed it, while many of those on the ground were say-ing quite another, and were eventually vindicated – with the notable exception of 'James' whose sensational claims, taken up by Ryan's opponents, were only discredited much later. Even Tim Priest, the main whistleblower, has sympathy for Ryan's predicament. 'I've never, ever criticised Peter Ryan,' he says. 'I said from the beginning he was poorly advised, and I believe he never recovered from that.' While Priest was, in turn, demonised by Ryan's supporters, he was never really an active part of the campaign to 'Get Peter Ryan'. He was purely a cop who cared passionately about his work and ended up being destroyed for speaking up against a hierarchy determined to stifle dissent. 'The New South Wales police force is one of the most venomous organisations in the world,' he says. 'Even the Taliban would be worried. It's the like the Magic Pudding, where every time you try and cut out [the poison], it just keeps on coming back.'

Academic Richard Basham was much more personally vindictive towards Ryan. Perhaps he sincerely believed what he was being told by his 'sources'. Perhaps he saw an opportunity to make a reputation for himself in an area in which he was generally considered a fairly minor figure. Or perhaps he simply became too drowned in the dark mire of conspiracy theory. Inviting him to comment for this book provided a startling insight into the world of rumour, innuendo and 'secret' unattributable information he seems to inhabit. Basham insisted he had it on 'several reliable journalist sources' that I had been working for 'several' years as the Ryans' personal publicist, continually pushing stories about them in the media. In truth, I'd written just five stories on them – well below the average for most journalists – before I was approached to write this biography. From the time I signed the contract in February 2000, I wrote only one other piece that mentioned Peter Ryan, and that was on Adrienne's book about miscarriage. Since the existence of the biography was a tightly held secret (known only, as far as I was aware, to my newspaper bosses) to have 'pushed stories' was inconceivable, as it would have meant revealing to other journalists that I knew the Ryans. Indeed, when I was ordered to write an 'insider' newspaper story on Ryan's departure, because of the conflict of interest I felt that represented, I resigned from my job on principle. None of this will make any difference to Basham and his supporters who look awestruck by what they have achieved. Like small boys who throw stones at speeding trucks, they have caused an almighty crash and then seemed suddenly both surprised and frightened by the destruction they wrought.

As for Ryan's other 'enemies', no one will probably ever know their real motivations for sure. Undoubtedly, it was in the Liberal Party's interests to try to destroy a police chief appointed and championed by their political adversaries, particularly one whose popularity consistently undermined the traditional strength of their own law-and-order platform. Some of Ryan's most vocal detractors had links with the Liberal Party, including Gary Sturgess, Alan Jones and John Marsden. Even Geoff Schuberg was once referred to in the press as a possible future Liberal candidate, after addressing a meeting in southern Sydney organised by local Liberal MP Malcolm Kerr. Kerry Chikarovski, the woman who led the Liberal Party through most of Ryan's time, denies, however, there having been a political conspiracy. 'There are all sorts of people in all sorts of positions in the Liberals,' she says. 'I can't be sure that none of those people had any role in what happened. But I met Geoff Schuberg twice. He is a nice man with a lot to offer, but to be suggesting that somehow we were being influenced by that is a nonsense.' A highly placed non-partisan onlooker agrees that a systematic Liberal plot to destabilise Ryan is unlikely. 'The Liberals couldn't possibly organise anything so complex,' he says. 'They have no policies on anything. The most they can do is snipe at what everyone else is doing.'

The police service, however, is a different matter. Complex, pressured, political and high profile, it is riddled with conflicting loyalties, networks and agendas that, at times, seek powerful expression. With Ryan cutting great swathes through the service, sacking senior officers, pushing others into retirement, demoting some and promoting others, he had, quite probably, more enemies than any other single person in Australia. Even if he had become paranoid, he had every reason to believe that somewhere, someone was plotting against him. 'It was the people shaking his hand, smiling at him and agreeing with him, then stabbing him in the back, who were the ones who killed him,' says Priest. 'The insiders brought him down. The person who does that job should be paid a million dollars a year; it's such a venomous, dirty task, with so many people out to discredit them. And now, with Ryan gone, it's about to start all over again . . .' In among the enemies Ryan made, there are those who honestly felt he wasn't the best man for the job, and who sincerely believed that, as an outsider, he couldn't possibly get to grips with a foreign culture. There will have been some who felt the mistakes he made might not have been made by those with an equal claim on the job. And there are many who were simply out to get him. The difficulty lies in separating legitimate criticism from genuine hostility.

Certainly, Ryan has his flaws, just like anyone else. He did make errors, as he confesses, in Cabramatta, and in failing to trust others, and then in trusting too much. It was a huge challenge to understand another culture under the most trying of circumstances. 'In a 100-yard race, he probably started twenty yards behind the start line,' says Moroney. 'He knew which way he was running, where the finishing line was and how much effort and energy it would take, but catching up would take a toll on anyone.' He may well have become beguiled by his position, at one stage, as the most popular figure in the entire State. And he would have had no idea of either the relish in Australia with which tall poppies are routinely torn down or the vigour of public life. 'It's a country built on the culture of mutiny against authority,' says his friend, Geoff Officer. 'The whole State is driven on the fact that people came out here and had to fight for their existence. We love to cut down the dignity of office.'

In addition, Ryan confesses he had no notion before he arrived of the intense media, public and political scrutiny the police service was under. Over his six years, there were, on average, more than 500 newspaper reports on him alone per month. He never got used to it, or learned how to deal with it.

Bob Carr used to tell me to ignore the buggers, but in the end even he had to admit that it was extraordinary, their constant, unending attacks on me. I think it's because I had become a well-known figure. Mention Ryan and you get a headline. They thought they had a public figure who was too big for his boots, a bit of a show-off, and they wanted to bring him down a peg or two. I was an easy target for everyone. I didn't sue. I didn't fight back. I wouldn't even talk to them. Maybe they were all mistakes, but I never had a top media advisor to help me. The police service couldn't afford one and, because we were trying to save money, I tried to do that on the cheap. I didn't want people to be

able to say that I was paying money to help my media profile.
But, in hindsight, that was a mistake.

Radio host and friend Stan Zemanek warned him about that often.
'He had idiots telling him not to speak to the press. They were just
stonewalling the media all the time. People got frustrated. Peter
needed to have answered their questions.'

Eventually, that was to prove Ryan's downfall. With a press constantly looking for new angles on the police, enthusiastically
pursuing those lurid tales of corruption, drug dealing and bribes,
and eager to chart the rise and falls of the charismatic, dapper Commissioner with his magnificently quotable quotes, the police
suddenly became the sexiest story in town. The frustration when he
refused to play ball by dishing up meaty tales or providing ready
access quickly became palpable. Far less coy were those more-
established, often disillusioned, police officers with an axe to grind
against him. Similarly, police union officials, resenting his pursuit of
industrial reforms, were also eager to feed those in hungry pursuit of
scraps. Ryan's signing of a new contract in the run-up to the 1999
election for a salary many considered unjustifiably, even obscenely,
generous, provided a godsend.

The bad press rapidly became a downward spiral, in which truth
and objectivity were often trampled in the rush for column inches,
especially in the absence of any voice refuting the tall tales. Radio host
Alan Jones added enormous momentum, with his calls for Ryan's head
and by striking fear and doubt into the hearts of both listeners and the
politicians who craved their votes. Was the $40-million broadcaster
part of a Liberal plot? Was he at the very heart of a disgruntled cabal
intent on getting revenge, whatever the cost? Did he simply recognise
what good radio such bitter conflict over the number one issue of the
day would make? Or was he a man looking for that elusive cause, who
had an earnest belief in what he was being told by those with the
motivation to call him on air, sincerely convinced he was doing the
right thing by his 'battlers'?

There are many who believe Jones is credited with wielding far
more power over politicians and his media colleagues than he actually deserves. 'Who are his main constituency?' asks one. 'The

unemployed and the unemployable, who have little else to do but sit at home in the mornings and listen to him. His influence is totally overestimated by some, particularly politicians, who really should know better.' Yet there is little doubt that he can make a formidable adversary. Forceful, persuasive, with a compelling command of the English language and a seemingly unshakeable belief in his own convictions, it's a mix that can be utterly seductive. He is, without doubt, one of the best exponents in the world of the art of talkback radio. He also peddles, extremely convincingly, the line of having an unerring instinct for what the bloke in the street really thinks. Does he really have his finger on the pulse? Most, on both sides of the political divide, are too cowed to put it to the test.

Listening to Jones and reading the newspapers the Government was becoming anxious about its prospects in the forthcoming 2003 election. Consequently it was the Government which ended up doing Ryan the gravest disservice. They buckled to the press outcry over Ryan's planned closure of police stations, undermining him once more, even though their own report, at the beginning of his tenure, recommended doing away with a quarter of stations. When crime went up the Government successfully blamed Ryan for that too, even though local figures merely reflect the general upward trend in every other western democracy struggling with the onslaught of drugs, the wider availability of firearms, disaffected youth, widening income gaps between the rich and the poor, and the wind-back of State-provided services in favour of an often brutal user-pays system.

Most criminologists – with the obvious exception of people like Basham (who is actually an anthropologist and not a member of his university's highly regarded criminology department) – will admit that police have little control over crime figures, beyond trying to provide a deterrent and reducing the opportunities for crime. The real causes, of course, lie within the social and economic conditions that exist at the time, but for politicians to effectively transfer the responsibility for crime onto the police is a masterstroke. It means they can absolve themselves of much of the blame while the police chiefs – and the more acquiescent the better – become the perennial whipping boys. Those braying commentators on the Right dismiss any notion that better social policies reduce crime. But those who truly know, know better. And, for politicians, it's infinitely better to sacrifice a police commissioner than it is to lose an election. In Ryan's case they could not sack him – those voters who weren't appalled at his treatment would have been furious at the payout he could, and would, have demanded. The best they could do was make him want to leave.

While Ryan still will not say a word against Carr, for whatever reason, merely praising him as 'a superb politician, an excellent Premier and a man of enormous intellect', there's little doubt that Carr's decision to surrender him to the cause of electoral popularity sealed Ryan's fate. 'I was, frankly, quite amazed that he would put Costa into the police portfolio,' says Ryan.

Costa was an arrogant, difficult man, who had little idea about policing. But if he was put into that role to beat up the Commissioner, it was a bizarre twist. I was quite concerned. He's been responsible for the whole damn thing. He gave me no handshake, absolutely nothing at all when I finished. He didn't speak to me about it. I honestly didn't want to go, but I wanted to take control of my police force, and they wouldn't let me.

At the end of the day, I got out of the situation and in many respects, I've let the Government off the hook. There's no doubt that when Costa was put into Whelan's job, the aim was to get rid of me. Carr, I think, must have been backing Costa. I have heard it from so many sources. Senior business figures say that Carr had a high regard for me and my abilities and what I was doing. He didn't really want me to go but, because of the bad media, I was becoming a political embarrassment. I wasn't a lame-duck Commissioner, but I was one under constant attack, and people were treating me as if I were a de facto part of the Government. I had to go, but they didn't want to pay me the $1 million [two years' pay] that my contract stipulated if they sacked me without notice. So they decided, instead, to force me out.

The only observation Carr would make for this book was, 'I have always had a good working relationship with Peter Ryan, and I hope to see more of him in the future.' Ryan's one-time foe Chikarovski is blunter. She says it was generally known around the corridors of

Parliament that Costa's principal assignment was to 'get rid of Ryan', a 'despicable' way to treat him. Cabramatta publican Ross Treyvaud later admitted that Costa had pledged to 'sideline' Ryan at his meeting with his critics in November 2001.

So while Ryan's departure may well have saved the New South Wales Labor Party, the question remains: who, or what, will now save the New South Wales Police? Moroney, the man who took over from him, says the potent mix of politics and police reminds him of the scene in *The Godfather, Part II* where Michael's [Al Pacino] treacherous henchman, who tried to set him up to be killed by rival Mafia bosses, is being driven away to some unspeakable fate. 'He says, "Tell Michael it wasn't personal, it's just business,"' recounts Moroney. 'Politics in New South Wales is like that, and I suspect it will ever be thus.'

This politicisation of the police was, of course, the loudest warning bell rung by the Wood Royal Commission's recommendations for the future of policing. Justice James Wood declined to comment for this book, but one can imagine the alarm with which he must be watching this major corruption of the process. Many believe that when Costa openly stepped beyond his role of deciding on police policy into making so many operational decisions, he crossed a line that should be held sacrosanct. Professor David Dixon, Associate Dean of the Law Faculty of the University of New South Wales is one. 'Politicians can intrude inappropriately in police decisions,' he says. 'The Wood Royal Commission called for the relationship to be sorted out . . . It laid out the process of reform, but that has gone out of the window.' He warns darkly of a possible undermining of the whole reform process as a result, and a return to the old days of unbridled corruption within the police service. Director of Public Prosecutions Nicholas Cowdery is another. He too laments the lack of action on the key Commission recommendation of separating operational policing decisions from politics, and has warned of the menace of the dark times returning to haunt us all.

Ryan, having been a victim of this blurring of powers, feels this more keenly than most.

I just feel very concerned for the future of the police in New South Wales now. I'm worried about the reform process. We seem likely now to return to the times of the old squads which, just as in Britain and America, can be prone to corruption because they're self-controlling and self-reporting. To be safe, they have to be properly supervised, with the members rotating regularly to avoid them becoming involved in networks. I've been positively alarmed to see the media actually turning towards Roger Rogerson to ask his opinion about the squads and the police service. It's like asking Ned Kelly what he would do with troopers. I fear for the future of democracy in a country when people like Rogerson are asked for their views, and where a radio host can call the shots for a government. That's a clear threat to democracy.

As for Ryan himself, now aged 58, he's facing another major challenge in both his personal and professional lives. He'd been flattered to be approached by the Greek Olympic authorities while he was advising them on their security preparations on a voluntary basis, but had said he was in no position to take another job. But when it was announced that he'd reached agreement with the New South Wales Government to terminate his contract two years early, the two sides started talking again. He was torn between the prospect of another Games and staying in Sydney, however, and was still attending interviews for alternative jobs in Sydney up until the evening of Friday, 26 April, when he finally signed the Athens memorandum of understanding, and faxed it back.

He's going to be based there for most of the next two years, but the family will stay in Sydney. The irony is that, after all the misery they've endured, Adrienne doesn't want to leave or to disrupt the girls' schooling. 'I used to wish that we'd never come here, all the time,' says Georgina, aged 12. 'But now it's home. We're settled here. I don't want to move any more.' Elizabeth agrees. 'I lived in nine houses before we came here,' says the 14-year-old. 'I don't want to move again. I want to stay in Australia. All my friends are here now.' Says Adrienne, 41, who once felt so alone here, 'This is our home. It was all the crap that went with it that got to us.'

It's easy to understand why Ryan has now accepted the challenge of another Games. Despite the enormous pressures it will place on him, he needs to exorcise the ghosts of such an ignominious end to a previously stellar police career. He's too young to retire yet. He still has a lot to give.

Above all, he still *cares*. On the Saturday night after he was terminated by the New South Wales Government, but four days before he was officially due to quit his post, he was on his way out to dinner with friends when he received a phone call at his home about the death of Senior Constable Chris Thornton, the officer whose patrol car was sideswiped by another vehicle in Woy Woy and rammed into a power pole. Ryan was visibly moved at the news, and he immediately left home to drive to the Central Coast to pass on his sympathies to the 35-year-old man's family and colleagues. He had every excuse not to do so, but it never seemed to occur to him not to go. 'But he told his [Chris Thornton's] parents, sorry, but he didn't think he'd be able to come to the funeral, as there'd be a new Commissioner then,' says friend Loretta Henson.

There will be those who will say the 'Peter Ryan experiment' didn't work. There will be others who'll say he achieved more than anyone has so far been prepared to admit. At the moment, however, it does seem that the person who paid the highest price was Ryan himself. Sure, he was a proud man. Sure, he was an exceedingly ambitious man, driven from humble beginnings to make as much of himself as he possibly could. Sure, he may have become a victim of his own celebrity. And maybe, just maybe, he could have looked down from his pedestal more carefully to see the warning signs.

But he was certainly a man eminently qualified for leading the New South Wales police into the future, a man with a simple morality, a clear-cut sense of honour, a solid integrity and a determination to do the right thing. Only history will eventually judge whether his time should not have come so soon.

Index

Relationships to Peter Ryan are described in parentheses, for personal and childhood relationships only.

The title 'Sir' is presented in parentheses where the title had not been conferred at time of first mention in the book.

Richmond, David 278
Rigg, Angus 189–90
riots, Britain 66–74
Ritchie, James 285, 286, 287, 288–9, 299
Robb, Andrew 285
Robinson, Reg 36
Rogerson, Roger 65, 152, 335
Rotary Club exchange program, Ryan's participation 47–8
Round Table Club, Ryan's membership 53, 54
Royal Commission, NSW
  beginnings 65, 140, 141–2
  after-effects 177
  audit 296
  corruption evidence 145
  cost and duration 191, 199
  dealings with Ryan 176, 183, 186
  findings 164, 248, 304
  Graham 'Chook' Fowler 142, 145
  named officers 160, 165, 166, 169, 203, 268
  Implementation Unit 3–4
  recommendations 200, 202–4, 283, 309, 317, 325, 334
  sackings resulting from 159
  side effects 213
  sidetracked on pedophilia issue 200–1, 207–8
  submission to, from Police Board 164
Royal Commission, Britain 194
Royal Family
  protection 252
  the Queen 59, 265
  at Sandringham 129–30
  wedding of Charles and Diana 73, 75
Royal Lancaster Grammar school 18
RSPCA 16
Royal Ulster Constabulary 71, 79
Rushdie, Salman 129

Russell Reynolds Associates 143
Russian Mafia 265, 302
Ryan, Adrienne (nee Butterworth, wife)
  career 97–8, 106, 235, 294
  comments on Australians 293
  dating Ryan 83, 84, 92, 94, 95–7, 103–5
  friends, making 120, 226–7, 235, 294
  marriage 105–6, 107–10, 111
  media comments by 180, 229, 235
  miscarriages 113–16, 147, 148, 266, 328
  and Prince Charles 130
  relationship difficulties 260, 261, 272
  studies 147, 178, 215
  Sydney, feelings about move to 3, 5
Ryan, Christine (sister-in-law) 120, 121
Ryan, Geoffrey (brother)
  childhood 17–18
  relationship with Ryan 29, 115–16, 120–3
  views on Ryan 121, 122
Ryan, Georgina Clare (daughter)
  attitudes to Australia 335
  behaviour 261
  birth 120
  boarding school 294
  receipt of death threats 234–5
  receipt of pornographic emails 257
  response to rumours 179, 180–1, 321
  visit to Lakemba 243
Ryan, Elizabeth (daughter) 243
  attitudes to Australia 150, 335
  birth 117
  boarding school 260, 294
  on death threats 234–5
  on media attention 180
  relationship with Ryan 260–1, 272, 318, 321
  visit to Lakemba 243